THE GLOBAL BURDEN OF DISEASE

2004 UPDATE

WHO Library Cataloguing-in-Publication Data

The global burden of disease: 2004 update.

1.Cost of illness. 2.World health - statistics. 3.Mortality - trends. I.World Health Organization.

ISBN 978 92 4 156371 0
(NLM classification: W 74)

© World Health Organization 2008

Acknowledgements

This publication was produced by the Department of Health Statistics and Informatics in the Information, Evidence and Research Cluster of WHO. The 2004 update of the Global burden of disease was primarily carried out by Colin Mathers and Doris Ma Fat, in collaboration with other WHO staff, WHO technical programmes and UNAIDS. The report was written by Colin Mathers, Ties Boerma and Doris Ma Fat.

Valuable inputs were provided by WHO staff from many departments and by experts outside WHO. While it is not possible to name all those who contributed to this effort, we would like to note the assistance and inputs provided by Elisabeth Aahman, Steve Begg, Bob Black, Cynthia Boschi-Pinto, Somnath Chatterji, Richard Cibulskis, Simon Cousens, Chris Dye, Mercedes de Onis, Dirk Engels, Majid Ezzati, Eric Fevre, Marta Gacic Dobo, Marc Gastellu-Etchegorry, Biswas Gautam, Peter Ghys, Kim Iburg, Mie Inoue, Robert Jakob, Jean Jannin, Sherrie Kelly, Eline Korenremp, Andre L'Hours, Joy Lawn, Steve Lim, Silvio Mariotti, Erin McLean, Nirmala Naidoo, Mike Nathan, Donatella Pascolini, Annette Pruess-Ustun, Juergen Rehm, Serge Resnikoff, Lisa Rogers, Gojke Roglic, Alexander Rowe, Florence Rusciano, Robert Salvatella, Lale Say, Suzanne Scheele, Kenji Shibuya, Perez Simaro, Andrew Smith, Karen Stanecki, Kate Strong, Jose Suaya, Jos Vandelaer, Theo Vos, Catherine Watt, Brian Williams and Lara Wolfson.

Figures were prepared by Florence Rusciano and design and layout were by Reto Schürch.

Contents

Tables..v

Figures vi

Abbreviations vii

Part 1: Introduction   **1**

Overview of the Global Burden of Disease Study 2

What is new in this update for 2004? 3

Regional estimates for 2004.. 5

Part 2: Causes of death   **7**

1.   Deaths in 2004: who and where?.. 8

2.   Deaths by broad cause groups 8

3.   Leading causes of death 11

4.   Cancer mortality 12

5.   Causes of death among children aged under five years 14

6.   Causes of death among adults aged 15–59 years 17

7.   Years of life lost: taking age at death into account 21

8.   Projected trends in global mortality: 2004–2030... 22

Part 3: Disease incidence, prevalence and disability   **27**

9.   How many people become sick each year? 28

10. Cancer incidence by site and region 29

11. How many people are sick at any given time? 31

12. Prevalence of moderate and severe disability 31

13. Leading causes of years lost due to disability in 2004 36

Part 4: Burden of disease: DALYs   **39**

14. Broad cause composition.. 40

15. The age distribution of burden of disease 42

16. Leading causes of burden of disease 42

17. The disease and injury burden for women 46

18. The growing burden of noncommunicable disease.. 47

19. The unequal burden of injury 48

20. Projected burden of disease in 2030 49

Annex A: Deaths and DALYs 2004: Annex tables   **53**

Table A1: Deaths by cause, sex and income group in WHO regions, estimates for 2004 54

Table A2: Burden of disease in DALYs by cause, sex and income group in WHO regions, estimates for 2004 60

Table A3: Deaths by cause and broad age group, countries grouped by income per capita, 2004 66

Table A4: Burden of disease in DALYs by cause and broad age group, countries grouped by income per capita, 2004 69

Table A5: Deaths by cause, sex and age group, countries grouped by income per capita, 2004 72

Table A6: Burden of disease in DALYs by cause, sex and age group, countries grouped by income per capita, 2004.......................... 84

Annex B: Data sources and methods   **97**

B1. Population and all-cause mortality estimates for 2004 98

B2. Estimation of deaths by cause 98

B3. Causes of death for children aged under five years 103

B4. YLD revisions 106

B5. Cause-specific revisions and updates 106

B6. Prevalence of long-term disability 116

B7. Projections of mortality and burden of disease 117

B8. Uncertainty of estimates and projections 117

Annex C: Analysis categories and mortality data sources   **119**

Table C1: Countries grouped by WHO region and income per capita, 2004 120

Table C2: Countries grouped by income per capita, 2004 121

Table C3: GBD cause categories and ICD codes 122

Table C4: Data sources and methods for estimation of mortality by cause, age and sex 126

References   **133**

Tables

Table 1: Leading causes of death, all ages, 2004 11

Table 2: Leading causes of death by income group, 2004 12

Table 3: Ranking of most common cancers among men and women according to the number of deaths, by cancer site and region, 2004..... 13

Table 4: Distribution of child deaths for selected causes by selected WHO region, 2004 16

Table 5: Incidence of selected conditions by WHO region, 2004.. 28

Table 6 : Cancer incidence by site, by WHO region, 2004... 30

Table 7: Prevalence of selected conditions by WHO region, 2004... 32

Table 8: Disability classes for the GBD study, with examples of long-term disease and injury sequelae falling in each class 33

Table 9: Estimated prevalence of moderate and severe disability for leading disabling conditions by age,
for high-income and low- and middle-income countries, 2004.. 35

Table 10: Leading global causes of YLD by sex, 2004 37

Table 11: Leading global causes of YLD, high-income and low- and middle-income countries, 2004................ 37

Table 12: Leading causes of burden of disease (DALYs), all ages, 2004 43

Table 13: Leading causes of burden of disease (DALYs), countries grouped by income, 2004.......................... 44

Table 14: Leading causes of burden of disease (DALYs) by WHO region, 2004... 45

Table A1: Deaths by cause, sex and income group in WHO regions, estimates for 2004 54

Table A2: Burden of disease in DALYs by cause, sex and income group in WHO regions, estimates for 2004 60

Table A3: Deaths by cause and broad age group, countries grouped by income per capita, 2004 66

Table A4: Burden of disease in DALYs by cause and broad age group, countries grouped by income per capita, 2004 69

Table A5: Deaths by cause, sex and age group, countries grouped by income per capita, 2004 72

Table A5a: Deaths by age, sex, cause in the world, 2004 72

Table A5b: Deaths by age, sex, cause in high-income countries, 2004.. 75

Table A5c: Deaths by age, sex, cause in middle-income countries, 2004... 78

Table A5d: Deaths by age, sex, cause in low-income countries, 2004 81

Table A6: Burden of disease in DALYs by cause, sex and age group, countries grouped by income per capita, 2004.. 84

Table A6a: DALYs by age, sex, cause in the world, 2004 84

Table A6b: DALYs by age, sex, cause in high-income countries, 2004 87

Table A6c: DALYs by age, sex, cause in middle-income countries, 2004 90

Table A6d: DALYs by age, sex, cause in low-income countries, 2004 93

Table B1: Methods and data for cause-of-death estimation for 2004, by WHO region.................................... 100

Table B2: Distribution of deaths by stratum from the Chinese sample vital registration system (VR)
and the Disease Surveillance Points system (DSP) 101

Table B3: Mapping of severe neonatal infection deaths to GBD cause categories 105

Table B4: Data inputs and assumptions for estimation of postneonatal deaths by cause 105

Table B5: Estimated malaria cases (episodes of illness) by WHO region, 2004.. 109

Table C1: Countries grouped by WHO region and income per capita, 2004 120

Table C2: Countries grouped by income per capita, 2004... 121

Table C3: GBD cause categories and ICD codes.. 122

Table C4: Data sources and methods for estimation of mortality by cause, age and sex 126

Figures

Map 1: Low- and middle-income countries grouped by WHO region, 2004...5

Figure 1: Distribution of age at death and numbers of deaths, world, 2004 9

Figure 2: Per cent distribution of age at death by region, 2004 9

Figure 3: Distribution of deaths in the world by sex, 2004...10

Figure 4: Distribution of deaths by leading cause groups, males and females, world, 2004 10

Figure 5 : Distribution of causes of death among children aged under five years and within the neonatal period, 2004 14

Figure 6: Child mortality rates by cause and region, 2004 15

Figure 7: Adult mortality rates by major cause group and region, 2004 17

Figure 8: Mortality rates among men and women aged 15–59 years, region and cause-of-death group, 2004............................18

Figure 9: Adult mortality rates among those aged 15–59 years in the African Region, by sex and major cause group, 2004 19

Figure 10: Causes of injury deaths among men aged 15–59 years, Eastern Mediterranean Region, 2004......................................20

Figure 11: Adult mortality among those aged 15–59 years in the low- and middle-income countries of the European Region
by sex and major cause grouping, 2004..20

Figure 12: Adult mortality among those aged 15–59 years in the low- and middle-income countries of the Americas
by sex and major cause grouping, 2004..21

Figure 13: Comparison of the proportional distribution of deaths and YLL by region, 2004...22

Figure 14: Comparison of the proportional distribution of deaths and YLL by leading cause of death, 2004 23

Figure 15: Projected deaths by cause for high-, middle- and low-income countries...24

Figure 16: Projected global deaths for selected causes, 2004–2030...25

Figure 17: Decomposition of projected changes in annual numbers of deaths by income group, 2004-2030 26

Figure 18: Age-standardized incidence rates for cancers by WHO region, 2004 30

Figure 19: Estimated prevalence of moderate and severe disability by region, sex and age, global burden of disease estimates for 2004 33

Figure 20 : YLL, YLD and DALYs by region, 2004..41

Figure 21: Burden of disease by broad cause group and region, 2004 41

Figure 22: Age distribution of burden of disease by income group, 2004 42

Figure 23: Leading causes of disease burden for women aged 15–44 years, high-income countries,
and low- and middle-income countries, 2004 46

Figure 24: Major causes of disease burden for women aged 15–59 years, high-income countries,
and low- and middle-income countries by WHO region, 2004..47

Figure 25: Age-standardized DALYs for noncommunicable diseases by major cause group, sex and country income group, 2004...................48

Figure 26: Burden of injuries (DALYs) by external cause, sex and WHO region, 2004...49

Figure 27: Ten leading causes of burden of disease, world, 2004 and 2030 51

Figure B1: Comparison of major cause group proportional mortality for the WHO African Region, GBD 2004 and GBD 2002 101

Abbreviations

AIDS........... acquired immune deficiency syndrome
AMI............ acute myocardial infarction
CHERG........ Child Health Epidemiology Reference Group
CodMod...... GBD cause of death model
COPD.......... chronic obstructive pulmonary disease
DALY.......... disability-adjusted life year
DSP............ Disease Surveillance Points system (China)
GBD .... global burden of disease
HIV .... human immunodeficiency virus
IARC.......... International Agency for Research on Cancer
ICD............ International Classification of Diseases
INDEPTH   International Network for field sites with continuous Demographic
           Evaluation of Populations and Their Health in developing countries
MERG .... Malaria Epidemiology Reference Group
RBM........... Roll Back Malaria Partnership
STD .... sexually transmitted disease
TB.............. tuberculosis
UNAIDS....... Joint United Nations Programme on HIV/AIDS
UNICEF .... United Nations Children's Fund
VR.............. vital registration system
WHO .... World Health Organization
YLD .... years lost due to disability
YLL............. years of life lost (due to premature mortality)

Part 1

Introduction

Overview of the Global Burden of Disease Study   2

What is new in this update for 2004?   3

Regional estimates for 2004   5

Overview of the Global Burden of Disease Study

A consistent and comparative description of the burden of diseases and injuries, and risk factors that cause them, is an important input to health decision-making and planning processes. Information that is available on mortality and health in populations in all regions of the world is fragmentary and sometimes inconsistent. Thus, a framework for integrating, validating, analysing and disseminating such information is needed to assess the comparative importance of diseases and injuries in causing premature death, loss of health and disability in different populations.

The first Global Burden of Disease (GBD) Study quantified the health effects of more than 100 diseases and injuries for eight regions of the world in 1990 (1–3). It generated comprehensive and internally consistent estimates of mortality and morbidity by age, sex and region (4). The study also introduced a new metric – the disability-adjusted life year (DALY) – as a single measure to quantify the burden of diseases, injuries and risk factors (5). The DALY is based on years of life lost from premature death and years of life lived in less than full health; more information is given in Box 1.

Drawing on extensive databases and information provided by Member States, the World Health Organization (WHO) prepared updated burden of disease assessments for the years 2000–2002, the most recent version being published in the *World health report 2004 (6)*. Following a country consultation process, country-specific estimates for 2002 were also published on the WHO web site (7). The GBD results for the year 2001 also provided a framework for cost-effectiveness and priority setting analyses carried out for the Disease Control Priorities Project (DCPP), a joint project of the World Bank, WHO and the National Institutes of Health, funded by the Bill & Melinda Gates Foundation (8). The GBD results were documented in detail, with information on data sources and methods, and analyses of uncertainty and sensitivity, in a book published as part of the DCPP (9).

The production and dissemination of health information for health action at the country, regional and global levels are core WHO activities mandated by the Member States in the Constitution. In her speech to the World Health Assembly in May 2007, the WHO Director-General, Dr Margaret Chan, noted, "Reliable health data and statistics are the foundation of health policies, strategies, and evaluation and monitoring". She also noted, "Evidence is also the foundation for sound health information for the general public".

World Health Assembly Resolution 60.27 (WHA60.27), adopted at the Assembly in 2007, requested the WHO Director-General to "… strengthen the information and evidence culture of the Organization and to ensure the use of accurate and timely health statistics in order to generate evidence for major policy decisions and recommendations within WHO". As part of the response to this request, the WHO Department of Health Statistics and Informatics has undertaken an update of the 1990 GBD study to produce comprehensive, comparable and consistent estimates of mortality and burden of disease by cause for all regions of the world in 2004. This update builds on the previous GBD analysis for 2002; revisions, new data and methods are summarized below. The standard DALYs reported here use 3% discounting and non-uniform age weights and differ from the discounted but non-age-weighted DALYs used in the DCPP (9).

The Bill & Melinda Gates Foundation has provided funding for a new GBD 2005 study to be published in late 2010. The study is led by the Institute for Health Metrics and Evaluation at the University of Washington, with key collaborating institutions including WHO, Harvard University, Johns Hopkins University and the University of Queensland (10). The GBD 2005 study will develop improved methods to make full use of the increasing amount of health data, particularly from developing countries, and will include a comprehensive and consistent revision of disability weights. The study will also assess trends in the global burden of disease from 1990 to 2005.

What is new in this update for 2004?

This update for 2004 builds on previous analyses for 2002 (6). It does not include a complete review and revision of data inputs and estimates for every cause. The methods and data sources are described in more detail in Annex B. The main changes in the 2004 estimates are listed below.

- A complete update was undertaken for estimated deaths by age, sex and cause for all WHO Member States. There were 192 Member States in 2004. The update was based on:
  - all-cause mortality estimates from WHO life tables for 2004, adjusted for revisions in estimates for deaths from acquired immune deficiency syndrome (AIDS) resulting from infection with human immunodeficiency virus (HIV), wars, civil conflicts and natural disasters;
  - latest death registration data reported to WHO for 112 Member States;
  - updated country-level mortality estimates for all Member States for 17 specific causes: HIV/AIDS, tuberculosis (TB), diphtheria, measles, pertussis, poliomyelitis, tetanus, dengue, malaria, schistosomiasis, trypanosomiasis, Japanese encephalitis, Chagas disease, maternal conditions, abortion, cancers, war and conflict;
  - incorporation of cause-specific and multicause models – developed by the WHO Child Health Epidemiology Reference Group (CHERG) – for causes of child deaths under five years of age and for neonatal deaths (deaths within the first four weeks after birth), with model inputs updated for the year 2004; the resulting cause-specific estimates were adjusted country by country for consistency with estimated total deaths for neonates, infants and children aged under five years;
  - revision of cause-of-death models for countries without usable death registration data; regional patterns for detailed cause-of-death distributions were updated for African countries using a greater range of information on cause-of-death distributions in Africa.
- Estimates of years lost due to disability (YLD) were revised for 52 causes where updated information for incidence or prevalence was available. Revisions resulting in significant change are noted below. For other causes, YLD estimates from the GBD 2002 were projected from 2002 to 2004 (see Annex Section B5 for details).
- Incidence, prevalence and mortality for HIV/AIDS were based on the most recent estimates released by WHO and the Joint United

---

Box 1: The disability-adjusted life year

The disability-adjusted life year (DALY) extends the concept of potential years of life lost due to premature death to include equivalent years of "healthy" life lost by virtue of being in states of poor health or disability (3). One DALY can be thought of as one lost year of "healthy" life, and the burden of disease can be thought of as a measurement of the gap between current health status and an ideal situation where everyone lives into old age, free of disease and disability.

DALYs for a disease or injury cause are calculated as the sum of the years of life lost due to premature mortality (YLL) in the population and the years lost due to disability (YLD) for incident cases of the disease or injury. YLL are calculated from the number of deaths at each age multiplied by a global standard life expectancy for each age. YLD for a particular cause in a particular time period are estimated as follows:

YLD = number of incident cases in that period × average duration of the disease × weight factor

The weight factor reflects the severity of the disease on a scale from 0 (perfect health) to 1 (death). The weights used for the GBD 2004 are listed in Annex Table A6 of Mathers et al. (11).

In the standard DALYs reported here and in recent *World Health Reports*, calculations of YLL and YLD used an additional 3% time discounting and non-uniform age weights that give less weight to years lived at young and older ages (6). Using discounting and age weights, a death in infancy corresponds to 33 DALYs, and deaths at ages 5–20 years to around 36 DALYs.

Nations Programme on HIV/AIDS (UNAIDS) *(12)*. Advances in methodology, applied to an increased range of country data, have resulted in substantial changes in estimates. The global prevalence of HIV infections for 2004 was revised from the 38 million estimated in 2006 down to 32 million – a reduction of 16%. Similarly, the estimated global deaths due to HIV/AIDS were revised from 2.7 million to 2.0 million for 2004. YLD estimates for HIV/AIDS were also revised to take into account coverage of antiretroviral drugs and associated increased survival times.

- Updated estimates for vaccine-preventable childhood diseases were prepared by the WHO Department of Immunization, Vaccines and Biologicals using estimates for vaccine coverage in 2004 prepared by WHO and UNICEF (United Nations Children's Fund).

- Revised incidence and mortality estimates for all forms of malaria, and for *Plasmodium falciparum* specifically, were based on estimates and analyses prepared by the Roll Back Malaria (RBM) Partnership, CHERG and the Malaria Epidemiology Reference Group (MERG), together with data from national case reports. Estimates for mortality for ages five years and above were revised using a transmission-intensity-based model, resulting in an increased proportion of such deaths (21% globally in 2004, compared to 10% in the GBD 2002 estimates).

- Estimates for tropical diseases, including dengue fever and Japanese encephalitis, were revised to take into account the latest WHO data on populations at risk, levels of endemicity, reported cases, treatment coverage and case fatality.

- Recent WHO updates of country-level prevalences of underweight, stunting and wasting in children (based on the new WHO growth standards), and anaemia prevalence, were used to update estimates for protein–energy malnutrition and iron-deficiency anaemia.

- Site-specific cancer incidence and mortality estimates were updated using revised estimates of site-specific survival probabilities for 2004, together with site-specific incidence distributions from the Globocan 2002 database of the International Agency for Research on Cancer (IARC).

- Diabetes incidence and prevalence estimates were updated to take into account a number of recently published population surveys that used oral glucose tolerance tests and WHO criteria to measure diabetes prevalence.

- Incidence and prevalence estimates for alcohol dependence and problem use were revised based on a new review restricted to studies conducted after 1990 that used one of three high-quality survey instruments. Disability weights for alcohol use disorders were revised downwards from 0.18 to 0.122–0.137 (depending on age and sex), based on analyses of the WHO Multi-country Survey Study.

- Prevalence estimates for low vision and blindness due to specific disease and injury causes were revised to take into account WHO analysis of regional distributions for causes of blindness. A recent WHO analysis of surveys measuring presenting vision loss was used to estimate YLD for an additional cause – "refractive errors". Previous GBD estimates for vision loss based on "best corrected" vision did not include correctable refractive errors.

- For the calculation of YLD for ischaemic heart disease, the model used to estimate the incidence and prevalence of angina pectoris was revised using recent analyses in national burden of disease studies. These revisions resulted in an increase in the estimated global prevalence of angina pectoris from 25 million in 2002 to 54 million in 2004, and a corresponding 78% increase in YLD and 7% increase in DALYs for ischaemic heart disease.

- Data from two recent national burden of disease studies were used to recalibrate the long-term case fatality rates for stroke survivors, resulting in a reduction in the estimated prevalence of stroke survivors from 50 million to 30 million, and a 30% reduction in YLD for cerebrovascular disease.

- Population estimates for 2004 were based on the latest revisions by the United Nations Population Division *(13)*.

Regional estimates for 2004

This report presents estimates for regional groupings of countries (including the six WHO regions) and income groupings, with the countries grouped as high, medium or low income, depending on their gross national income per capita in 2004. The classification most commonly used for low- and middle-income countries in the report is the six WHO regions, with the high-income countries separated off as a seventh group (see map). Regional and income groupings are defined in Annex C (Tables C1 and C2). Detailed tables of GBD 2004 results by cause, age, sex and region are available on the WHO web site[a] for a range of different regional groupings, including:

- the six WHO regions
- the 14 subregions of the WHO regions (used in previous WHO reports)
- the World Bank geographical regions used in the Disease Control Priorities Project
- the United Nations regions used for monitoring progress to the Millennium Development Goals.

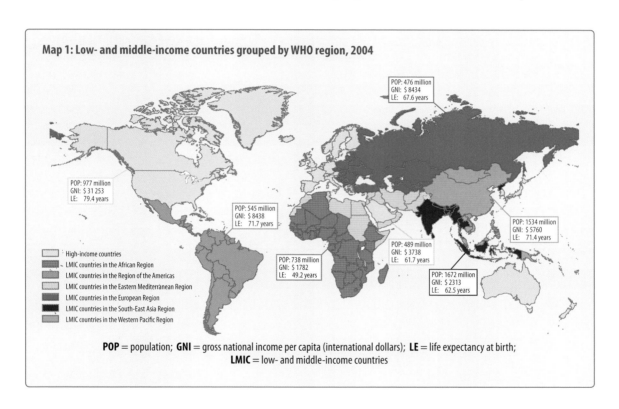

Map 1: Low- and middle-income countries grouped by WHO region, 2004

POP: 476 million
GNI: $ 8434
LE: 67.6 years

POP: 977 million
GNI: $ 31 253
LE: 79.4 years

POP: 545 million
GNI: $ 8438
LE: 71.7 years

POP: 1534 million
GNI: $ 5760
LE: 71.4 years

POP: 489 million
GNI: $ 3738
LE: 61.7 years

POP: 738 million
GNI: $ 1782
LE: 49.2 years

POP: 1672 million
GNI: $ 2313
LE: 62.5 years

- High-income countries
- LMIC countries in the African Region
- LMIC countries in the Region of the Americas
- LMIC countries in the Eastern Mediterranean Region
- LMIC countries in the European Region
- LMIC countries in the South-East Asia Region
- LMIC countries in the Western Pacific Region

POP = population; **GNI** = gross national income per capita (international dollars); **LE** = life expectancy at birth; **LMIC** = low- and middle-income countries

---

[a] http://www.who.int/evidence/bod

Part 2

Causes of death

1. Deaths in 2004: who and where? — 8
2. Deaths by broad cause groups — 8
3. Leading causes of death — 11
4. Cancer mortality — 12
5. Causes of death among children aged under five years — 14
6. Causes of death among adults aged 15–59 years — 17
7. Years of life lost: taking age at death into account — 21
8. Projected trends in global mortality: 2004–2030 — 22

1. Deaths in 2004: who and where?

Almost one in five of all deaths are of children aged under five years

In 2004, an estimated 58.8 million deaths occurred globally, of which 27.7 million were females and 31.1 million males. More than half of all deaths involved people 60 years and older, of whom 22 million were people aged 70 years and older, and 10.7 million were people aged 80 years and older. Almost one in five deaths in the world was of a child under the age of five years (Figure 1).

In Africa, death takes the young; in high-income countries, death takes the old

The distribution of deaths by age differs markedly between regions. In the African Region, 46% of all deaths were children aged under 15 years, whereas only 20% were people aged 60 years and over. In contrast, in the high-income countries, only 1% of deaths were children aged under 15 years, whereas 84% were people aged 60 years and older. There were also large differences in the Asia and Pacific regions. In the South-East Asia Region, 24% of deaths were of children aged under 15 years, compared with 8% in the low- and middle-income countries of the Western Pacific Region, where 67% of deaths were of people aged 60 years and older (Figure 2).

2. Deaths by broad cause groups

Out of every 10 deaths, 6 are due to noncommunicable conditions; 3 to communicable, reproductive or nutritional conditions; and 1 to injuries

The GBD study classifies disease and injury, causes of death and burden of disease into three broad cause groups:

- Group I – communicable, maternal, perinatal and nutritional conditions
- Group II – noncommunicable diseases
- Group III – injuries.

Group I causes are conditions that occur largely in poorer populations, and typically decline at a faster pace than all-cause mortality during the epidemiological transition (in which the pattern of mortality shifts from high death rates from Group I causes at younger ages to chronic diseases at older ages). Among both men and women, most deaths are due to noncommunicable conditions (Group II), and they account for about 6 out of 10 deaths globally. Communicable, maternal, perinatal and nutritional conditions are responsible for just under one third of deaths in both males and females. The largest difference between the sexes occurs for Group III, with injuries accounting for almost 1 in 8 male deaths and 1 in 14 female deaths (Figure 3).

Cardiovascular diseases are the leading cause of death

Figure 4 shows the distribution of deaths at all ages for 12 major cause groups (groups responsible for at least 2% of all deaths, plus maternal conditions). This illustrates the relative importance of the respective causes of death and of male–female differences. Cardiovascular diseases are the leading cause of death in the world, particularly among women; such diseases caused almost 32% of all deaths in women and 27% in men in 2004. Infectious and parasitic diseases are the next leading cause, followed by cancers, but these groupings show much smaller overall sex differentials. The largest differences between men and women are observed for intentional injuries (twice as high among men) and unintentional injuries. Maternal conditions account for 1.9% of all female deaths. The respiratory infections are treated by the GBD as a separate cause group from infectious and parasitic diseases, and are to be distinguished from respiratory diseases, which refers to noncommunicable respiratory diseases (refer to Annex Table C3).

1

2

3

4

Annex A

Annex B

Annex C

References

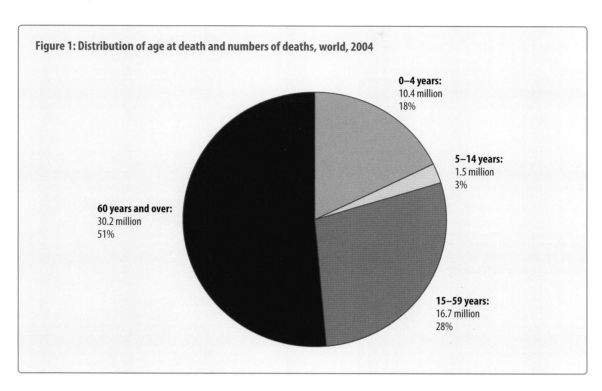

Figure 1: Distribution of age at death and numbers of deaths, world, 2004

0–4 years:
10.4 million
18%

5–14 years:
1.5 million
3%

60 years and over:
30.2 million
51%

15–59 years:
16.7 million
28%

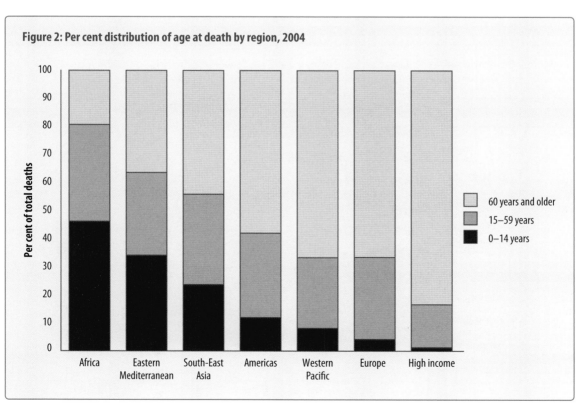

Figure 2: Per cent distribution of age at death by region, 2004

Per cent of total deaths

100
90
80
70
60
50
40
30
20
10
0

Africa | Eastern Mediterranean | South-East Asia | Americas | Western Pacific | Europe | High income

60 years and older
15–59 years
0–14 years

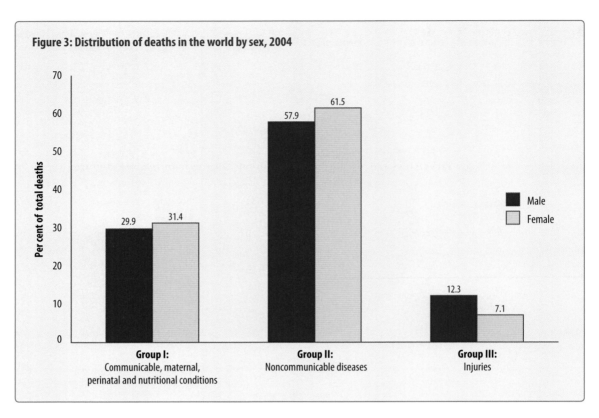

Figure 3: Distribution of deaths in the world by sex, 2004

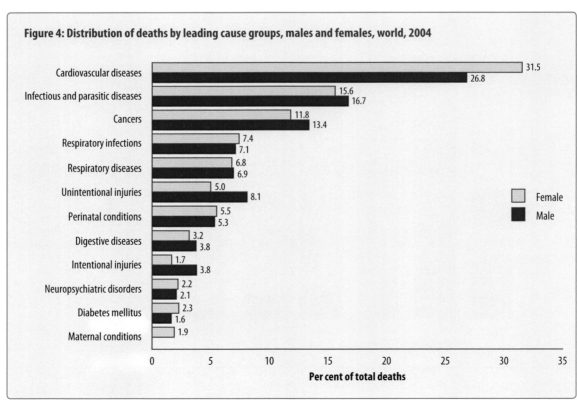

Figure 4: Distribution of deaths by leading cause groups, males and females, world, 2004

3. Leading causes of death

This report uses 136 categories for disease and injury causes. The 20 most frequent causes of death are shown in Table 1. Ischaemic heart disease and cerebrovascular disease are the leading causes of death, followed by lower respiratory infections (including pneumonia), chronic obstructive pulmonary disease and diarrhoeal diseases. HIV/AIDS and TB are the sixth and seventh most common causes of death

respectively, and together caused 3.5 million deaths in 2004.

As may be expected from the very different distributions of deaths by age and sex, there are major differences in the ranking of causes between high- and low-income countries (Table 2). In low-income countries, the dominant causes are infectious and parasitic diseases (including malaria), and perinatal conditions. In the high-income countries, 9 out of the 10 leading causes of death are noncommunicable conditions, including four types of cancer. In the middle-income countries, the 10 leading causes of death are again dominated by noncommunicable conditions; they also include road traffic accidents as the sixth most common cause.

Table 1: Leading causes of death, all ages, 2004

	Disease or injury	Deaths (millions)	Per cent of total deaths
1	Ischaemic heart disease	7.2	12.2
2	Cerebrovascular disease	5.7	9.7
3	Lower respiratory infections	4.2	7.1
4	COPD	3.0	5.1
5	Diarrhoeal diseases	2.2	3.7
6	HIV/AIDS	2.0	3.5
7	Tuberculosis	1.5	2.5
8	Trachea, bronchus, lung cancers	1.3	2.3
9	Road traffic accidents	1.3	2.2
10	Prematurity and low birth weight	1.2	2.0
11	Neonatal infections[a]	1.1	1.9
12	Diabetes mellitus	1.1	1.9
13	Hypertensive heart disease	1.0	1.7
14	Malaria	0.9	1.5
15	Birth asphyxia and birth trauma	0.9	1.5
16	Self-inflicted injuries[b]	0.8	1.4
17	Stomach cancer	0.8	1.4
18	Cirrhosis of the liver	0.8	1.3
19	Nephritis and nephrosis	0.7	1.3
20	Colon and rectum cancers	0.6	1.1

COPD, chronic obstructive pulmonary disease.

[a] This category also includes other non-infectious causes arising in the perinatal period, apart from prematurity, low birth weight, birth trauma and asphyxia. These non-infectious causes are responsible for about 20% of deaths shown in this category.
[b] Self-inflicted injuries resulting in death can also be referred to as suicides.

Table 2: Leading causes of death by income group, 2004

	Disease or injury	Deaths (millions)	Per cent of total deaths		Disease or injury	Deaths (millions)	Per cent of total deaths
	World				*Low-income countries*[a]		
1	Ischaemic heart disease	7.2	12.2	1	Lower respiratory infections	2.9	11.2
2	Cerebrovascular disease	5.7	9.7	2	Ischaemic heart disease	2.5	9.4
3	Lower respiratory infections	4.2	7.1	3	Diarrhoeal diseases	1.8	6.9
4	COPD	3.0	5.1	4	HIV/AIDS	1.5	5.7
5	Diarrhoeal diseases	2.2	3.7	5	Cerebrovascular disease	1.5	5.6
6	HIV/AIDS	2.0	3.5	6	COPD	0.9	3.6
7	Tuberculosis	1.5	2.5	7	Tuberculosis	0.9	3.5
8	Trachea, bronchus, lung cancers	1.3	2.3	8	Neonatal infections[b]	0.9	3.4
9	Road traffic accidents	1.3	2.2	9	Malaria	0.9	3.3
10	Prematurity and low birth weight	1.2	2.0	10	Prematurity and low birth weight	0.8	3.2
	Middle-income countries				*High-income countries*		
1	Cerebrovascular disease	3.5	14.2	1	Ischaemic heart disease	1.3	16.3
2	Ischaemic heart disease	3.4	13.9	2	Cerebrovascular disease	0.8	9.3
3	COPD	1.8	7.4	3	Trachea, bronchus, lung cancers	0.5	5.9
4	Lower respiratory infections	0.9	3.8	4	Lower respiratory infections	0.3	3.8
5	Trachea, bronchus, lung cancers	0.7	2.9	5	COPD	0.3	3.5
6	Road traffic accidents	0.7	2.8	6	Alzheimer and other dementias	0.3	3.4
7	Hypertensive heart disease	0.6	2.5	7	Colon and rectum cancers	0.3	3.3
8	Stomach cancer	0.5	2.2	8	Diabetes mellitus	0.2	2.8
9	Tuberculosis	0.5	2.2	9	Breast cancer	0.2	2.0
10	Diabetes mellitus	0.5	2.1	10	Stomach cancer	0.1	1.8

COPD, chronic obstructive pulmonary disease.

[a] Countries grouped by gross national income per capita – low income ($825 or less), high income ($10 066 or more). Note that these high-income groups differ slightly from those used in the Disease Control Priorities Project (see Annex C, Table C2).
[b] This category also includes other non-infectious causes arising in the perinatal period, which are responsible for about 20% of deaths shown in this category.

4. Cancer mortality

The relative importance of the most common cancers, in terms of numbers of deaths at all ages, is summarized in Table 3. Globally, lung cancers (including trachea and bronchus cancers) are the most common cause of death from cancer among men, and this is also the case in five of the seven regional groupings of countries. Lung cancers are the second most common cause of male cancer deaths in the low- and middle-income countries of

the Americas, and the fifth most common cause in the African Region. For males, stomach cancer mortality is second overall, being a leading cause in all regions, whereas liver cancer is the second leading cause of cancer death in the African Region. Colon and rectum cancers are the fourth leading cause and oesophagus cancer the fifth leading cause globally. Prostate cancer is sixth globally, but is the leading cause of cancer deaths in the African Region and in the low- and middle-income countries of the Region of the Americas. In the South-East Asia Region, cancers of the mouth and oropharynx are the second leading cause of cancer deaths.

For women, 15 cancers are ranked for each of the regions. The most common cancer at the global level is breast cancer, followed by cancers of the trachea, bronchus and lung, and stomach cancer. Breast cancer is the leading cause in four of the seven regions, second in two regions and fifth in the Western Pacific Region. Stomach cancer is the main cause of cancer death among women in that Region, followed by lung cancer and liver cancer. Cervix uteri cancer is the number one cause of cancer deaths in the South-East Asia Region and the African Region. Other cancers of the female reproductive system are the eighth (ovary) and thirteenth (corpus uteri) leading causes of cancer deaths globally.

Table 3: Ranking of most common cancers among men and women according to the number of deaths, by cancer site and region, 2004

	World	High income	Africa	Americas	Eastern Mediterranean	Europe	South-East Asia	Western Pacific
Men								
Trachea, bronchus, lung cancers	1	1	5	2	1	1	1	1
Stomach cancer	2	4	6	3	4	2	5	2
Liver cancer	3	5	2	10	10	10	6	3
Colon and rectum cancers	4	2	8	4	8	3	7	5
Oesophagus cancer	5	8	3	8	6	9	3	4
Prostate cancer	6	3	1	1	9	4	8	11
Mouth and oropharynx cancers	7	11	7	7	5	5	2	7
Lymphomas and multiple myeloma	8	6	4	5	3	11	4	9
Leukaemia	9	10	10	6	7	8	9	6
Bladder cancer	10	9	9	11	2	6	10	10
Pancreas cancer	11	7	11	9	11	7	11	8
Melanoma and other skin cancers	12	12	12	12	12	12	12	12
Women								
Breast cancer	1	1	2	1	1	1	2	5
Trachea, bronchus, lung cancers	2	2	11	5	10	4	5	2
Stomach cancer	3	6	5	3	5	3	8	1
Colon and rectum cancers	4	3	7	4	8	2	6	6
Cervix uteri cancer	5	10	1	2	6	5	1	7
Liver cancer	6	8	3	10	12	11	11	3
Oesophagus cancer	7	13	6	12	2	12	4	4
Ovary cancer	8	7	8	8	9	6	7	10
Lymphomas and multiple myeloma	9	5	4	6	4	10	9	12
Pancreas cancer	10	4	12	7	14	7	12	9
Leukaemia	11	9	10	9	3	8	10	8
Mouth and oropharynx cancers	12	15	9	14	7	15	3	11
Corpus uteri cancer	13	11	15	11	13	9	14	14
Bladder cancer	14	12	13	13	11	14	13	13
Melanoma and other skin cancers	15	14	14	15	15	13	15	15

5. Causes of death among children aged under five years

Six causes of death account for 73% of the 10.4 million deaths among children under the age of five years worldwide (Figure 5):

- acute respiratory infections, mainly pneumonia (17%)
- diarrhoeal diseases (17%)
- prematurity and low birth weight (11%)
- neonatal infections such as sepsis (9%)

- birth asphyxia and trauma (8%)
- malaria (7%).

The four communicable disease categories above account for one half (50%) of all child deaths. Under-nutrition is an underlying cause in an estimated 30% of all deaths among children under five (14). In this analysis, "undernutrition" refers to childhood malnutrition resulting in stunting and wasting, together with micronutrient deficiencies (iron, iodine, vitamin A and zinc). If the effects of suboptimal breast-feeding are also included, an estimated 35% of child deaths are due to undernutrition.

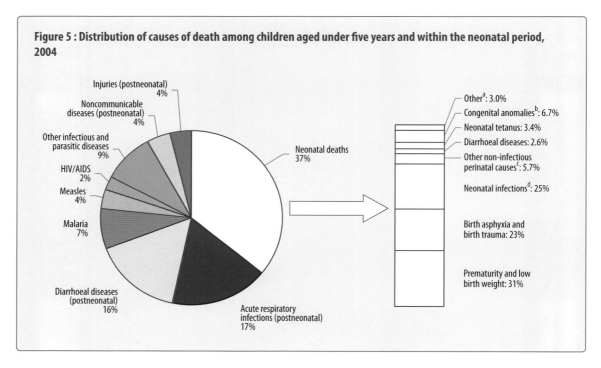

Figure 5 : Distribution of causes of death among children aged under five years and within the neonatal period, 2004

[a] Includes other non-communicable diseases (1%) and injuries (0.3%).
[b] ICD-10 codes Q00-Q99. Another 1.2% of neonatal deaths are due to genetic conditions classified elsewhere.
[c] Other non-infectious causes arising in the perinatal period.
[d] Includes all neonatal infections except diarrhoeal diseases and neonatal tetanus.

Deaths in the neonatal period (0–27 days) account for more than one third of all deaths in children. Among neonatal deaths, three main causes account for 80% of all neonatal deaths: prematurity and low birth weight (31%), neonatal infections (mainly sepsis and pneumonia and excluding diarrhoeal diseases) (26%) and birth asphyxia and birth trauma (23%).

Several analyses have shown that the decline in mortality in children aged under five years is falling behind the Millennium Development Goal 4 of reducing child mortality by two thirds from 1990 levels (15, 16). For some causes – notably for measles and diarrhoeal diseases – there is evidence of a substantial decline. The GBD analysis by cause of death also shows that renewed efforts will be needed to prevent and control pneumonia and diarrhoea, and to address the underlying cause of undernutrition

in all WHO regions (Figure 6). In the WHO African Region, increased efforts to prevent and control malaria are essential. Deaths in the neonatal period must also be addressed in all regions to achieve the Millennium Development Goal 4. In general, neonatal mortality becomes more important as mortality levels in children aged under five years decline. Cost-effective interventions are available for all major causes of death (17).

Deaths in the neonatal period – including prematurity and low birth weight, birth asphyxia and birth trauma, and other perinatal conditions based on the GBD cause list – represent between 42% and 54% of child deaths in all regions apart from the African Region, where the proportion of neonatal deaths (25%) is depressed by high numbers of postneonatal deaths, particularly those due to malaria (Figure 6).

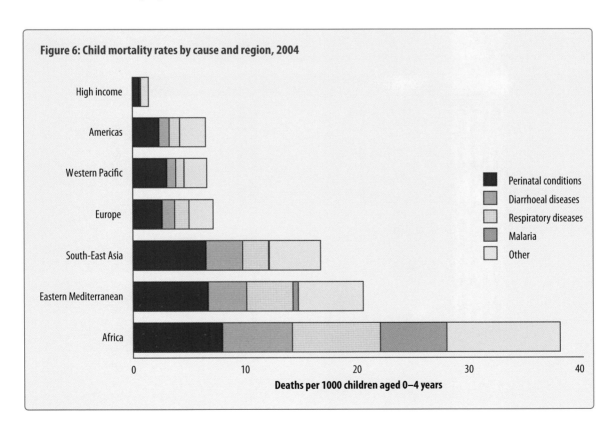

Figure 6: Child mortality rates by cause and region, 2004

Legend:
- Perinatal conditions
- Diarrhoeal diseases
- Respiratory diseases
- Malaria
- Other

Regions (top to bottom): High income, Americas, Western Pacific, Europe, South-East Asia, Eastern Mediterranean, Africa

Deaths per 1000 children aged 0–4 years

Among the 10.4 million deaths in children aged under five years worldwide, 4.7 million (45%) occur in the African Region, and an additional 3.1 million (30%) occur in the South-East Asia Region. The death rate per 1000 children aged 0–4 years in the African Region is almost double that of the region with the next highest rate, the Eastern Mediterranean, and more than double that of any other region (**Figure 6**). The two leading communicable disease killers in all regions are diarrhoeal diseases and respiratory infections. Deaths directly attributable to malaria occur almost entirely in the African Region, representing 16% of all under-five deaths in that region.

HIV/AIDS and measles are important causes of death summarized in the "other" category. Globally, estimates suggest that 2.5% of all child deaths are associated with HIV infection. In the African Region, however – where more than 9 out of 10 of the total global number of child deaths due to HIV/AIDS in 2004 occurred – 5% of all child deaths are associated with HIV. Measles mortality, which has declined considerably in recent years, is estimated to be responsible for 4% of deaths among children aged under five years worldwide and also 4% of such deaths in the African Region.

More than 7 out of every 10 child deaths are in Africa and South-East Asia

Further analyses of under-five deaths by cause show a burden distribution that is heavily skewed toward Africa (**Table 4**). More than 9 out of 10 child deaths directly attributable to malaria, 9 out of 10 child deaths due to HIV/AIDS, 4 out of 10 child deaths due to diarrhoeal diseases and 5 out of 10 child deaths due to pneumonia occur in the WHO African Region.

Table 4: Distribution of child deaths for selected causes by selected WHO region, 2004

    = about 10% of the world's child deaths due to a specific cause;   = about 5%.

6. Causes of death among adults aged 15–59 years

The ranking of regions by mortality rates among adults aged 15–59 years differs markedly from the rankings by child mortality. The European Region (low- and middle-income countries) is the WHO region with the second highest mortality level for adults aged 15–59 years; the mortality level is lower than for the African Region but higher than that for the South-East Asia Region (Figure 7). The Eastern Mediterranean Region drops to fourth place for this age group.

The difference between the high-income countries and other regions is less pronounced for adult mortality than for child mortality, due in part to the population structure – high-income countries have a higher proportion of people in the 15–59 years age group, and a higher proportion of people at the older end of this range, than lower income countries. These rankings are overshadowed by adult mortality in the African Region, which is 40% higher than for the next highest mortality region, and nearly four times higher than for high-income countries.

The mortality rate due to noncommunicable diseases is highest in Europe, where nearly two thirds of all deaths at ages 15–59 years for low- and middle-income countries are associated with cardiovascular diseases, cancers and other noncommunicable diseases. Mortality rates due to noncommunicable diseases are second highest in the African Region, followed by the Eastern Mediterranean and South-East Asia regions, and lowest in the high-income countries. Injury mortality ranges from 0.5 (high-income countries) to 1.5 (European Region) per 1000 adults aged 15–59 years. The proportion of deaths in this age group due to injuries ranges from 22% (high-income countries) to 29% (the Americas) of all deaths at ages 15–59, except in Africa, where it is 13%.

Group I causes of death – which include infectious and parasitic diseases, and maternal and nutritional conditions – account for more than one fifth of all deaths in adults aged 15–59 years in two regions: South-East Asia (29%) and Africa (62%). This includes 35% of the adult deaths due to HIV/

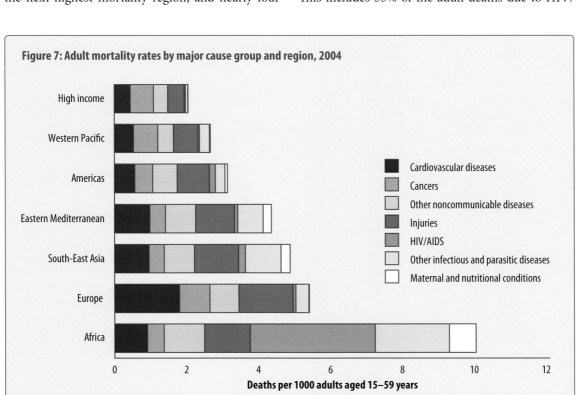

Figure 7: Adult mortality rates by major cause group and region, 2004

Legend:
- Cardiovascular diseases
- Cancers
- Other noncommunicable diseases
- Injuries
- HIV/AIDS
- Other infectious and parasitic diseases
- Maternal and nutritional conditions

Regions (top to bottom): High income, Western Pacific, Americas, Eastern Mediterranean, South-East Asia, Europe, Africa

x-axis: 0, 2, 4, 6, 8, 10, 12
Deaths per 1000 adults aged 15–59 years

AIDS in Africa. In fact, the mortality rate among adults due to HIV/AIDS alone in Africa is higher than mortality at 15–59 years due to all causes in three other regions: high-income countries, the Americas and the Western Pacific Region.

Mortality is high among adult men in Eastern Europe

There are major differences in adult mortality by sex and major cause grouping (Figure 8). Overall, mortality is highest among men and women in the African Region, mainly because of high mortality due to Group I causes. Men in the European Region (excluding high-income countries) had the second highest mortality rates at ages 15–59 years, considerably higher than mortality in South-East Asia, the Eastern Mediterranean and the Americas. In all regions, men had higher mortality rates than women. The largest differences were observed in Europe (male mortality 2.7 times as high as the female mortality rate), the Americas (2.0 times as high) and high-income countries (1.9 times as high).

HIV/AIDS is the main cause of adult mortality in Africa

In the African Region, mortality among men is slightly higher than among women, due entirely to higher mortality through injuries. Women have higher mortality due to Group I causes. Figure 9 presents a more detailed look at the mortality rates in the African Region, by sex, for major cause groupings. At ages 15–59 years, women have much higher mortality than men for HIV/AIDS, which causes more than half of all deaths in Group I and 40% of all female deaths. Maternal conditions were associated with 14% of all deaths.

In the South-East Asia Region, differences between male and female mortality were relatively small, with similar levels of mortality due to Group I causes, and somewhat higher mortality for men due to Group II and III causes. The Eastern Mediterranean Region presents a different picture, with much higher mortality among men, due almost entirely to Group III causes; that is, injuries. Figure 10 shows the distribution of male deaths due to Group III causes

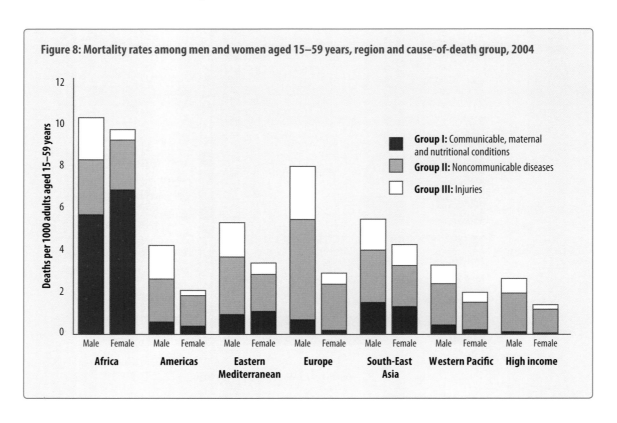

Figure 8: Mortality rates among men and women aged 15–59 years, region and cause-of-death group, 2004

in the Eastern Mediterranean. War and violence caused almost 40% of these deaths, followed by road traffic accidents (31%).

Injuries and cardiovascular diseases are leading causes of death among men in Europe

Figure 11 illustrates the high levels of mortality among men in the low- and middle-income countries of the European Region. The main reason is the high mortality rates due to cardiovascular diseases and injuries, each associated with a mortality rate exceeding 2.5 per 1000 adults aged 15–59 years, and together

being responsible for almost two thirds of overall male mortality in this age group.

Injuries are the main cause of death for adult men in Latin America and the Caribbean

The most striking data from the low- and middle-income countries of the Americas relate to injury mortality, which is about 1.6 per 1000 men aged 15–59 years, making it the leading cause group (Figure 12). Intentional injuries account for 57% of adult mortality due to injuries, while motor vehicle accidents account for 25% of adult mortality due to injuries.

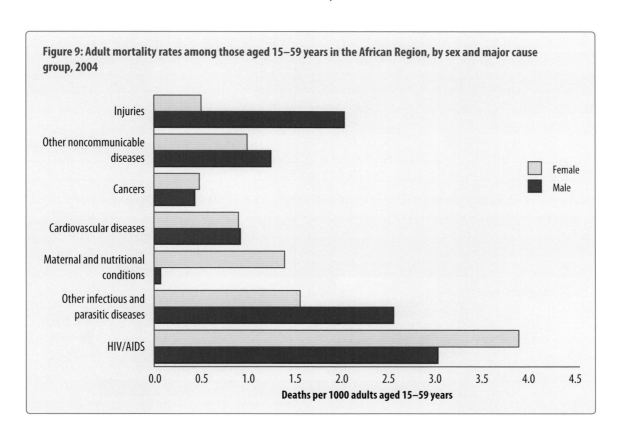

Figure 9: Adult mortality rates among those aged 15–59 years in the African Region, by sex and major cause group, 2004

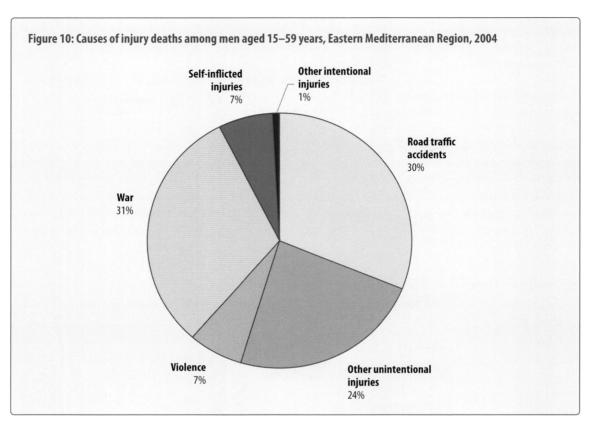

Figure 10: Causes of injury deaths among men aged 15–59 years, Eastern Mediterranean Region, 2004

Self-inflicted injuries 7%

Other intentional injuries 1%

Road traffic accidents 30%

War 31%

Violence 7%

Other unintentional injuries 24%

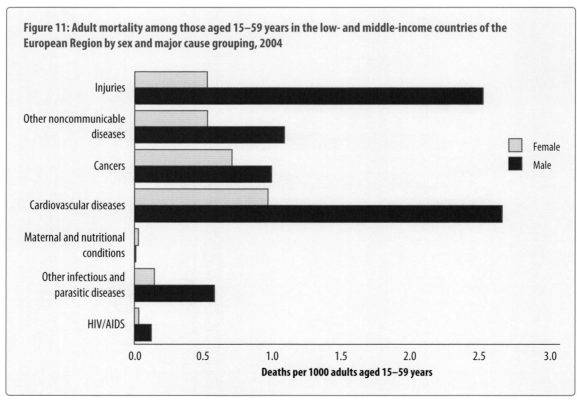

Figure 11: Adult mortality among those aged 15–59 years in the low- and middle-income countries of the European Region by sex and major cause grouping, 2004

Injuries

Other noncommunicable diseases

Cancers

Cardiovascular diseases

Maternal and nutritional conditions

Other infectious and parasitic diseases

HIV/AIDS

□ Female
■ Male

0.0   0.5   1.0   1.5   2.0   2.5   3.0

Deaths per 1000 adults aged 15–59 years

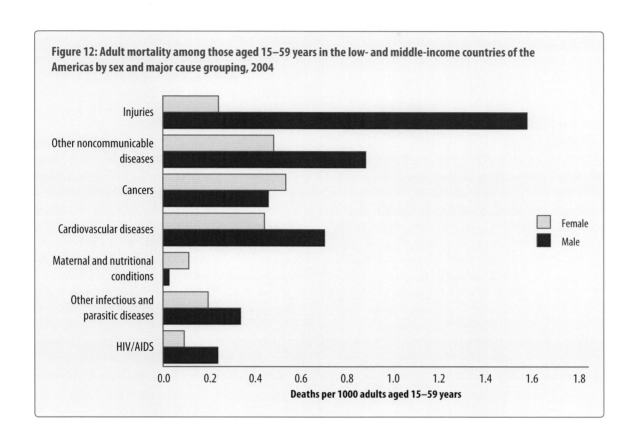

Figure 12: Adult mortality among those aged 15–59 years in the low- and middle-income countries of the Americas by sex and major cause grouping, 2004

1

2

3

4

Annex A

Annex B

Annex C

References

7. Years of life lost: taking age at death into account

The years of life lost (YLL) measure is a measure of premature mortality that takes into account both the frequency of deaths and the age at which death occurs, and is an important input in the calculation of the DALYs for a disease or health condition (see Box 1, page 3). YLL are calculated from the number of deaths at each age multiplied by a global standard life expectancy for the age at which death occurs.

Taking into account the age at death causes major shifts in the proportion of deaths occurring in each of the WHO Regions (Figure 13). Based on the distribution of the world's 58.8 million deaths in 2004, the South-East Asia Region has the highest proportion of deaths (26%), followed by the African Region (19%), the Western Pacific Region (18%) and high-income countries (14%). Based on the YLL, however, the African Region accounts for 32% of all YLL, followed by South-East Asia (30%), the Western Pacific

(13%) and the Eastern Mediterranean (9%) regions. Using the YLL increases the relative importance of Africa and South-East Asia in the global picture, because people from these regions die at a relatively young age. The relative importance of the Eastern Mediterranean and the Americas change little, and the remaining three regions decline in relative importance.

Noncommunicable diseases become less important

Figure 14 presents similar data on the proportional distribution of deaths and YLL for the leading causes of death. Taking the age at death into account causes major shifts in the relative importance of the major causes. The two most common causes of death – ischaemic heart disease (12.2% of all deaths) and cerebrovascular conditions (9.7% of all deaths) – are responsible for only 5.8% and 4.2% of YLL, respectively. The main causes of YLL are perinatal conditions (prematurity and low birth weight, birth asphyxia and birth trauma, and other perinatal conditions), lower respiratory infections, diarrhoeal diseases and HIV/AIDS.

8. Projected trends in global mortality: 2004–2030

WHO has previously published projections of mortality from 2002 to 2030 based on the GBD 2002 estimates and using projection methods similar to those used in the original GBD 1990 study (18, 19). These projections have been updated (Figure 15) using the GBD 2004 estimates as a starting-point, together with updated projections of HIV deaths prepared by UNAIDS and WHO (20), and updated forecasts of economic growth by region published by the World Bank (21) (see Annex B7 for further information).

Large declines in mortality between 2004 and 2030 are projected for all of the principal communicable, maternal, perinatal and nutritional causes,

including HIV/AIDS, TB and malaria. Global HIV/AIDS deaths are projected to rise from 2.2 million in 2008 to a maximum of 2.4 million in 2012, and then to decline to 1.2 million in 2030, under a baseline scenario that assumes that coverage with antiretroviral drugs continues to rise at current rates.

Ageing of populations in low- and middle-income countries will result in significantly increasing total deaths due to most noncommunicable diseases over the next 25 years. Global cancer deaths are projected to increase from 7.4 million in 2004 to 11.8 million in 2030, and global cardiovascular deaths from 17.1 million in 2004 to 23.4 million in 2030. Overall, noncommunicable conditions are projected to account for just over three quarters of all deaths in 2030.

The projected 28% increase in global deaths due to injury between 2004 and 2030 is predominantly due to the increasing numbers of road traffic accident deaths, and increases in population numbers are projected to more than offset small declines in age-specific death rates for other causes of injury.

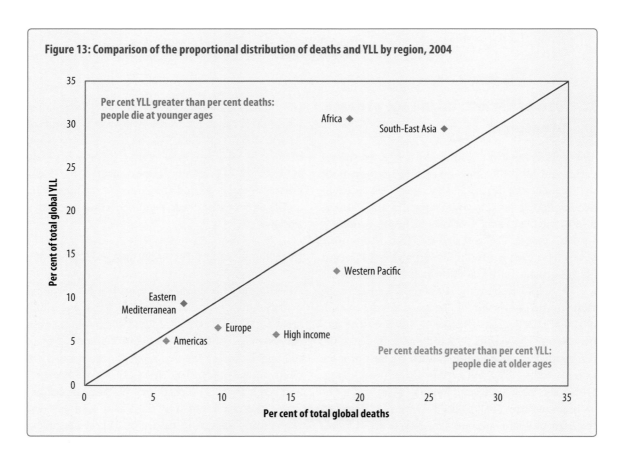

Figure 13: Comparison of the proportional distribution of deaths and YLL by region, 2004

Road traffic accident deaths are projected to increase from 1.3 million in 2004 to 2.4 million in 2030, primarily due to the increased motor vehicle ownership and use associated with economic growth in low- and middle-income countries.

Leading causes of death in 2030

The four leading causes of death globally in 2030 are projected to be ischaemic heart disease, cerebrovascular disease (stroke), chronic obstructive pulmonary disease and lower respiratory infections (mainly pneumonia). Total tobacco-attributable deaths are projected to rise from 5.4 million in 2004 to 8.3 million in 2030, at which point they will represent almost 10% of all deaths globally.

Apart from lower respiratory infections, the 10 main causes of death in 2004 included three other communicable diseases: diarrhoeal diseases, HIV/AIDS and TB. HIV/AIDS deaths are projected to decrease by 2030, but will remain the tenth leading cause of death globally. Deaths due to other communicable diseases are projected to decline at a faster rate: TB will drop to the twentieth leading cause and diarrhoeal diseases to twenty-third. Population ageing will result in significant increases in the rankings for most noncommunicable diseases, particularly cancers. Increasing levels of tobacco smoking in many middle- and low-income countries will contribute to increased deaths from cardiovascular disease, chronic obstructive pulmonary disease and some cancers. Road traffic accidents are projected to rise from the ninth leading cause of death globally in 2004 to the fifth in 2030.

Figure 16 shows projected trends in total numbers of global deaths for selected causes of death. This figure clearly illustrates the projected increases in numbers of deaths for important noncommunicable causes, and the projected declines for leading Group I causes.

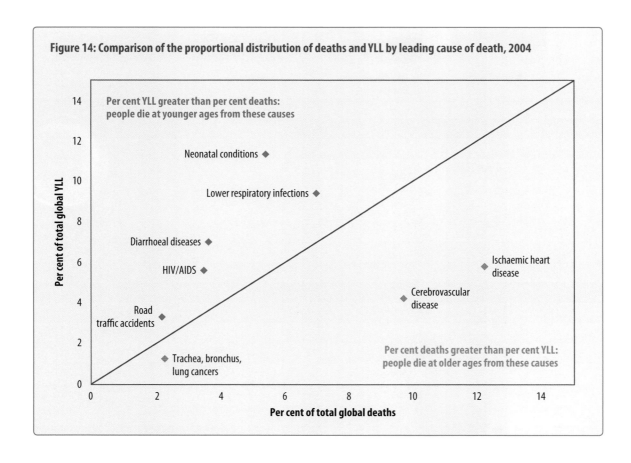

Figure 14: Comparison of the proportional distribution of deaths and YLL by leading cause of death, 2004

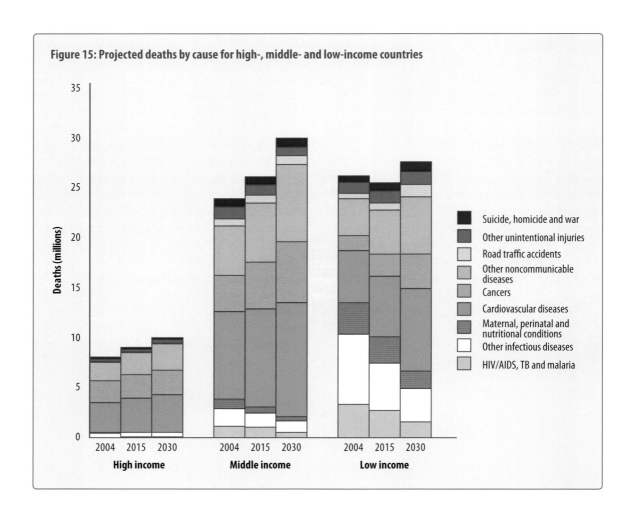

Figure 15: Projected deaths by cause for high-, middle- and low-income countries

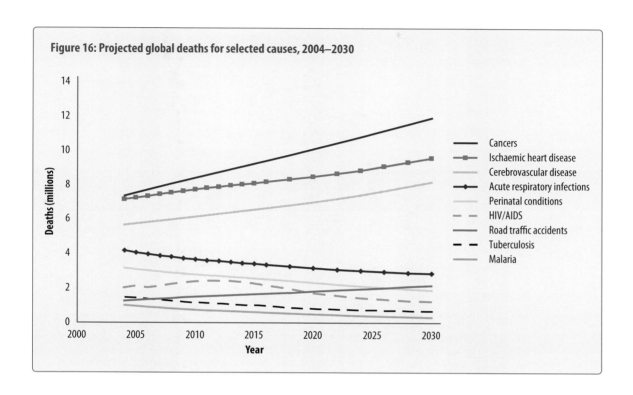

Figure 16: Projected global deaths for selected causes, 2004–2030

Legend:
- Cancers
- Ischaemic heart disease
- Cerebrovascular disease
- Acute respiratory infections
- Perinatal conditions
- HIV/AIDS
- Road traffic accidents
- Tuberculosis
- Malaria

Decomposition of projected changes in cause-specific deaths

Projected changes in numbers of deaths may be due to changes in age-specific disease and injury death rates, or due to demographic changes that alter the size and age composition of the population, or both. Death rates are strongly age dependent for most causes, so changes in the age structure of a population may result in substantial changes in the number of deaths, even when the age-specific rates remain unchanged.

The relative impact of demographic and epidemiological change on the projected numbers of deaths by cause is shown in Figure 17. The change in the projected numbers of deaths globally from 2004 to 2030 can be divided into three components. The first is *population growth*, which shows the expected increase in deaths due to the increase in the total size of the global population, assuming there are no changes in age distribution. The second is *population ageing*, which shows the additional increase in deaths resulting from the projected changes in the age distribution of the population from 2004 to 2030. Both the population-related components are

calculated assuming that the age- and sex-specific death rates for causes remain at 2004 levels. The final component, *epidemiological change*, shows the increase or decrease in numbers of deaths occurring in the 2030 population due to the projected change from 2004 to 2030 in the age- and sex-specific death rates for each cause.

For most Group I causes, the projected reduction in global deaths from 2004 to 2030 is due mostly to epidemiological change, offset to some extent by population growth. Population ageing has little effect. For noncommunicable diseases, demographic changes in all regions will tend to increase total deaths substantially, even though age- and sex-specific death rates are projected to decline for most causes, other than for lung cancer. The impact of population ageing is generally much more important than that of population growth. For injuries, demographic change also dominates the epidemiological change. The total epidemiological change for injuries is small in most regions, because the projected increase in road traffic fatalities is offset by projected decreases in death rates for other unintentional injuries.

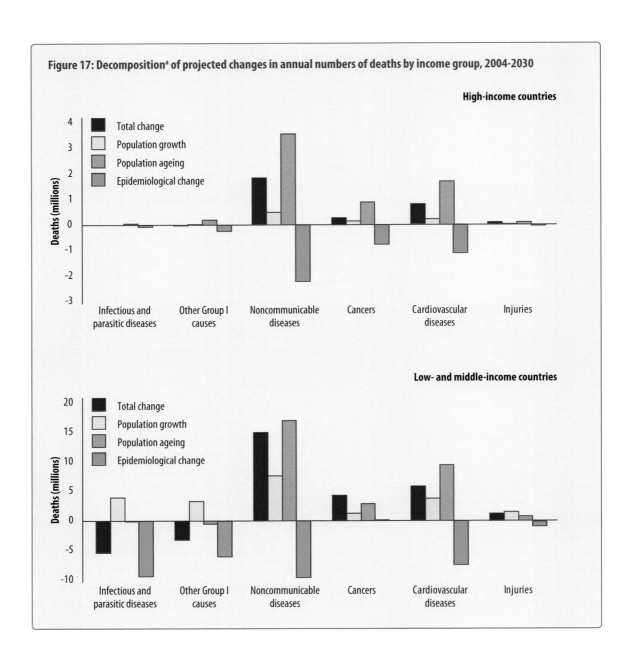

Figure 17: Decomposition[a] of projected changes in annual numbers of deaths by income group, 2004-2030

a The dark blue bars show the total projected change in the annual numbers of deaths (in millions) from 2004 to 2030 for a given cause group. The dark orange bars show the change in the annual numbers of deaths that would have occurred due to epidemiological change only (changes in age- and sex-specific death rates) if the population size and age structure had remained unchanged. The light orange bars show the change that would have occurred due to population growth only, if the age structure had remained unchanged, and age- and sex-specific death rates had also remained unchanged. The purple bars show the change that would have occurred due to changes in the age distribution of the population only, if the size of the population had remained constant, and the age- and sex-specific death rates also remained unchanged.

Part 3

Disease incidence, prevalence and disability

9.	How many people become sick each year?	28
10.	Cancer incidence by site and region	29
11.	How many people are sick at any given time?	31
12.	Prevalence of moderate and severe disability	31
13.	Leading causes of years lost due to disability in 2004	36

9. How many people become sick each year?

The "incidence" of a condition is the number of new cases in a period of time – usually one year (Table 5). For most conditions in this table, the figure given is the number of individuals who developed the illness or problem in 2004. However, for some conditions, such as diarrhoeal disease or malaria, it is common for individuals to be infected repeatedly and have several episodes. For such conditions, the number given in the table is the number of disease episodes, rather than the number of individuals affected.

It is important to remember that the incidence of a disease or condition measures how many people are affected by it for the first time over a period of

Table 5: Incidence (millions) of selected conditions by WHO region, 2004

	World	Africa	The Americas	Eastern Mediter-ranean	Europe	South-East Asia	Western Pacific
Tuberculosis[a]	7.8	1.4	0.4	0.6	0.6	2.8	2.1
HIV infection[a]	2.8	1.9	0.2	0.1	0.2	0.2	0.1
Diarrhoeal disease[b]	4 620.4	912.9	543.1	424.9	207.1	1 276.5	1 255.9
Pertussis[b]	18.4	5.2	1.2	1.6	0.7	7.5	2.1
Measles[a]	27.1	5.3	0.0[e]	1.0	0.2	17.4	3.3
Tetanus[a]	0.3	0.1	0.0	0.1	0.0	0.1	0.0
Meningitis[b]	0.7	0.3	0.1	0.1	0.0	0.2	0.1
Malaria[b]	241.3	203.9	2.9	8.6	0.0	23.3	2.7
Dengue[b]	9.0	0.1	1.4	0.5	0.0	4.6	2.3
Lower respiratory infections[b]	429.2	131.3	45.4	52.7	19.0	134.6	46.2
Complications of pregnancy:							
– maternal haemorrhage	12.0	3.0	1.2	1.6	0.7	4.0	1.4
– maternal sepsis	5.2	1.2	0.6	0.7	0.3	1.7	0.6
– hypertensive disorders	8.4	2.1	0.8	1.2	0.5	2.8	1.1
– obstructed labour	4.0	1.1	0.1	0.5	0.0	1.9	0.4
– unsafe abortion	20.4	4.8	4.0	2.9	0.5	7.4	0.8
Malignant neoplasms – all sites	11.4	0.7	2.3	0.5	3.1	1.7	3.2
Congestive heart failure[c]	5.7	0.5	0.8	0.4	1.3	1.4	1.3
Stroke, first-ever	9.0	0.7	0.9	0.4	2.0	1.8	3.3
Injuries[d] due to:							
– road traffic accidents	24.3	4.7	2.2	2.8	1.8	8.6	4.1
– falls	37.3	2.8	3.3	3.6	5.3	14.4	8.0
– fires	10.9	1.7	0.3	1.5	0.8	5.9	0.7
– violence	17.2	4.5	5.9	2.0	1.6	2.2	1.0

[a] New cases.
[b] Episodes of illness.
[c] Incidence of congestive heart failure due to rheumatic heart disease, hypertensive heart disease, ischaemic heart disease or inflammatory heart diseases.
[d] Incidence of injuries severe enough to require medical attention.
[e] An entry of 0.0 in the table refers to an incidence of less than 0.05 million (less than 50 000).

time (mostly one year). Incidence does not measure how many people have a disease at any given moment (this is "prevalence") or how badly their lives are affected. A health problem or disease can have a relatively low incidence but cause death or disability, and will therefore result in a high burden of disease or many life years lost. Conversely, some common illnesses may cause a much smaller burden of disease or fewer life years lost. Data on the contribution of various conditions and diseases to the burden of disease in a community are given in later sections.

Diarrhoeal disease is the most common cause of illness

Of the diseases listed in Table 5, diarrhoeal disease affects far more individuals than any other illness, even in regions that include high-income countries. Pneumonia and other lower respiratory tract infections are the second most common cause of illness globally, and in all regions except Africa. Other common illnesses – such as upper respiratory tract infections (including the common cold) and allergic rhinitis (hay fever) – have not been included in Table 5.

10. Cancer incidence by site and region

11.4 million people were diagnosed with cancer in 2004

More cancers occur in high-income countries than in low- and middle-income countries. Cervix cancer is the only type of cancer more common in the African and South-East Asia regions than in high-income countries. In part, this is due to the age of the populations in different regions, because most cancers affect older adults; also, some cancers, such as prostate cancer, are much more common in older men than in younger men. Another factor contributing to the distribution of a type of cancer is the number of people exposed to causes, such as cigarette smoking in the case of lung cancer, and hepatitis B virus in the case of liver cancer. Globally, lung cancer is the most common cancer (Table 6), followed

by breast cancer, then colon and rectum cancer, and stomach cancer. Lung cancer is also the leading cancer in the Western Pacific Region, but is less common than colon and rectum cancers or breast cancers in most other regions. Cervix cancer is the cancer with the highest incidence in the African and South-East Asia regions, even though it occurs only in women.

Variations across regions in the risk of cancer are best shown using age-standardized incidence rates that apply the estimated age- and sex-specific incidence rates for cancers in each region to the WHO World Standard Population (22). This estimates how many cases of cancer would occur in that population if it experienced the cancer incidence rates of a given region (Figure 18).

Table 6 : Cancer incidence (thousands) by site, by WHO region, 2004

	World	Africa	The Americas	Eastern Mediter-ranean	Europe	South-East Asia	Western Pacific
Lung cancer	1 448	27	264	34	401	164	558
Stomach cancer	933	38	89	25	182	78	521
Colon and rectum cancers	1 080	32	217	23	409	106	293
Liver cancer	632	65	38	13	67	64	386
Cervix cancer	489	95	95	15	81	180	73
Breast cancer	1 100	72	310	54	326	154	184
Prostate cancer	605	77	236	13	180	45	54
Lymphomas and multiple myeloma	479	56	102	39	113	91	79
Leukaemia	375	20	68	28	86	72	101
Other cancers	5 187	234	874	226	1 214	773	919
All sites (excluding non-melanoma skin cancer)	11 474	716	2 294	470	3 058	1 726	3 166

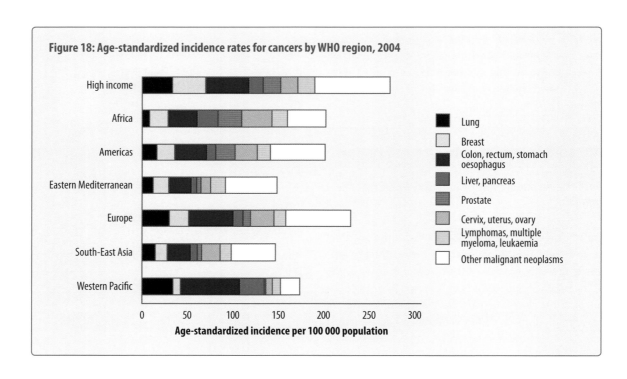

Figure 18: Age-standardized incidence rates for cancers by WHO region, 2004

11. How many people are sick at any given time?

The prevalence of an illness or condition is the number of individuals who have the condition at any moment. In some cases, such as epilepsy or migraine, individuals will not have symptoms most of the time, but still have the condition. The effects of the illness and the loss of health will vary from one individual to another. The result may be serious impairments and disability affecting a person's ability to work or take part in family and community activities, or only mild impairments or disability. Prevalence data therefore do not capture the burden of disease experienced by individuals in terms of lost health.

Anaemia, hearing loss and migraine are the three most prevalent conditions

The conditions that affect the largest number of individuals at any given moment are not dramatic, and are thus easily overlooked and underestimated (Table 7). Worldwide, at any given moment, more individuals have iron-deficiency anaemia than any other health problem. Even in high-income countries, iron deficiency anaemia is common. Other very common conditions, with varying levels of severity, include asthma, arthritis, vision and hearing problems, migraine, major depressive episodes and intestinal worms.

12. Prevalence of moderate and severe disability

The previous sections presented estimates of numbers of new and current cases for various diseases and injuries. A disease or injury may have multiple disabling effects of various levels of severity, and cause varying degrees of health problems. The GBD links average loss of health to disease and injury causes through the disability weights (see Box 1, page 3). The term *disability* has a number of different meanings and, in particular, is not seen by some

as a synonym or proxy for "loss of health". However, the GBD uses the term *disability* to refer to *loss of health*, where health is conceptualized in terms of functioning capacity in a set of health domains such as mobility, cognition, hearing and vision.

The original GBD study established severity weights for approximately 500 disabling sequelae of diseases and injury, in a formal study involving health workers from all regions of the world. These weights were then grouped into seven classes, where class I has a weight between 0 and 0.02, and class VII a weight between 0.7 and 1 (Table 8). Participants in the study estimated distributions across the seven classes for each sequela. Distributions across disability classes were estimated separately for treated and untreated cases where relevant; distributions could also vary by age group and sex.

These distributions were applied to prevalence estimates from the GBD 2004 study to estimate the prevalence of disability by severity class in 2004. Results are presented here for the prevalence of:
- "severe" disability, defined as severity classes VI and VII (the equivalent of having blindness, Down syndrome, quadriplegia, severe depression or active psychosis) – see Table 8;
- "moderate and severe" disability, defined as severity classes III and greater (the equivalent of having angina, arthritis, low vision or alcohol dependence).

Prevalence estimates were restricted to sequelae lasting, on average, six months or more.

The GBD prevalence estimates cannot be added easily, because they were calculated without regard for multiple pathologies or comorbidities; thus, a given individual would be counted more than once if they had more than one diagnosis. Overall disability prevalence estimates presented here were adjusted for comorbidity using a method that takes account of the increased probability of having certain pairs of conditions (23). Limited self-reported data were available on comorbidity levels in populations, so the adjusted disability prevalences presented here have quite high levels of uncertainty.

Table 7: Prevalence (millions) of selected conditions by WHO region, 2004

	World	Africa	The Americas	Eastern Mediter-ranean	Europe	South-East Asia	Western Pacific
Tuberculosis	13.9	3.0	0.5	1.1	0.6	5.0	3.8
HIV infection	31.4	21.7	2.8	0.5	2.0	3.3	1.0
Intestinal nematodes							
– high intensity infection	150.9	57.6	5.8	8.5	0.0	37.7	41.1
Protein-energy malnutrition:							
– wasting (ages 0-4)	56.2	13.7	1.4	6.5	0.9	27.0	6.7
– stunting (ages 0-4)	182.7	51.9	9.5	18.6	4.0	76.5	22.0
Iron-deficiency anaemia	1159.3	193.8	66.4	88.5	77.7	462.4	269.0
Diabetes mellitus	220.5	9.7	46.4	17.9	45.4	44.7	56.0
Unipolar depressive disorders	151.2	13.4	22.7	12.4	22.2	40.9	39.3
Bipolar affective disorder	29.5	2.7	4.1	2.1	4.4	7.2	8.9
Schizophrenia	26.3	2.1	3.9	1.9	4.4	6.2	7.9
Epilepsy	40.0	7.7	8.6	2.8	4.1	9.8	7.0
Alcohol use disorders	125.0	3.8	24.2	1.1	26.9	21.5	47.3
Alzheimer and other dementias	24.2	0.6	5.0	0.6	7.6	2.8	7.4
Parkinson disease	5.2	0.2	1.2	0.2	2.0	0.7	1.0
Migraine[a]	324.1	12.6	59.7	16.2	77.3	70.3	87.5
Low vision[b]	272.4	22.2	26.6	18.7	27.9	82.3	94.3
Blindness[c]	42.7	7.6	2.9	4.1	2.3	15.7	10.1
Hearing loss:							
– moderate or greater[d]	275.7	37.6	31.0	19.5	44.5	89.8	52.9
– mild[e]	360.8	18.6	45.7	25.2	75.8	88.5	106.3
Angina pectoris	54.0	2.0	6.3	4.1	17.2	16.0	8.2
Stroke survivors	30.7	1.6	4.8	1.1	9.6	4.5	9.1
COPD, symptomatic cases	63.6	1.5	13.2	3.3	11.3	13.9	20.2
Asthma	234.9	30.0	53.3	15.4	28.8	45.7	61.2
Rheumatoid arthritis	23.7	1.2	4.6	1.3	6.2	4.4	6.0
Osteoarthritis	151.4	10.1	22.3	6.0	40.2	27.4	45.0

COPD, chronic obstructive pulmonary disease.

[a] Prevalence of migraine sufferers, not of episodes.
[b] Low vision (presenting visual acuity <6/18 and ≥3/60) due to glaucoma, cataracts, macular degeneration or refractive errors.
[c] Blindness (<3/60 presenting visual acuity) due to glaucoma, cataracts, macular degeneration or refractive errors.
[d] Hearing loss threshold in the better ear of 41 decibels or greater (measured average for 0.5, 1, 2, 4 kHz).
[e] Hearing loss threshold in the better ear of 26–40 decibels (measured average for 0.5, 1, 2, 4 kHz).

Table 8: Disability classes for the GBD study, with examples of long-term disease and injury sequelae falling in each class[a]

Disability class	Severity weights	Conditions[b]
I	0.00–0.02	Stunting due to malnutrition, schistosomiasis infection, long-term scarring due to burns (less than 20% of body)
II	0.02–0.12	Amputated finger, asthma case, edentulism, mastectomy, severe anaemia, stress incontinence
III	0.12–0.24	Angina, HIV not progressed to AIDS, infertility, alcohol dependence and problem use, low vision (<6/18, >3/60), rheumatoid arthritis
IV	0.24–0.36	Amputated arm, congestive heart failure, deafness, drug dependence, Parkinson disease, tuberculosis
V	0.36–0.50	Bipolar affective disorder, mild mental retardation, neurological sequelae of malaria, recto-vaginal fistula
VI	0.50–0.70	AIDS cases not on antiretroviral drugs, Alzheimer and other dementias, blindness, Down syndrome
VII	0.70–1.00	Active psychosis, severe depression, severe migraine, quadriplegia, terminal stage cancer

[a] Based on average severity weight globally for both sexes and all ages in the GBD 2004 update.
[b] Conditions are listed in the disability class for their global average weight. Most conditions will have distributions of severity spanning more than one disability class, potentially up to all seven.

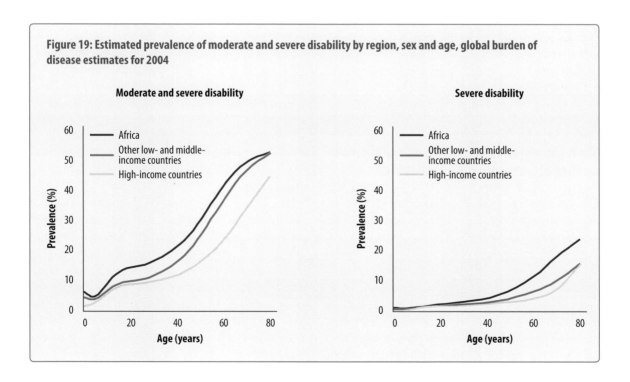

Figure 19: Estimated prevalence of moderate and severe disability by region, sex and age, global burden of disease estimates for 2004

Almost 19 million people were severely disabled in 2004

Of the world's population of nearly 6.5 billion in 2004, 18.6 million (2.9%) were severely disabled and another 79.7 million (12.4%) had moderate long-term disability, according to the definitions given above. Disability prevalences rise strongly with age (Figure 19). The average global prevalence of moderate and severe disability ranges from 5% in children aged 0–14 years, to 15% in adults aged 15–59 years, and 46% in adults aged 60 years and older. At all ages, both moderate and severe levels of disability are higher in low- and middle-income countries than in high-income countries; they are also higher in Africa than in other low- and middle-income countries (Figure 19). Older people make up a greater proportion of the population in high-income countries, but have lower levels of disability than their counterparts in low- and middle-income countries. Disability is also more common among children in the low- and middle-income countries. Moderate disability rates are similar for males and females in high-income countries, but females have somewhat higher rates of severe disability. In low- and middle-income countries, male and female disability rates are similar, although females aged 15–59 years tend to have higher levels of moderate disability in Africa, the Eastern Mediterranean and the Western Pacific.

Hearing loss, vision problems and mental disorders are the most common causes of disability

The most common causes of disability globally are adult-onset hearing loss and refractive errors. Mental disorders such as depression, alcohol use disorders and psychoses (e.g. bipolar disorder and schizophrenia) are also among the 20 leading causes of disability (Table 9). The pattern differs between the high-income countries and the low- and middle-income countries. In the lower income countries, many more people are disabled due to preventable causes such as unintentional injuries and infertility arising from unsafe abortion and maternal sepsis. The data also demonstrate the lack of interventions for easily treated conditions such as hearing loss, refractive errors and cataracts in low-income countries.

Disability due to mental disorders is more common among people aged 0–59 years, whereas chronic diseases such as dementias, chronic obstructive pulmonary disease and cerebrovascular disease are more common in older populations. In low-income countries, disability due to unintentional injuries, among the younger population, and cataracts, among the older population, are far more common.

Much uncertainty around the disability estimates

The GBD prevalence estimates are based on systematic assessments of the available data on incidence, prevalence, duration and severity of a wide range of conditions. However, these assessments are often based on inconsistent, fragmented and partial data from different studies, meaning that there are still substantial data gaps and uncertainties. Improving the population-level information on the incidence, prevalence and states of health associated with major health conditions remains a major priority for national and international health and statistical agencies. Clinically and conceptually, it is not usual practice to infer disability from diagnoses. In future revisions of the GBD study, increased effort will be devoted to direct estimation of the prevalences of impairments and disabilities, and to ensuring consistency with the estimates for disease- and injury-specific sequelae.

Population survey data on disability prevalence are limited in availability and comparability. The estimates derived from the GBD have the virtue of comprehensiveness, and at least some grounding in disease prevalence. However, they are very much approximations, and are subject to very clear limitations in the way they were compiled. These estimates are presented to give an indication of the regional prevalences of long-term disability implied by the GBD analyses.

Table 9: Estimated prevalence of moderate and severe disability[a] (millions) for leading disabling conditions by age, for high-income and low- and middle-income countries, 2004

	Disabling condition[c]	High-income countries[b]		Low- and middle-income countries		World
		0–59 years	60 years and over	0–59 years	60 years and over	All ages
1	Hearing loss[d]	7.4	18.5	54.3	43.9	124.2
2	Refractive errors[e]	7.7	6.4	68.1	39.8	121.9
3	Depression	15.8	0.5	77.6	4.8	98.7
4	Cataracts	0.5	1.1	20.8	31.4	53.8
5	Unintentional injuries	2.8	1.1	35.4	5.7	45.0
6	Osteoarthritis	1.9	8.1	14.1	19.4	43.4
7	Alcohol dependence and problem use	7.3	0.4	31.0	1.8	40.5
8	Infertility due to unsafe abortion and maternal sepsis	0.8	0.0	32.5	0.0	33.4
9	Macular degeneration[f]	1.8	6.0	9.0	15.1	31.9
10	COPD	3.2	4.5	10.9	8.0	26.6
11	Ischaemic heart disease	1.0	2.2	8.1	11.9	23.2
12	Bipolar disorder	3.3	0.4	17.6	0.8	22.2
13	Asthma	2.9	0.5	15.1	0.9	19.4
14	Schizophrenia	2.2	0.4	13.1	1.0	16.7
15	Glaucoma	0.4	1.5	5.7	7.9	15.5
16	Alzheimer and other dementias	0.4	6.2	1.3	7.0	14.9
17	Panic disorder	1.9	0.1	11.4	0.3	13.8
18	Cerebrovascular disease	1.4	2.2	4.0	4.9	12.6
19	Rheumatoid arthritis	1.3	1.7	5.9	3.0	11.9
20	Drug dependence and problem use	3.7	0.1	8.0	0.1	11.8

COPD, chronic obstructive pulmonary disease.

[a] GBD disability classes III and above.
[b] High-income countries are those with 2004 gross national income per capita of $10 066 or more, as estimated by the World Bank.
[c] Disease and injury causes of disability. Conditions are listed in descending order by global all-age prevalence.
[d] Includes adult-onset hearing loss, excluding that due to infectious causes; adjusted for availability of hearing aids.
[e] Includes presenting refractive errors; adjusted for availability of glasses and other devices for correction.
[f] Includes other age-related causes of vision loss apart from glaucoma, cataracts and refractive errors.

13. Leading causes of years lost due to disability in 2004

The data presented in the sections above concern the number of new cases of diseases and injuries (incidence), and the number of individuals living with diseases or injuries and their sequelae (prevalence). These counts of incidence or prevalence of diseases in populations do not take into account the relative severity or health loss associated with different conditions, and hence do not capture the burden of disease experienced by individuals. The disability weights used in the GBD convert the years lived with various health conditions to equivalent lost years of full health. The disability weights used in the GBD 2004 are listed in detail elsewhere (24).

As explained in Box 1 (see page 3), YLD measure the equivalent years of healthy life lost through time spent in states of less than full health. When all the years of life with reduced capability for all the sufferers of each condition are added up and weighted by the disability weight, a total of YLD for each condition is obtained. YLD estimates are restricted to loss of health experienced by individuals, and do not take into account other aspects of quality of life or well-being, or the impacts of a person's health condition on other people (except as far as they experience directly assessed losses of health themselves).

Neuropsychiatric disorders cause one third of YLD

The 10 leading causes of YLD are shown in Table 10 for males and females, and in Table 11 for high-income and low- and middle-income countries. The overall burden of non-fatal disabling conditions is dominated by a relatively short list of causes, particularly a number of neuropsychiatric conditions and sense organ disorders. In all regions, neuropsychiatric conditions are the most important causes of disability, accounting for around one third of YLD among adults aged 15 years and over.

Depression is particularly common among women

The disabling burden of neuropsychiatric conditions is almost the same for males and females, but the major contributing causes are different. While depression is the leading cause for both males and

females, the burden of depression is 50% higher for females than males. Females also have a higher burden from anxiety disorders, migraine and Alzheimer and other dementias. In contrast, the male burden for alcohol and drug use disorders is nearly seven times higher than that for females, and accounts for almost one third of the male neuropsychiatric burden. In both low- and middle-income countries, and high-income countries, alcohol use disorders are among the 10 leading causes of YLD. This includes only the direct burden of alcohol dependence and problem use. The total attributable burden of disability due to alcohol use is much larger.

One in four adults aged 45 years and older have hearing loss

Curable disorders of vision (cataracts and refractive errors) cause 9% of YLD in men and women aged 15 years and over; adult-onset hearing loss accounts for another 6.5% in men and 5.6% in women. Adult-onset hearing loss is extremely prevalent – more than 27% of males and 24% of females aged 45 years and over experience mild hearing loss or greater (hearing threshold of 26 decibels or greater in the better ear). The GBD 2004 has estimated only the burden of moderate or greater hearing loss (hearing threshold of 41 decibels or greater in the better ear). Childhood-onset hearing loss is not included in this cause category because most childhood hearing loss is due to congenital causes, infectious diseases, or other diseases or injury. It is included as sequelae for such causes in the estimation of burden of disease.

Ninety per cent of the burden of non-fatal health outcomes is in low- and middle-income countries

Perhaps surprisingly, around 90% of global non-fatal health outcomes (as measured by YLD) occur in low- and middle-income countries, and nearly half (44%) of all YLD fall in low-income countries. Although the prevalence of disabling conditions such as dementia and musculoskeletal disease are higher in countries with long life expectancies, this is offset by lower contributions to disability from conditions such as cardiovascular disease, chronic respiratory diseases and long-term sequelae of communicable diseases and nutritional deficiencies. In other words, people living in developing countries not only face lower life expectancies (higher risk of premature death) than those in developed countries but also live a higher proportion of their lives in poor health.

Table 10: Leading global causes of YLD by sex, 2004

	Males				Females		
	Cause	YLD (millions)	Per cent of total YLD		Cause	YLD (millions)	Per cent of total YLD
1	Unipolar depressive disorders	24.3	8.3	1	Unipolar depressive disorders	41.0	13.4
2	Alcohol use disorders	19.9	6.8	2	Refractive errors	14.0	4.6
3	Hearing loss, adult onset	14.1	4.8	3	Hearing loss, adult onset	13.3	4.3
4	Refractive errors	13.8	4.7	4	Cataracts	9.9	3.2
5	Schizophrenia	8.3	2.8	5	Osteoarthritis	9.5	3.1
6	Cataracts	7.9	2.7	6	Schizophrenia	8.0	2.6
7	Bipolar disorder	7.3	2.5	7	Anaemia	7.4	2.4
8	COPD	6.9	2.4	8	Bipolar disorder	7.1	2.3
9	Asthma	6.6	2.2	9	Birth asphyxia and birth trauma	6.9	2.3
10	Falls	6.3	2.2	10	Alzheimer and other dementias	5.8	1.9

COPD, chronic obstructive pulmonary disease.

Table 11: Leading global causes of YLD, high-income and low- and middle-income countries, 2004

	Low- and middle-income countries				High-income countries		
	Cause	YLD (millions)	Per cent of total YLD		Cause	YLD (millions)	Per cent of total YLD
1	Unipolar depressive disorders	55.3	10.4	1	Unipolar depressive disorders	10.0	14.6
2	Refractive errors	25.0	4.7	2	Hearing loss, adult onset	4.2	6.2
3	Hearing loss, adult onset	23.2	4.4	3	Alcohol use disorders	3.9	5.7
4	Alcohol use disorders	18.4	3.5	4	Alzheimer and other dementias	3.7	5.4
5	Cataracts	17.4	3.3	5	Osteoarthritis	2.8	4.1
6	Schizophrenia	14.8	2.8	6	Refractive errors	2.7	4.0
7	Birth asphyxia and birth trauma	12.9	2.4	7	COPD	2.4	3.5
8	Bipolar disorder	12.9	2.4	8	Diabetes mellitus	2.3	3.4
9	Osteoarthritis	12.8	2.4	9	Asthma	1.8	2.6
10	Iron-deficiency anaemia	12.6	2.4	10	Drug use disorders	1.7	2.4

COPD, chronic obstructive pulmonary disease.

Part 4

Burden of disease: DALYs

14.	Broad cause composition	40
15.	The age distribution of burden of disease	42
16.	Leading causes of burden of disease	42
17.	The disease and injury burden for women	46
18.	The growing burden of noncommunicable disease	47
19.	The unequal burden of injury	48
20.	Projected burden of disease in 2030	49

14. Broad cause composition

The measures of ill-health used so far (incidence, prevalence and YLL) do not give a good indication of the burden of disease borne by individuals in different communities. The summary measure used to give an indication of the burden of disease is the DALY (see Box 1, page 3). One DALY represents the loss of the equivalent of one year of full health. Using DALYs, the burden of diseases that cause early death but little disability (eg. drowning or measles) can be compared to that of diseases that do not cause death but do cause disability (e.g. cataract causing blindness).

Globally, 60% of DALYs are due to premature mortality

As described in the Introduction, DALYs for 2004 combine the following:

- YLL for years of life lost due to deaths in 2004
- YLD for equivalent healthy years of life lost through living in states of less than full health for cases of disease and injury incident in 2004.

The global average burden of disease across all regions in 2004 was 237 DALYs per 1000 population, of which about 60% was due to premature death and 40% to non-fatal health outcomes.

DALYs in Africa are at least two times higher than in any other region

The contribution of premature death varied dramatically across regions, with YLL rates seven times higher in Africa than in high-income countries (Figure 20). In contrast, the YLD rates were less varied, with Africa having 80% higher rates than high-income countries. South-East Asia and Africa together bore 54% of the total global burden of disease in 2004, although they account for only about 40% of the world's population. The Western Pacific

Region has the "healthiest" low- and middle-income countries, with countries such as China now having life expectancies similar to those of many Latin American countries, and higher than those in some European countries.

The greatest variation between regions is for Group I conditions

The high levels of burden of disease for the WHO African, South-East Asia and Eastern Mediterranean regions compared to other regions are predominantly due to Group I conditions (communicable diseases, and maternal, perinatal and nutritional conditions), although injury DALY rates are also higher than in other regions (Figure 21). European low- and middle-income countries have a substantially higher noncommunicable disease burden than high-income countries (Figure 21). They also have a higher burden due to Group I causes and Group III causes (injuries). In fact, these countries have the highest proportion of burden due to injuries (16%) of all the regions, followed by the low- and middle-income countries of the Americas.

Noncommunicable diseases now cause almost half of the burden of disease in low- and middle-income countries

Almost one half of the disease burden in low- and middle-income countries is now from noncommunicable diseases. Ischaemic heart disease and stroke are the largest sources of this burden, especially in the low- and middle-income countries of Europe, where cardiovascular diseases account for more than one quarter of the total disease burden. Injuries accounted for 17% of the disease burden in adults aged 15–59 years in 2004. In the low- and middle-income countries of the Americas, Europe and the Eastern Mediterranean Region, more than 30% of the entire disease and injury burden among men aged 15–44 years was from injuries.

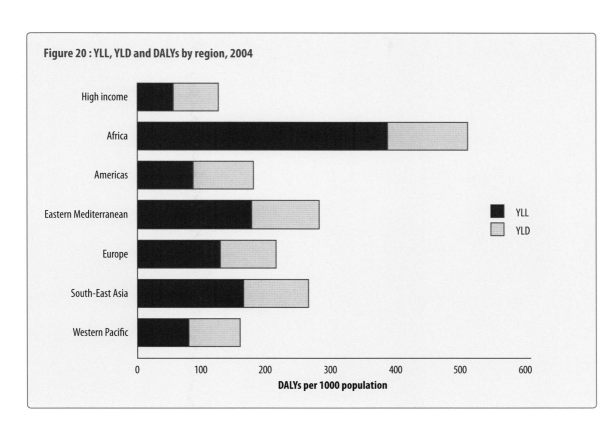

Figure 20 : YLL, YLD and DALYs by region, 2004

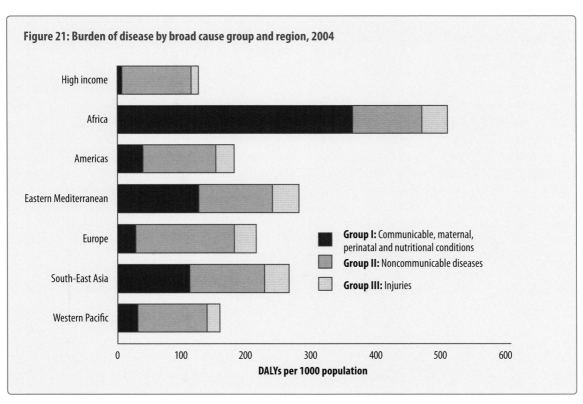

Figure 21: Burden of disease by broad cause group and region, 2004

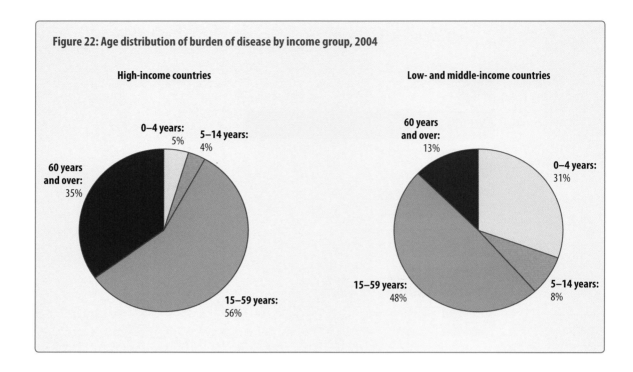

Figure 22: Age distribution of burden of disease by income group, 2004

High-income countries

0–4 years: 5%

5–14 years: 4%

60 years and over: 35%

15–59 years: 56%

Low- and middle-income countries

60 years and over: 13%

0–4 years: 31%

5–14 years: 8%

15–59 years: 48%

15. The age distribution of burden of disease

Children bear more than half of the disease burden in low-income countries

Measured in DALYs, 36% of the total disease and injury burden for the world in 2004 involved children aged less than 15 years, and almost 50% involved adults aged 15–59 years. The disease burden for children falls almost entirely in low- and middle-income countries (Figure 22). While the proportion of the total burden of disease borne by adults aged 15–59 years is similar in both groups of countries, the remaining burden is predominantly among those aged 60 years and older in high-income countries.

DALYs are attributed to the age at which the disease, injury or death occurred. Some of the YLD associated with DALYs for children will be lived at older ages.

16. Leading causes of burden of disease

Four non-fatal conditions are in the 20 leading causes of burden of disease

While the two leading causes of death – ischaemic heart disease and cerebrovascular disease – remain among the top six causes of burden of disease (Table 12), four primarily non-fatal conditions are also among the 20 leading causes of burden of disease; these are unipolar depressive disorders, adult-onset hearing loss, refractive errors and alcohol use disorders. This again illustrates the importance of taking non-fatal conditions into account, as well as deaths, when assessing the causes of loss of health in populations.

Income levels are associated with major differences in burden of disease

The two leading causes of burden of disease in the world are infectious diseases – lower respiratory infections and diarrhoeal diseases. HIV/AIDS is

Table 12: Leading causes of burden of disease (DALYs), all ages, 2004

	Disease or injury	DALYs (millions)	Per cent of total DALYs
1	Lower respiratory infections	94.5	6.2
2	Diarrhoeal diseases	72.8	4.8
3	Unipolar depressive disorders	65.5	4.3
4	Ischaemic heart disease	62.6	4.1
5	HIV/AIDS	58.5	3.8
6	Cerebrovascular disease	46.6	3.1
7	Prematurity and low birth weight	44.3	2.9
8	Birth asphyxia and birth trauma	41.7	2.7
9	Road traffic accidents	41.2	2.7
10	Neonatal infections and other[a]	40.4	2.7
11	Tuberculosis	34.2	2.2
12	Malaria	34.0	2.2
13	COPD	30.2	2.0
14	Refractive errors	27.7	1.8
15	Hearing loss, adult onset	27.4	1.8
16	Congenital anomalies	25.3	1.7
17	Alcohol use disorders	23.7	1.6
18	Violence	21.7	1.4
19	Diabetes mellitus	19.7	1.3
20	Self-inflicted injuries	19.6	1.3

COPD, chronic obstructive pulmonary disease.

[a] This category also includes other non-infectious causes arising in the perinatal period apart from prematurity, low birth weight, birth trauma and asphyxia. These non-infectious causes are responsible for about 20% of DALYs shown in this category.

now the fifth cause of burden of disease globally, and three other infectious diseases also appear in the top 15 causes (Table 12).

The leading causes of burden of disease in low-income countries were broadly similar to those for the world in 2004, apart from malaria and TB (Table 13). Of the top 10 causes, 8 were Group I, but the leading causes in high-income countries were all noncommunicable diseases, with the exception of road traffic accidents (tenth leading cause). The leading causes in high-income countries included

three diseases (unipolar major depression, adult-onset hearing loss and alcohol use disorders) for which direct mortality is low.

Unipolar depression makes a large contribution to the burden of disease, being at third place worldwide and eighth place in low-income countries, but at first place in middle- and high-income countries. Effective treatments for depression are available, suggesting that this burden could be reduced.

Cigarette smoking is a major and entirely preventable cause of burden of disease in middle- and high-income countries. Chronic obstructive pulmonary disease is in fifth place in middle-income countries and seventh place in high-income countries, and lung cancer is in ninth place in high-income countries. Cigarette smoking also contributes to the burden of disease from ischaemic heart disease and cerebrovascular disease, and affects communities in low-income countries as well. Alcohol use disorders are another important preventable contributor to burden of disease in middle- and high-income countries.

Considerable variation between regions in the burden of disease

The WHO regions fall into two groups – those in which the burden of disease is dominated by infectious disease, and those in which the burden of disease is dominated by vascular disease and depression (Table 14).

In Africa, HIV/AIDS, lower respiratory infections and diarrhoeal disease are the leading causes of burden of disease, whereas in the Eastern Mediterranean and in South-East Asia, lower respiratory infections and diarrhoeal disease are the two leading causes. In all three of these regions, problems during pregnancy and childbirth are important and preventable causes of burden of disease. The role of road traffic accidents in these regions, and of war and conflict in the Eastern Mediterranean, should also be noted.

Unipolar depression is one of the three leading causes of burden of disease in the WHO regions of the Americas, Europe and the Western Pacific. Ischaemic heart disease or cerebrovascular disease are also consistently leading causes of death in these regions. The role of violence in the Americas as the second leading cause of burden of disease, and the role of chronic obstructive pulmonary disease in the Western Pacific as the third leading cause, are also notable. Alcohol use and road traffic accidents, consistently causing about 6% of DALYs, are also important in these regions.

The leading 10 causes of the burden of disease in 2004 included 4 communicable diseases. HIV/AIDS was the fifth leading cause of the burden of disease globally in 2004 and the leading cause in the WHO African Region, where it was followed by lower respiratory infections, diarrhoeal diseases and malaria. The WHO regions of South-East Asia, the Eastern Mediterranean and Africa are affected by a dual burden of disease (Table 14). These WHO regions are much more heavily burdened by infectious disease and conditions related to pregnancy and childbirth than other regions, but they also suffer severely from the problems that affect people in high-income countries – cardiovascular disease, depression and injury.

Table 13: Leading causes of burden of disease (DALYs), countries grouped by income, 2004

	Disease or injury	DALYs (millions)	Per cent of total DALYs		Disease or injury	DALYs (millions)	Per cent of total DALYs
	World				**Low-income countries[a]**		
1	Lower respiratory infections	94.5	6.2	1	Lower respiratory infections	76.9	9.3
2	Diarrhoeal diseases	72.8	4.8	2	Diarrhoeal diseases	59.2	7.2
3	Unipolar depressive disorders	65.5	4.3	3	HIV/AIDS	42.9	5.2
4	Ischaemic heart disease	62.6	4.1	4	Malaria	32.8	4.0
5	HIV/AIDS	58.5	3.8	5	Prematurity and low birth weight	32.1	3.9
6	Cerebrovascular disease	46.6	3.1	6	Neonatal infections and other[b]	31.4	3.8
7	Prematurity and low birth weight	44.3	2.9	7	Birth asphyxia and birth trauma	29.8	3.6
8	Birth asphyxia and birth trauma	41.7	2.7	8	Unipolar depressive disorders	26.5	3.2
9	Road traffic accidents	41.2	2.7	9	Ischaemic heart disease	26.0	3.1
10	Neonatal infections and other[b]	40.4	2.7	10	Tuberculosis	22.4	2.7
	Middle-income countries				**High-income countries**		
1	Unipolar depressive disorders	29.0	5.1	1	Unipolar depressive disorders	10.0	8.2
2	Ischaemic heart disease	28.9	5.0	2	Ischaemic heart disease	7.7	6.3
3	Cerebrovascular disease	27.5	4.8	3	Cerebrovascular disease	4.8	3.9
4	Road traffic accidents	21.4	3.7	4	Alzheimer and other dementias	4.4	3.6
5	Lower respiratory infections	16.3	2.8	5	Alcohol use disorders	4.2	3.4
6	COPD	16.1	2.8	6	Hearing loss, adult onset	4.2	3.4
7	HIV/AIDS	15.0	2.6	7	COPD	3.7	3.0
8	Alcohol use disorders	14.9	2.6	8	Diabetes mellitus	3.6	3.0
9	Refractive errors	13.7	2.4	9	Trachea, bronchus, lung cancers	3.6	3.0
10	Diarrhoeal diseases	13.1	2.3	10	Road traffic accidents	3.1	2.6

COPD, chronic obstructive pulmonary disease.

[a] Countries grouped by gross national income per capita (see Annex C, Table C2).
[b] This category also includes other non-infectious causes arising in the perinatal period apart from prematurity, low birth weight, birth trauma and asphyxia. These non-infectious causes are responsible for about 20% of DALYs shown in this category.

Table 14: Leading causes of burden of disease (DALYs) by WHO region, 2004

	Disease or injury	DALYs (millions)	Per cent of total DALYs		Disease or injury	DALYs (millions)	Per cent of total DALYs
	African Region				**Region of the Americas**		
1	HIV/AIDS	46.7	12.4	1	Unipolar depressive disorders	10.8	7.5
2	Lower respiratory infections	42.2	11.2	2	Violence	6.6	4.6
3	Diarrhoeal diseases	32.2	8.6	3	Ischaemic heart disease	6.5	4.6
4	Malaria	30.9	8.2	4	Alcohol use disorders	4.8	3.4
5	Neonatal infections and other[a]	13.4	3.6	5	Road traffic accidents	4.6	3.2
6	Birth asphyxia and birth trauma	13.4	3.6	6	Diabetes mellitus	4.1	2.9
7	Prematurity and low birth weight	11.3	3.0	7	Cerebrovascular disease	4.0	2.8
8	Tuberculosis	10.8	2.9	8	Lower respiratory infections	3.6	2.5
9	Road traffic accidents	7.2	1.9	9	COPD	3.1	2.2
10	Protein-energy malnutrition	7.1	1.9	10	Congenital anomalies	2.9	2.1
	Eastern Mediterranean Region				**European Region**		
1	Lower respiratory infections	12.1	8.5	1	Ischaemic heart disease	16.8	11.1
2	Diarrhoeal diseases	8.3	5.9	2	Cerebrovascular disease	9.5	6.3
3	Ischaemic heart disease	6.2	4.3	3	Unipolar depressive disorders	8.4	5.6
4	Neonatal infections and other[a]	6.1	4.3	4	Alcohol use disorders	5.0	3.3
5	Birth asphyxia and birth trauma	5.5	3.9	5	Hearing loss, adult onset	3.9	2.6
6	Prematurity and low birth weight	5.3	3.8	6	Road traffic accidents	3.7	2.4
7	Unipolar depressive disorders	5.2	3.7	7	Trachea, bronchus, lung cancers	3.3	2.2
8	Road traffic accidents	5.1	3.6	8	Osteoarthritis	3.1	2.1
9	War and conflict	3.8	2.7	9	Cirrhosis of the liver	3.1	2.0
10	Congenital anomalies	3.7	2.6	10	Self-inflicted injuries	3.1	2.0
	South-East Asia Region				**Western Pacific Region**		
1	Lower respiratory infections	28.3	6.4	1	Cerebrovascular disease	15.8	6.0
2	Diarrhoeal diseases	23.0	5.2	2	Unipolar depressive disorders	15.2	5.7
3	Ischaemic heart disease	21.6	4.9	3	COPD	11.9	4.5
4	Unipolar depressive disorders	21.1	4.8	4	Refractive errors	10.6	4.0
5	Prematurity and low birth weight	18.3	4.1	5	Road traffic accidents	9.6	3.6
6	Neonatal infections and other[a]	14.3	3.2	6	Alcohol use disorders	8.6	3.2
7	Birth asphyxia and birth trauma	13.9	3.1	7	Ischaemic heart disease	7.9	3.0
8	Tuberculosis	12.4	2.8	8	Hearing loss, adult onset	7.0	2.6
9	Road traffic accidents	11.0	2.5	9	Birth asphyxia and birth trauma	5.7	2.1
10	Cerebrovascular disease	9.6	2.2	10	Tuberculosis	5.6	2.1

COPD, chronic obstructive pulmonary disease.

[a] This category also includes other non-infectious causes arising in the perinatal period apart from prematurity, low birth weight, birth trauma and asphyxia. These non-infectious causes are responsible for about 20% of DALYs shown in this category.

17. The disease and injury burden for women

Depression is the leading cause among young adult women

Mental disorders are an important source of lost years of healthy life for women aged 15–44 years. They make up 3 of the 10 leading causes of disease burden in low- and middle-income countries, and 4 of the leading 10 in high-income countries; self-inflicted injuries are also in the leading 10 causes for low- and middle-income countries (Figure 23). Depression is the leading cause of disease burden for women in both high-income and low- and middle-income countries. Injuries are also important for women aged 15–44 years, although road traffic accidents are the eighth leading cause globally, followed by self-inflicted injuries in ninth place.

Maternal conditions are important causes of disease and injury for women of reproductive age

Although injuries become more important for boys beyond infancy, the causes of burden of disease are broadly similar for boys and girls. However, striking sex differences emerge in adulthood (ages 15–59 years). The burden of reproductive problems is almost entirely confined to low- and middle-income countries, but it is so great that maternal conditions make up 2 out of the 10 leading causes of disease burden in women aged 15–44 years. Together with HIV/AIDS, maternal conditions are a major contributor to the high burden of disease for women in Africa relative to other regions. The burden of maternal conditions in the African and South-East Asia regions is responsible for 8% of the total global burden of disease for women aged 15–59 years. Almost all of this loss of healthy years of life is avoidable.

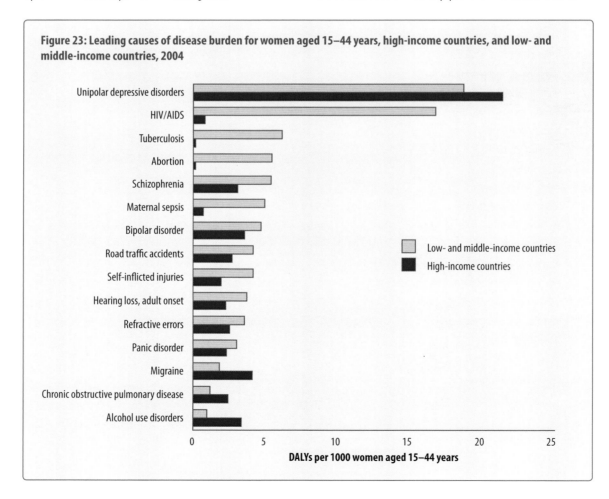

Figure 23: Leading causes of disease burden for women aged 15–44 years, high-income countries, and low- and middle-income countries, 2004

Worldwide, and particularly in low-income countries, better care for women in pregnancy and childbirth could make a large contribution to reducing the burden of disease. The Millennium Development Goal of giving all women access to a skilled birth attendant when they give birth is directed at substantially reducing the burden of disease by avoiding preventable maternal and neonatal deaths.

HIV/AIDS, neuropsychiatric conditions and sense organ disorders are the three main causes of burden of disease in women

HIV/AIDS is the most important single cause of burden of disease for women aged 15–59 years in Africa (Figure 24), and the per capita burden of HIV is 40% higher for women than for men. Neuropsychiatric conditions are responsible for 22% of global DALYs for women aged 15–59 years, the largest cause group in all regions outside Africa. Sense organ disorders

are another important cause group, responsible for 8% of global DALYs for women aged 15–59 years. Causes of vision loss are responsible for more than two thirds of the DALYs for sense organ disorders in women; causes of hearing loss account for most of the rest.

18. The growing burden of noncommunicable disease

The burden of noncommunicable diseases now accounts for nearly half of the global burden of disease (all ages). Surprisingly, almost 45% of the adult disease burden in low- and middle-income countries globally is now attributable to noncommunicable disease. Population ageing and changes in the distribution of risk factors have accelerated the noncommunicable disease share of total disease burden in many developing countries.

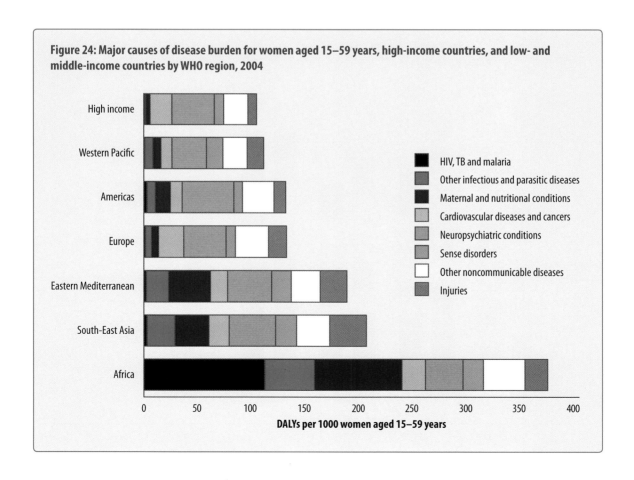

Figure 24: Major causes of disease burden for women aged 15–59 years, high-income countries, and low- and middle-income countries by WHO region, 2004

Legend:
- HIV, TB and malaria
- Other infectious and parasitic diseases
- Maternal and nutritional conditions
- Cardiovascular diseases and cancers
- Neuropsychiatric conditions
- Sense disorders
- Other noncommunicable diseases
- Injuries

Regions: High income, Western Pacific, Americas, Europe, Eastern Mediterranean, South-East Asia, Africa

x-axis: DALYs per 1000 women aged 15–59 years (0 to 400)

Noncommunicable disease risks are higher in low- and middle-income countries

Noncommunicable diseases dominate the disease burden of high-income countries, and in the past they have often been seen as a health priority mainly for high-income countries. In part this reflects the older population structure of the high-income countries, because noncommunicable disease risks generally increase with age. If the effects of different age distributions of populations are controlled for through age-standardization of DALY rates, it becomes apparent that noncommunicable disease risks, as measured by age-standardized DALY rates, are higher in low- and middle-income countries than in high-income countries (Figure 25). This is mainly due to cardiovascular diseases, principally ischaemic heart disease and stroke, whose age-standardized burden is substantially higher in low- and middle-income countries than in high-income countries. The burden of sense disorders, principally

vision impairment and hearing loss, is also greater in low- and middle-income countries than in high-income countries.

19. The unequal burden of injury

One sixth of the disease burden in adults is caused by injuries

Injuries accounted for 17% of the disease burden in adults aged 15–59 years in 2004. In the low- and middle-income countries of the Americas, Europe and the Eastern Mediterranean Region, more than 30% of the entire disease and injury burden among men aged 15–44 years was from injuries. Globally for both sexes, road traffic accidents are the third leading cause of burden in that age–sex group, preceded only by HIV/AIDS and unipolar depression. The burden of road traffic accidents is increasing – especially in the developing countries of sub-Saharan

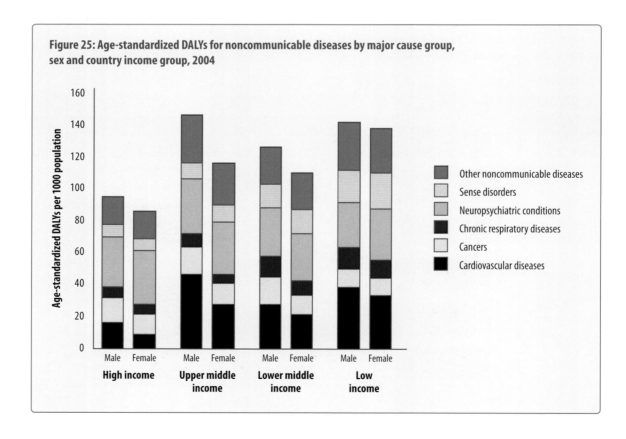

Figure 25: Age-standardized DALYs for noncommunicable diseases by major cause group, sex and country income group, 2004

Africa, southern Asia and South-East Asia – and particularly affects males. Violence and self-inflicted injuries are also in the leading 10 causes of burden of disease for people aged 15–44 years, at sixth and eighth position respectively.

Relative importance of intentional injuries varies between regions

The category of intentional injuries includes self-inflicted injuries and suicide, violence and war. This type of injury accounts for an increasing share of the burden, especially among economically productive young adults. In developed countries, suicides are the largest source of intentional injury burden, whereas in developing regions violence and war are the larger source. Countries of the former Soviet Union and other high-mortality countries of Eastern Europe have rates of injury, death and disability among males that are similar to those in sub-Saharan Africa (Figure 26). The death rate due to poisoning is much higher in the low- and middle-income countries of Europe than in any other region of the world. Alcohol overdose deaths are likely to be a primary contributor to this situation. The death rate for injuries due to fire is much higher for women in South-East Asia than for men or women in any other region of the world.

20. Projected burden of disease in 2030

Global burden of disease per capita is projected to decrease

Global DALYs are projected to decrease from 1.53 billion in 2004 to 1.36 billion in 2030, an overall decline of about 10%. Since the population increase is projected to be 25% over the same period, this represents a significant reduction in the global per capita burden. The DALY rate decreases at a faster rate than the overall death rate because of the shift

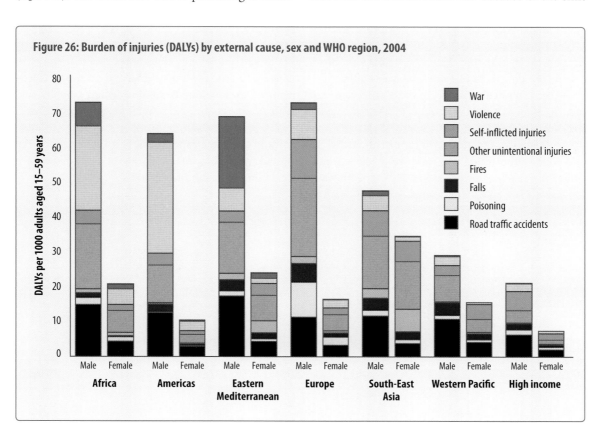

Figure 26: Burden of injuries (DALYs) by external cause, sex and WHO region, 2004

Legend:
- War
- Violence
- Self-inflicted injuries
- Other unintentional injuries
- Fires
- Falls
- Poisoning
- Road traffic accidents

Y-axis: DALYs per 1000 adults aged 15–59 years

Regions: Africa, Americas, Eastern Mediterranean, Europe, South-East Asia, Western Pacific, High income (each Male / Female)

in age at death to older ages, associated with fewer YLL. Even assuming that the age-specific burden for most non-fatal causes remains constant into the future, and hence that the overall burden for these conditions increases with the ageing of the population, there is still an overall projected decrease in the global burden of disease per capita of 30% from 2004 to 2030. This decrease is largely driven by projected levels of economic growth in the projection model. If economic growth is slower than in recent World Bank projections, or risk factor trends in low- and middle-income regions are adverse, then the global burden of disease will fall more slowly than projected.

Halving the contribution of Group I causes

The proportional contribution of the three major cause groups to the total disease burden is projected to change substantially. Group I causes are projected to account for 20% of total DALYs lost in 2030, compared with just under 40% in 2004. The noncommunicable disease (Group II) burden is projected to increase to 66% in 2030, and to represent a greater burden of disease than Group I conditions in all income groups, including low-income countries.

Figure 27 shows the changes in the leading causes of DALYs globally from 2004 to 2030. The three leading causes of DALYs in 2030 are projected to be unipolar depressive disorders, ischaemic heart disease and road traffic accidents. Lower respiratory infections drop from leading cause in 2004 to sixth leading cause, and HIV/AIDS drops from fifth leading

cause in 2004 to ninth leading cause in 2030.

Lower respiratory infections, perinatal conditions and diarrhoeal diseases are all projected to decline substantially in importance. On the other hand, diabetes mellitus, road traffic accidents, chronic obstructive pulmonary disease, hearing loss and refractive errors are all projected to move up three or more places in the rankings. Ischaemic heart disease, cerebrovascular disease and unipolar depressive disorders move up two places in the rankings to become three of the four leading causes of disease and injury burden in 2030.

These projections represent a vision of an improving future for population health under:

- an explicit set of assumptions
- specific projections of income and human capital
- specific projections of future trends in tobacco smoking, HIV/AIDS transmission and survival, and overweight and obesity.

Under these projections, people in all regions of the world will live longer and with lower levels of disability, particularly from infectious, maternal, perinatal and nutritional conditions. But if there is no sustained and additional effort to address Millennium Development Goals, neglected tropical diseases, tobacco smoking and other chronic disease risks, or if economic growth in low-income countries is lower than the forecasts used here, then the world may achieve slower progress and experience widening of health inequalities.

Figure 27: Ten leading causes of burden of disease, world, 2004 and 2030

2004 Disease or injury	As % of total DALYs	Rank		Rank	As % of total DALYs	2030 Disease or injury
Lower respiratory infections	6.2	1		1	6.2	Unipolar depressive disorders
Diarrhoeal diseases	4.8	2		2	5.5	Ischaemic heart disease
Unipolar depressive disorders	4.3	3		3	4.9	Road traffic accidents
Ischaemic heart disease	4.1	4		4	4.3	Cerebrovascular disease
HIV/AIDS	3.8	5		5	3.8	COPD
Cerebrovascular disease	3.1	6		6	3.2	Lower respiratory infections
Prematurity and low birth weight	2.9	7		7	2.9	Hearing loss, adult onset
Birth asphyxia and birth trauma	2.7	8		8	2.7	Refractive errors
Road traffic accidents	2.7	9		9	2.5	HIV/AIDS
Neonatal infections and other[a]	2.7	10		10	2.3	Diabetes mellitus
COPD	2.0	13		11	1.9	Neonatal infections and other[a]
Refractive errors	1.8	14		12	1.9	Prematurity and low birth weight
Hearing loss, adult onset	1.8	15		15	1.9	Birth asphyxia and birth trauma
Diabetes mellitus	1.3	19		18	1.6	Diarrhoeal diseases

COPD, chronic obstructive pulmonary disease.

[a] This category also includes other non-infectious causes arising in the perinatal period apart from prematurity, low birth weight, birth trauma and asphyxia. These non-infectious causes are responsible for about 20% of DALYs shown in this category.

Annex A

Deaths and DALYs 2004: Annex tables

Table A1: Deaths by cause, sex and income group in WHO regions, estimates for 2004   54

Table A2: Burden of disease in DALYs by cause, sex and income group in WHO regions, estimates for 2004   60

Table A3: Deaths by cause and broad age group, countries grouped by income per capita, 2004   66

Table A4: Burden of disease in DALYs by cause and broad age group, countries grouped by income per capita, 2004   69

Table A5: Deaths by cause, sex and age group, countries grouped by income per capita, 2004   72

Table A6: Burden of disease in DALYs by cause, sex and age group, countries grouped by income per capita, 2004   84

Table A1: Deaths by cause, sex and income group in WHO regions,[a] estimates for 2004

Cause[b]	Sex[c]						Africa	South East Asia	The Americas		
	Both sexes		Males		Females		Low and middle income	Low and middle income	Total	High income	Low and middle income
Population (millions)	6 437		3 244		3 193		738	1 672	874	329	545
	(000)	% total	(000)	% total	(000)	% total	(000)	(000)	(000)	(000)	(000)
Total deaths	58 772	100	31 082	100	27 690	100	11 248	15 279	6 158	2 695	3 464
Communicable, maternal, perinatal and nutritional conditions	*17 971*	*30.6*	*9 284*	*29.9*	*8 687*	*31.4*	*7 682*	*5 636*	*835*	*165*	*669*
Infectious and parasitic diseases	**9 519**	**16.2**	**5 198**	**16.7**	**4 321**	**15.6**	**4 849**	**2 674**	**350**	**72**	**278**
Tuberculosis	1 464	2.5	969	3.1	494	1.8	405	519	46	1	45
STDs excluding HIV	128	0.2	71	0.2	57	0.2	44	58	2	0	2
Syphilis	99	0.2	60	0.2	39	0.1	36	42	1	0	1
Chlamydia	9	0.0	0	0.0	9	0.0	0	8	0	0	0
Gonorrhoea	1	0.0	0	0.0	0	0.0	0	0	0	0	0
HIV/AIDS	2 040	3.5	1 027	3.3	1 013	3.7	1 651	206	74	14	60
Diarrhoeal diseases	2 163	3.7	1 127	3.6	1 037	3.7	1 005	684	70	5	64
Childhood-cluster diseases	847	1.4	458	1.5	390	1.4	356	363	6	0	6
Pertussis	254	0.4	129	0.4	125	0.5	102	116	4	0	4
Poliomyelitis[d]	1	0.0	1	0.0	1	0.0	0	0	0	0	0
Diphtheria	5	0.0	3	0.0	3	0.0	2	2	0	0	0
Measles	424	0.7	220	0.7	204	0.7	182	191	0	0	0
Tetanus	163	0.3	105	0.3	58	0.2	69	54	1	0	1
Meningitis	340	0.6	181	0.6	159	0.6	156	103	13	1	12
Hepatitis B[e]	105	0.2	74	0.2	31	0.1	12	37	5	1	4
Hepatitis C[e]	54	0.1	36	0.1	18	0.1	5	14	8	5	3
Malaria	889	1.5	456	1.5	433	1.6	806	36	2	0	2
Tropical-cluster diseases	152	0.3	94	0.3	58	0.2	95	32	13	0	13
Trypanosomiasis	52	0.1	33	0.1	19	0.1	50	0	0	0	0
Chagas disease	11	0.0	7	0.0	5	0.0	0	0	11	0	11
Schistosomiasis	41	0.1	26	0.1	15	0.1	36	0	1	0	1
Leishmaniasis	47	0.1	29	0.1	18	0.1	9	32	0	0	0
Lymphatic filariasis	0	0.0	0	0.0	0	0.0	0	0	0	0	0
Onchocerciasis	0	0.0	0	0.0	0	0.0	0	0	0	0	0
Leprosy	5	0.0	4	0.0	1	0.0	1	3	0	0	0
Dengue	18	0.0	9	0.0	9	0.0	0	11	2	0	2
Japanese encephalitis	11	0.0	5	0.0	6	0.0	0	8	0	0	0
Trachoma	0	0.0	0	0.0	0	0.0	0	0	0	0	0
Intestinal nematode infections	6	0.0	4	0.0	3	0.0	0	3	1	0	1
Ascariasis	2	0.0	1	0.0	1	0.0	0	1	0	0	0
Trichuriasis	2	0.0	1	0.0	1	0.0	0	1	0	0	0
Hookworm disease	0	0.0	0	0.0	0	0.0	0	0	0	0	0
Respiratory infections	**4 259**	**7.2**	**2 207**	**7.1**	**2 052**	**7.4**	**1 437**	**1 416**	**261**	**68**	**193**
Lower respiratory infections	4 177	7.1	2 163	7.0	2 014	7.3	1 417	1 395	258	68	190
Upper respiratory infections	77	0.1	41	0.1	36	0.1	17	20	2	0	2
Otitis media	5	0.0	3	0.0	2	0.0	3	1	0	0	0
Maternal conditions	**527**	**0.9**	**0**	**0.0**	**527**	**1.9**	**259**	**169**	**16**	**1**	**16**
Maternal haemorrhage	140	0.2	0	0.0	140	0.5	62	52	3	0	3
Maternal sepsis	62	0.1	0	0.0	62	0.2	30	23	1	0	1
Hypertensive disorders of pregnancy	62	30.1	0	0.0	62	0.2	22	24	4	0	4
Obstructed labour	34	0.1	0	0.0	34	0.1	13	17	0	0	0
Abortion	68	0.1	0	0.0	68	0.2	36	21	2	0	2
Perinatal conditions[f]	**3 180**	**5.4**	**1 657**	**5.3**	**1 523**	**5.5**	**977**	**1 198**	**150**	**17**	**133**
Prematurity and low birth weight	1 179	2.0	612	2.0	567	2.0	309	478	68	8	60
Birth asphyxia and birth trauma	857	1.5	446	1.4	411	1.5	285	312	28	3	26
Neonatal infections and other conditions[g]	1 144	1.9	599	1.9	546	2.0	382	408	54	7	47

Cause^b	Eastern Mediterranean			Europe			Western Pacific		
	Total	High income	Low and middle income	Total	High income	Low and middle income	Total	High income	Low and middle income
Population (millions)	520	31	489	883	407	476	1 738	204	1 534
	(000)	(000)	(000)	(000)	(000)	(000)	(000)	(000)	(000)
Total deaths	4 306	113	4 194	9 493	3 809	5 683	12 191	1 478	10 714
Communicable, maternal, perinatal and nutritional conditions	*1 664*	*18*	*1 646*	*567*	*198*	*368*	*1 568*	*151*	*1 417*
Infectious and parasitic diseases	**716**	**7**	**709**	**219**	**56**	**164**	**700**	**32**	**668**
Tuberculosis	111	1	109	77	4	74	305	9	296
STDs excluding HIV	18	0	18	1	0	1	5	0	5
Syphilis	15	0	15	0	0	0	4	0	4
Chlamydia	1	0	1	0	0	0	0	0	0
Gonorrhoea	0	0	0	0	0	0	0	0	0
HIV/AIDS	31	0	31	31	6	25	45	0	45
Diarrhoeal diseases	256	2	254	39	5	35	108	2	106
Childhood-cluster diseases	102	0	102	1	0	1	20	0	20
Pertussis	31	0	31	0	0	0	1	0	1
Poliomyelitis^d	0	0	0	0	0	0	0	0	0
Diphtheria	0	0	0	0	0	0	0	0	0
Measles	44	0	44	0	0	0	7	0	7
Tetanus	27	0	27	0	0	0	12	0	12
Meningitis	29	0	29	11	2	9	27	0	27
Hepatitis B^e	15	0	15	7	3	4	28	2	25
Hepatitis C^e	7	0	7	5	3	1	15	5	11
Malaria	39	0	39	0	0	0	5	0	5
Tropical-cluster diseases	10	0	10	0	0	0	2	0	2
Trypanosomiasis	2	0	2	0	0	0	0	0	0
Chagas disease	0	0	0	0	0	0	0	0	0
Schistosomiasis	4	0	3	0	0	0	0	0	0
Leishmaniasis	5	0	5	0	0	0	1	0	1
Lymphatic filariasis	0	0	0	0	0	0	0	0	0
Onchocerciasis	0	0	0	0	0	0	0	0	0
Leprosy	0	0	0	0	0	0	1	0	1
Dengue	1	0	1	0	0	0	5	0	5
Japanese encephalitis	0	0	0	0	0	0	3	0	3
Trachoma	0	0	0	0	0	0	0	0	0
Intestinal nematode infections	1	0	1	0	0	0	1	0	1
Ascariasis	0	0	0	0	0	0	0	0	0
Trichuriasis	0	0	0	0	0	0	0	0	0
Hookworm disease	0	0	0	0	0	0	0	0	0
Respiratory infections	**421**	**5**	**416**	**244**	**124**	**120**	**475**	**112**	**363**
Lower respiratory infections	414	5	410	235	120	114	452	112	340
Upper respiratory infections	6	0	6	9	3	5	22	0	22
Otitis media	0	0	0	0	0	0	0	0	0
Maternal conditions	**61**	**0**	**60**	**3**	**0**	**3**	**18**	**0**	**18**
Maternal haemorrhage	17	0	17	1	0	1	6	0	6
Maternal sepsis	6	0	6	0	0	0	1	0	1
Hypertensive disorders of pregnancy	8	0	8	0	0	0	3	0	3
Obstructed labour	3	0	3	0	0	0	1	0	1
Abortion	7	0	7	0	0	0	2	0	2
Perinatal conditions^f	**416**	**5**	**411**	**88**	**10**	**77**	**348**	**3**	**345**
Prematurity and low birth weight	135	3	132	39	5	35	149	1	148
Birth asphyxia and birth trauma	109	1	107	22	2	19	99	1	99
Neonatal infections and other conditions^g	172	1	171	27	4	23	99	1	98

(Table A1 continued)

Cause[b]	Sex[c]						Africa	South East Asia	The Americas		
	Both sexes		Males		Females		Low and middle income	Low and middle income	Total	High income	Low and middle income
Population (millions)	6 437		3 244		3 193		738	1 672	874	329	545
	(000)	% total	(000)	% total	(000)	% total	(000)	(000)	(000)	(000)	(000)
Total deaths	58 772	100	31 082	100	27 690	100	11 248	15 279	6 158	2 695	3 464
Nutritional deficiencies	**487**	**0.8**	**223**	**0.7**	**264**	**1.0**	**159**	**179**	**57**	**7**	**50**
Protein-energy malnutrition	251	0.4	127	0.4	124	0.4	111	55	39	3	36
Iodine deficiency	5	0.0	3	0.0	2	0.0	2	1	0	0	0
Vitamin A deficiency	17	0.0	9	0.0	8	0.0	13	2	0	0	0
Iron-deficiency anaemia	153	0.3	55	0.2	98	0.4	27	83	15	3	12
II. Noncommunicable conditions	***35 017***	***59.6***	***17 985***	***57.9***	***17 032***	***61.5***	***2 797***	***7 695***	***4 737***	***2 347***	***2 390***
Malignant neoplasms	**7 424**	**12.6**	**4 154**	**13.4**	**3 270**	**11.8**	**480**	**1 195**	**1 180**	**642**	**537**
Mouth and oropharynx cancers	335	0.6	239	0.8	96	0.3	22	158	25	10	15
Oesophagus cancer	508	0.9	331	1.1	177	0.6	32	97	32	17	15
Stomach cancer	803	1.4	499	1.6	304	1.1	32	70	77	16	61
Colon and rectum cancer	639	1.1	336	1.1	303	1.1	21	73	112	70	42
Liver cancer	610	1.0	418	1.3	192	0.7	60	58	36	17	19
Pancreas cancer	265	0.5	137	0.4	128	0.5	10	23	57	36	21
Trachea, bronchus and lung cancers	1 323	2.3	943	3.0	381	1.4	25	154	244	182	62
Melanoma and other skin cancers	68	0.1	37	0.1	31	0.1	7	4	20	13	7
Breast cancer	519	0.9	2	0.0	517	1.9	43	94	100	53	47
Cervix uteri cancer	268	0.5	0	0.0	268	1.0	50	102	39	7	31
Corpus uteri cancer	55	0.1	0	0.0	55	0.2	2	7	12	7	5
Ovary cancer	144	0.2	0	0.0	144	0.5	9	34	28	17	11
Prostate cancer	308	0.5	308	1.0	0	0.0	51	31	93	38	56
Bladder cancer	187	0.3	138	0.4	49	0.2	14	27	29	17	12
Lymphomas and multiple myeloma	332	0.6	191	0.6	142	0.5	37	67	69	43	26
Leukaemia	277	0.5	154	0.5	123	0.4	14	53	50	27	23
Other neoplasms	**163**	**0.3**	**83**	**0.3**	**80**	**0.3**	**17**	**20**	**30**	**16**	**14**
Diabetes mellitus	**1 141**	**1.9**	**508**	**1.6**	**633**	**2.3**	**172**	**280**	**258**	**84**	**173**
Endocrine disorders	**303**	**0.5**	**141**	**0.5**	**162**	**0.6**	**67**	**36**	**67**	**34**	**34**
Neuropsychiatric disorders	**1 263**	**2.1**	**647**	**2.1**	**616**	**2.2**	**126**	**275**	**280**	**201**	**79**
Unipolar depressive disorders	15	0.0	7	0.0	8	0.0	0	10	1	1	0
Bipolar affective disorder	1	0.0	0	0.0	1	0.0	0	0	0	0	0
Schizophrenia	30	0.1	15	0.0	14	0.1	3	15	1	1	0
Epilepsy	142	0.2	82	0.3	60	0.2	47	32	9	2	8
Alcohol use disorders	88	0.1	75	0.2	13	0.0	4	17	23	8	15
Alzheimer and other dementias	492	0.8	181	0.6	312	1.1	20	92	153	132	21
Parkinson disease	110	0.2	58	0.2	52	0.2	4	11	27	21	6
Multiple sclerosis	17	0.0	7	0.0	11	0.0	1	1	5	4	1
Drug use disorders	91	0.2	75	0.2	16	0.1	3	27	9	5	4
Post-traumatic stress disorder	0	0.0	0	0.0	0	0.0	0	0	0	0	0
Obsessive-compulsive disorder	0	0.0	0	0.0	0	0.0	0	0	0	0	0
Panic disorder	0	0.0	0	0.0	0	0.0	0	0	0	0	0
Insomnia (primary)	0	0.0	0	0.0	0	0.0	0	0	0	0	0
Migraine	0	0.0	0	0.0	0	0.0	0	0	0	0	0
Sense organ disorders	**4**	**0.0**	**2**	**0.0**	**2**	**0.0**	**1**	**1**	**0**	**0**	**0**
Glaucoma	0	0.0	0	0.0	0	0.0	0	0	0	0	0
Cataracts	0	0.0	0	0.0	0	0.0	0	0	0	0	0
Refractive errors	0	0.0	0	0.0	0	0.0	0	0	0	0	0
Hearing loss, adult onset	0	0.0	0	0.0	0	0.0	0	0	0	0	0
Macular degeneration and other[h]	4	0.0	2	0.0	2	0.0	1	1	0	0	0

Cause[b]	Eastern Mediterranean			Europe			Western Pacific		
	Total	High income	Low and middle income	Total	High income	Low and middle income	Total	High income	Low and middle income
Population (millions)	520	31	489	883	407	476	1 738	204	1 534
	(000)	(000)	(000)	(000)	(000)	(000)	(000)	(000)	(000)
Total deaths	4 306	113	4 194	9 493	3 809	5 683	12 191	1 478	10 714
Nutritional deficiencies	**50**	**0**	**50**	**13**	**8**	**5**	**27**	**3**	**24**
Protein-energy malnutrition	26	0	26	5	4	1	14	2	13
Iodine deficiency	2	0	2	0	0	0	0	0	0
Vitamin A deficiency	2	0	2	0	0	0	0	0	0
Iron-deficiency anaemia	12	0	12	7	4	4	9	1	8
II. Noncommunicable conditions	*2 157*	*76*	*2 081*	*8 137*	*3 425*	*4 711*	*9 428*	*1 208*	*8 220*
Malignant neoplasms	**296**	**12**	**283**	**1 862**	**1 042**	**820**	**2 398**	**458**	**1 940**
Mouth and oropharynx cancers	22	1	21	51	23	28	56	8	48
Oesophagus cancer	22	0	22	50	29	21	275	15	260
Stomach cancer	23	1	22	155	59	96	446	69	377
Colon and rectum cancer	16	1	15	238	137	101	178	57	121
Liver cancer	12	1	11	65	39	25	377	50	327
Pancreas cancer	5	0	5	93	56	37	77	29	48
Trachea, bronchus and lung cancers	33	1	31	371	207	164	495	87	408
Melanoma and other skin cancers	2	0	2	28	17	12	6	4	2
Breast cancer	29	1	28	158	90	69	93	17	76
Cervix uteri cancer	7	0	7	34	11	23	36	6	30
Corpus uteri cancer	2	0	2	25	11	13	7	3	4
Ovary cancer	6	0	5	46	25	21	22	6	15
Prostate cancer	8	0	8	97	69	28	26	14	12
Bladder cancer	21	0	21	62	37	25	33	8	25
Lymphomas and multiple myeloma	25	2	24	79	55	24	55	19	37
Leukaemia	20	1	19	67	39	29	71	11	60
Other neoplasms	**22**	**0**	**22**	**41**	**32**	**9**	**33**	**12**	**20**
Diabetes mellitus	**61**	**6**	**55**	**155**	**98**	**58**	**210**	**33**	**176**
Endocrine disorders	**29**	**2**	**27**	**37**	**30**	**8**	**65**	**11**	**55**
Neuropsychiatric disorders	**95**	**2**	**93**	**287**	**211**	**76**	**197**	**38**	**159**
Unipolar depressive disorders	1	0	1	2	2	0	0	0	0
Bipolar affective disorder	0	0	0	0	0	0	0	0	0
Schizophrenia	2	0	2	3	1	2	7	1	6
Epilepsy	11	0	10	15	7	8	27	2	25
Alcohol use disorders	3	0	3	26	13	14	16	2	14
Alzheimer and other dementias	14	0	14	137	125	12	74	19	55
Parkinson disease	3	0	3	29	25	4	36	6	30
Multiple sclerosis	1	0	1	8	4	3	2	0	2
Drug use disorders	34	0	34	15	4	11	3	0	3
Post-traumatic stress disorder	0	0	0	0	0	0	0	0	0
Obsessive-compulsive disorder	0	0	0	0	0	0	0	0	0
Panic disorder	0	0	0	0	0	0	0	0	0
Insomnia (primary)	0	0	0	0	0	0	0	0	0
Migraine	0	0	0	0	0	0	0	0	0
Sense organ disorders	**1**	**0**	**1**	**1**	**0**	**0**	**0**	**0**	**0**
Glaucoma	0	0	0	0	0	0	0	0	0
Cataracts	0	0	0	0	0	0	0	0	0
Refractive errors	0	0	0	0	0	0	0	0	0
Hearing loss, adult onset	0	0	0	0	0	0	0	0	0
Macular degeneration and other[h]	1	0	1	1	0	0	0	0	0

(Table A1 continued)

Cause[b]	Sex[c] Both sexes (000)	% total	Males (000)	% total	Females (000)	% total	Africa Low and middle income (000)	South East Asia Low and middle income (000)	The Americas Total (000)	High income (000)	Low and middle income (000)
Population (millions)	6 437		3 244		3 193		738	1 672	874	329	545
Total deaths	58 772	100	31 082	100	27 690	100	11 248	15 279	6 158	2 695	3 464
Cardiovascular diseases	**17 073**	**29.0**	**8 338**	**26.8**	**8 735**	**31.5**	**1 175**	**3 875**	**1 969**	**982**	**987**
Rheumatic heart disease	298	0.5	127	0.4	171	0.6	11	129	10	4	6
Hypertensive heart disease	987	1.7	457	1.5	530	1.9	78	156	151	49	103
Ischaemic heart disease	7 198	12.2	3 827	12.3	3 371	12.2	346	2 011	925	532	394
Cerebrovascular disease	5 712	9.7	2 661	8.6	3 051	11.0	425	1 074	461	176	285
Inflammatory heart diseases[i]	440	0.7	229	0.7	211	0.8	53	74	69	35	33
Respiratory diseases	**4 036**	**6.9**	**2 155**	**6.9**	**1 881**	**6.8**	**310**	**1 057**	**398**	**188**	**210**
Chronic obstructive pulmonary disease	3 025	5.1	1 620	5.2	1 405	5.1	121	821	240	132	108
Asthma	287	0.5	151	0.5	136	0.5	63	101	16	4	11
Digestive diseases	**2 045**	**3.5**	**1 166**	**3.8**	**879**	**3.2**	**216**	**515**	**307**	**98**	**209**
Peptic ulcer disease	270	0.5	163	0.5	107	0.4	26	105	19	4	15
Cirrhosis of the liver	772	1.3	510	1.6	262	0.9	28	210	113	30	83
Appendicitis	22	0.0	13	0.0	9	0.0	2	8	3	1	3
Diseases of the genitourinary system	**928**	**1.6**	**493**	**1.6**	**435**	**1.6**	**100**	**279**	**152**	**68**	**85**
Nephritis and nephrosis	739	1.3	385	1.2	354	1.3	88	229	115	49	65
Benign prostatic hypertrophy	39	0.1	39	0.1	0	0.0	2	20	3	1	3
Skin diseases	**68**	**0.1**	**27**	**0.1**	**41**	**0.1**	**16**	**16**	**13**	**5**	**9**
Musculoskeletal diseases	**127**	**0.2**	**45**	**0.1**	**81**	**0.3**	**18**	**18**	**30**	**17**	**14**
Rheumatoid arthritis	26	0.0	8	0.0	18	0.1	2	4	6	3	3
Osteoarthritis	7	0.0	2	0.0	4	0.0	2	1	2	1	1
Congenital abnormalities	**440**	**0.7**	**225**	**0.7**	**215**	**0.8**	**96**	**126**	**51**	**12**	**39**
Oral diseases	**3**	**0.0**	**2**	**0.0**	**2**	**0.0**	**1**	**1**	**1**	**0**	**0**
Dental caries	0	0.0	0	0.0	0	0.0	0	0	0	0	0
Periodontal disease	0	0.0	0	0.0	0	0.0	0	0	0	0	0
Edentulism	0	0.0	0	0.0	0	0.0	0	0	0	0	0
III. Injuries	***5 784***	***9.8***	***3 812***	***12.3***	***1 972***	***7.1***	***769***	***1 949***	***586***	***182***	***404***
Unintentional	**3 906**	**6.6**	**2 520**	**8.1**	**1 386**	**5.0**	**496**	**1 331**	**342**	**126**	**216**
Road traffic accidents	1 275	2.2	944	3.0	331	1.2	205	306	152	48	103
Poisonings	346	0.6	222	0.7	124	0.4	42	96	25	22	3
Falls	424	0.7	260	0.8	164	0.6	19	126	41	22	20
Fires	310	0.5	120	0.4	190	0.7	48	186	8	4	5
Drownings	388	0.7	263	0.8	125	0.5	62	100	22	4	19
Other unintentional injuries	1 163	2.0	711	2.3	452	1.6	121	517	93	26	67
Intentional	**1 642**	**2.8**	**1 181**	**3.8**	**461**	**1.7**	**273**	**392**	**238**	**57**	**181**
Self-inflicted injuries	844	1.4	529	1.7	316	1.1	50	252	69	37	32
Violence	600	1.0	485	1.6	115	0.4	182	115	155	18	137
War and conflict	184	0.3	155	0.5	29	0.1	40	20	11	1	10

a See Annex Table C1 for a list of Member States by WHO region and income category.
b Estimates for specific causes may not sum to broader cause groupings due to omission of residual categories.
c World totals for males and females include residual populations living outside WHO Member States.
d For the Americas, Europe and Western Pacific regions, these figures include late effects of polio cases with onset prior to regional certification of polio eradication in 1994, 2000 and 2002, respectively.
e Does not include liver cancer and cirrhosis deaths resulting from chronic hepatitis virus infection.
f This category includes 'Causes arising in the perinatal period' as defined in the International Classification of Diseases, and does not include all deaths occurring in the perinatal period.
g Includes severe neonatal infections and other non-infectious causes arising in the perinatal period.
h Includes macular degeneration and other age-related causes of vision loss not correctable by provision of glasses or contact lenses, together with deaths due to other sense organ disorders.
i Includes myocarditis, pericarditis, endocarditis and cardiomyopathy.

Cause[b]	Eastern Mediterranean			Europe			Western Pacific		
	Total	High income	Low and middle income	Total	High income	Low and middle income	Total	High income	Low and middle income
Population (millions)	520	31	489	883	407	476	1 738	204	1 534
	(000)	*(000)*	*(000)*	*(000)*	*(000)*	*(000)*	*(000)*	*(000)*	*(000)*
Total deaths	4 306	113	4 194	9 493	3 809	5 683	12 191	1 478	10 714
Cardiovascular diseases	**1 163**	**42**	**1 121**	**4 767**	**1 520**	**3 247**	**4 094**	**467**	**3 627**
Rheumatic heart disease	25	0	24	30	10	19	93	3	90
Hypertensive heart disease	103	10	93	179	69	110	316	16	300
Ischaemic heart disease	579	20	559	2 296	622	1 674	1 029	151	878
Cerebrovascular disease	254	5	249	1 364	380	984	2 128	196	1 932
Inflammatory heart diseases[i]	33	0	33	123	33	90	87	9	78
Respiratory diseases	**164**	**3**	**161**	**374**	**203**	**171**	**1 728**	**79**	**1 649**
Chronic obstructive pulmonary disease	99	1	97	234	122	112	1 508	30	1 478
Asthma	23	0	22	36	8	28	49	8	41
Digestive diseases	**160**	**3**	**156**	**420**	**182**	**238**	**422**	**62**	**360**
Peptic ulcer disease	13	0	13	37	15	22	70	5	65
Cirrhosis of the liver	69	1	68	185	60	125	166	25	141
Appendicitis	1	0	1	2	1	1	5	0	4
Diseases of the genitourinary system	**89**	**3**	**86**	**117**	**67**	**50**	**187**	**33**	**154**
Nephritis and nephrosis	74	3	71	80	45	35	152	29	123
Benign prostatic hypertrophy	3	0	3	5	1	4	6	0	6
Skin diseases	**6**	**1**	**5**	**12**	**8**	**3**	**5**	**2**	**3**
Musculoskeletal diseases	**4**	**0**	**4**	**28**	**22**	**6**	**28**	**8**	**20**
Rheumatoid arthritis	1	0	1	6	3	2	8	2	5
Osteoarthritis	0	0	0	2	2	0	0	0	0
Congenital abnormalities	**69**	**3**	**67**	**36**	**11**	**24**	**61**	**4**	**56**
Oral diseases	**0**	**0**	**0**	**0**	**0**	**0**	**0**	**0**	**0**
Dental caries	0	0	0	0	0	0	0	0	0
Periodontal disease	0	0	0	0	0	0	0	0	0
Edentulism	0	0	0	0	0	0	0	0	0
III. Injuries	*485*	*19*	*466*	*789*	*186*	*604*	*1 196*	*119*	*1 077*
Unintentional	**321**	**16**	**305**	**564**	**131**	**432**	**846**	**68**	**778**
Road traffic accidents	146	7	139	129	38	91	336	21	314
Poisonings	17	0	17	107	6	101	59	2	57
Falls	24	2	23	79	40	38	134	12	122
Fires	29	0	29	23	3	20	16	2	14
Drownings	30	2	28	34	4	30	139	7	132
Other unintentional injuries	76	5	71	191	40	152	163	23	140
Intentional	**163**	**3**	**160**	**226**	**54**	**171**	**348**	**51**	**297**
Self-inflicted injuries	36	2	35	151	49	102	286	49	236
Violence	25	1	24	65	5	60	57	2	55
War and conflict	99	0	99	10	0	9	2	0	2

Table A2: Burden of disease in DALYs by cause, sex and income group in WHO regions,[a] estimates for 2004

Cause[b]	Sex[c] Both sexes (000)	% total	Males (000)	% total	Females (000)	% total	Africa Low and middle income (000)	South East Asia Low and middle income (000)	The Americas Total (000)	High income (000)	Low and middle income (000)
Population (millions)	6 437		3 244		3 193		738	1 672	874	329	545
Total DALYs	1 523 259	100	796 133	100	727 126	100	376 525	442 979	143 233	45 116	98 116
Communicable, maternal, perinatal and nutritional conditions	*603 993*	*39.7*	*294 075*	*36.9*	*309 918*	*42.6*	*267 725*	*184 876*	*24 544*	*2 707*	*21 837*
Infectious and parasitic diseases	**302 144**	**19.8**	**159 741**	**20.1**	**142 403**	**19.6**	**159 817**	**82 900**	**9 650**	**1 102**	**8 548**
Tuberculosis	34 217	2.2	21 658	2.7	12 558	1.7	10 827	12 386	893	10	882
STDs excluding HIV	10 425	0.7	3 558	0.4	6 866	0.9	3 449	4 072	637	65	572
Syphilis	2 846	0.2	1 531	0.2	1 316	0.2	1 340	841	78	1	77
Chlamydia	3 748	0.2	320	0.0	3 428	0.5	842	1 600	313	51	262
Gonorrhoea	3 550	0.2	1 554	0.2	1 996	0.3	1 186	1 501	231	12	219
HIV/AIDS	58 513	3.8	28 569	3.6	29 944	4.1	46 653	6 097	2 147	388	1 759
Diarrhoeal diseases	72 777	4.8	37 905	4.8	34 872	4.8	32 203	22 987	2 576	107	2 469
Childhood-cluster diseases	30 226	2.0	16 221	2.0	14 005	1.9	12 549	12 994	254	19	235
Pertussis	9 882	0.6	5 009	0.6	4 873	0.7	3 815	4 463	217	18	199
Poliomyelitis[d]	34	0.0	19	0.0	15	0.0	22	3	3	2	1
Diphtheria	174	0.0	86	0.0	88	0.0	79	72	3	0	3
Measles	14 853	1.0	7 699	1.0	7 154	1.0	6 336	6 706	0	0	0
Tetanus	5 283	0.3	3 409	0.4	1 875	0.3	2 297	1 750	31	0	31
Meningitis	11 426	0.8	5 891	0.7	5 536	0.8	5 334	3 314	458	30	428
Hepatitis B[e]	2 068	0.1	1 437	0.2	630	0.1	355	704	102	13	89
Hepatitis C[e]	955	0.1	653	0.1	302	0.0	155	260	118	77	41
Malaria	33 976	2.2	17 340	2.2	16 636	2.3	30 928	1 341	89	0	89
Tropical-cluster diseases	12 113	0.8	8 264	1.0	3 850	0.5	6 077	4 789	529	0	529
Trypanosomiasis	1 673	0.1	1 041	0.1	631	0.1	1 609	0	0	0	0
Chagas disease	430	0.0	231	0.0	199	0.0	0	0	426	0	426
Schistosomiasis	1 707	0.1	1 021	0.1	686	0.1	1 502	0	46	0	46
Leishmaniasis	1 974	0.1	1 227	0.2	748	0.1	328	1 264	45	0	45
Lymphatic filariasis	5 941	0.4	4 521	0.6	1 420	0.2	2 263	3 525	10	0	10
Onchocerciasis	389	0.0	223	0.0	166	0.0	375	0	1	0	1
Leprosy	194	0.0	116	0.0	78	0.0	25	118	16	0	16
Dengue	670	0.0	336	0.0	334	0.0	9	391	73	0	73
Japanese encephalitis	681	0.0	330	0.0	351	0.0	0	492	0	0	0
Trachoma	1 334	0.1	338	0.0	997	0.1	601	88	15	0	15
Intestinal nematode infections	4 013	0.3	2 052	0.3	1 961	0.3	1 528	1 076	180	0	180
Ascariasis	1 851	0.1	943	0.1	908	0.1	915	404	60	0	60
Trichuriasis	1 012	0.1	525	0.1	487	0.1	236	372	73	0	73
Hookworm disease	1 092	0.1	551	0.1	541	0.1	377	286	20	0	20
Respiratory infections	**97 786**	**6.4**	**51 266**	**6.4**	**46 520**	**6.4**	**43 058**	**29 078**	**3 877**	**365**	**3 512**
Lower respiratory infections	94 511	6.2	49 542	6.2	44 969	6.2	42 203	28 321	3 616	316	3 301
Upper respiratory infections	1 787	0.1	952	0.1	835	0.1	534	323	88	14	74
Otitis media	1 488	0.1	772	0.1	716	0.1	322	434	173	35	137
Maternal conditions	**38 936**	**2.6**	**0**	**0.0**	**38 936**	**5.4**	**14 906**	**12 892**	**2 252**	**290**	**1 962**
Maternal haemorrhage	4 439	0.3	0	0.0	4 439	0.6	1 986	1 623	93	1	91
Maternal sepsis	6 535	0.4	0	0.0	6 535	0.9	2 010	2 327	524	75	449
Hypertensive disorders of pregnancy	1 888	0.1	0	0.0	1 888	0.3	707	727	126	2	124
Obstructed labour	2 882	0.2	0	0.0	2 882	0.4	913	1 367	67	2	65
Abortion	7 424	0.5	0	0.0	7 424	1.0	2 864	2 957	354	1	353
Perinatal conditions[f]	**126 423**	**8.3**	**64 633**	**8.1**	**61 791**	**8.5**	**38 191**	**46 503**	**6 471**	**794**	**5 677**
Prematurity and low birth weight	44 307	2.9	22 624	2.8	21 683	3.0	11 317	18 323	2 529	350	2 179
Birth asphyxia and birth trauma	41 684	2.7	21 051	2.6	20 633	2.8	13 433	13 858	1 971	171	1 800
Neonatal infections and other conditions[g]	40 433	2.7	20 957	2.6	19 476	2.7	13 441	14 322	1 970	273	1 697

Cause[b]	Eastern Mediterranean			Europe			Western Pacific		
	Total	High income	Low and middle income	Total	High income	Low and middle income	Total	High income	Low and middle income
Population (millions)	520	31	489	883	407	476	1 738	204	1 534
	(000)	(000)	(000)	(000)	(000)	(000)	(000)	(000)	(000)
Total DALYs	141 993	4 379	137 614	151 461	49 331	102 130	264 772	22 305	242 466
Communicable, maternal, perinatal and nutritional conditions	*62 440*	*790*	*61 650*	*15 391*	*2 297*	*13 094*	*48 409*	*1 383*	*47 027*
Infectious and parasitic diseases	**23 691**	**241**	**23 450**	**6 041**	**838**	**5 203**	**19 763**	**490**	**19 272**
Tuberculosis	2 720	33	2 686	1 735	40	1 695	5 631	94	5 537
STDs excluding HIV	1 290	29	1 261	366	77	290	595	38	557
Syphilis	478	1	477	16	3	13	89	1	87
Chlamydia	437	19	417	237	58	179	313	28	285
Gonorrhoea	344	9	335	98	14	83	185	9	176
HIV/AIDS	920	8	912	1 180	196	983	1 453	15	1 439
Diarrhoeal diseases	8 349	100	8 249	1 393	114	1 279	5 225	106	5 119
Childhood-cluster diseases	3 567	5	3 562	67	20	47	772	7	765
Pertussis	1 158	2	1 156	48	18	30	175	7	169
Poliomyelitis[d]	3	0	3	3	2	1	0	0	0
Diphtheria	17	0	17	1	0	1	1	0	1
Measles	1 533	0	1 533	12	1	12	252	0	252
Tetanus	856	2	854	3	0	2	343	0	343
Meningitis	1 068	12	1 056	333	50	284	910	13	897
Hepatitis B[e]	281	6	275	136	32	104	487	30	457
Hepatitis C[e]	121	2	119	71	34	37	229	40	188
Malaria	1 412	1	1 411	4	1	3	169	0	169
Tropical-cluster diseases	574	11	563	7	0	7	128	0	128
Trypanosomiasis	62	0	62	0	0	0	0	0	0
Chagas disease	0	0	0	0	0	0	0	0	0
Schistosomiasis	145	8	136	0	0	0	13	0	13
Leishmaniasis	281	3	278	6	0	6	51	0	51
Lymphatic filariasis	75	0	75	1	0	1	65	0	65
Onchocerciasis	11	0	11	0	0	0	0	0	0
Leprosy	22	0	22	0	0	0	13	0	13
Dengue	28	6	22	0	0	0	169	0	169
Japanese encephalitis	0	0	0	4	0	4	186	2	183
Trachoma	208	0	208	0	0	0	419	0	419
Intestinal nematode infections	269	0	269	0	0	0	955	22	933
Ascariasis	162	0	161	0	0	0	308	5	303
Trichuriasis	61	0	61	0	0	0	269	6	264
Hookworm disease	43	0	43	0	0	0	364	11	353
Respiratory infections	**12 421**	**110**	**12 311**	**2 907**	**488**	**2 419**	**6 363**	**390**	**5 973**
Lower respiratory infections	12 060	101	11 959	2 618	424	2 194	5 616	361	5 256
Upper respiratory infections	211	2	209	196	29	167	434	10	425
Otitis media	151	8	143	94	35	58	313	20	293
Maternal conditions	**5 081**	**99**	**4 982**	**862**	**171**	**691**	**2 901**	**95**	**2 805**
Maternal haemorrhage	541	3	538	19	1	18	173	1	172
Maternal sepsis	824	15	809	232	38	194	612	14	598
Hypertensive disorders of pregnancy	238	1	237	13	1	12	76	1	76
Obstructed labour	325	3	322	9	2	7	197	6	190
Abortion	977	22	955	38	5	33	225	0	225
Perinatal conditions[f]	**16 958**	**258**	**16 699**	**3 687**	**515**	**3 173**	**14 463**	**170**	**14 293**
Prematurity and low birth weight	5 345	99	5 246	1 490	221	1 269	5 249	61	5 188
Birth asphyxia and birth trauma	5 472	107	5 366	1 230	150	1 080	5 661	52	5 609
Neonatal infections and other conditions[g]	6 141	53	6 088	967	143	824	3 552	57	3 495

1

2

3

4

Annex A

Annex B

Annex C

References

(Table A2 continued)

Cause[b]	Sex[c]						Africa	South East Asia	The Americas		
	Both sexes		Males		Females		Low and middle income	Low and middle income	Total	High income	Low and middle income
Population (millions)	6 437		3 244		3 193		738	1 672	874	329	545
	(000)	% total	(000)	% total	(000)	% total	(000)	(000)	(000)	(000)	(000)
Total DALYs	1 523 259	100	796 133	100	727 126	100	376 525	442 979	143 233	45 116	98 116
Nutritional deficiencies	**38 703**	**2.5**	**18 436**	**2.3**	**20 268**	**2.8**	**11 753**	**13 503**	**2 294**	**155**	**2 139**
Protein-energy malnutrition	17 462	1.1	8 925	1.1	8 536	1.2	7 095	5 568	1 134	35	1 099
Iodine deficiency	3 529	0.2	1 789	0.2	1 740	0.2	1 198	635	134	0	134
Vitamin A deficiency	629	0.0	339	0.0	291	0.0	478	82	1	0	1
Iron-deficiency anaemia	16 152	1.1	6 918	0.9	9 234	1.3	2 850	6 821	980	117	863
II. Noncommunicable conditions	*731 652*	*48.0*	*378 693*	*47.6*	*352 959*	*48.5*	*79 142*	*195 285*	*98 884*	*37 917*	*60 967*
Malignant neoplasms	**77 812**	**5.1**	**41 893**	**5.3**	**35 919**	**4.9**	**5 913**	**14 139**	**11 461**	**5 672**	**5 788**
Mouth and oropharynx cancers	3 790	0.2	2 790	0.4	999	0.1	277	1 714	270	97	174
Oesophagus cancer	4 768	0.3	3 121	0.4	1 647	0.2	316	960	273	135	139
Stomach cancer	7 491	0.5	4 683	0.6	2 808	0.4	355	717	689	124	565
Colon and rectum cancer	5 874	0.4	3 207	0.4	2 666	0.4	252	778	1 004	610	394
Liver cancer	6 712	0.4	4 726	0.6	1 986	0.3	773	677	324	150	174
Pancreas cancer	2 219	0.1	1 228	0.2	992	0.1	102	230	436	263	173
Trachea, bronchus and lung cancers	11 766	0.8	8 312	1.0	3 454	0.5	259	1 499	1 960	1 384	576
Melanoma and other skin cancers	706	0.0	389	0.0	317	0.0	81	47	206	132	74
Breast cancer	6 629	0.4	18	0.0	6 611	0.9	568	1 222	1 293	685	608
Cervix uteri cancer	3 719	0.2	0	0.0	3 719	0.5	631	1 428	586	125	461
Corpus uteri cancer	745	0.0	0	0.0	745	0.1	28	81	151	84	68
Ovary cancer	1 745	0.1	0	0.0	1 745	0.2	131	437	306	161	145
Prostate cancer	1 843	0.1	1 843	0.2	0	0.0	329	179	570	253	317
Bladder cancer	1 451	0.1	1 079	0.1	372	0.1	123	196	229	144	85
Lymphomas and multiple myeloma	4 284	0.3	2 660	0.3	1 624	0.2	667	989	686	324	362
Leukaemia	4 944	0.3	2 805	0.4	2 139	0.3	276	1 189	712	232	479
Other neoplasms	**1 953**	**0.1**	**1 016**	**0.1**	**937**	**0.1**	**318**	**343**	**270**	**100**	**170**
Diabetes mellitus	**19 705**	**1.3**	**9 046**	**1.1**	**10 659**	**1.5**	**2 125**	**4 892**	**4 095**	**1 475**	**2 620**
Endocrine disorders	**10 446**	**0.7**	**4 793**	**0.6**	**5 653**	**0.8**	**3 063**	**889**	**2 518**	**851**	**1 667**
Neuropsychiatric disorders	**199 280**	**13.1**	**98 328**	**12.4**	**100 952**	**13.9**	**19 403**	**52 279**	**33 759**	**12 846**	**20 914**
Unipolar depressive disorders	65 472	4.3	24 392	3.1	41 080	5.6	4 667	21 103	10 764	4 568	6 196
Bipolar affective disorder	14 425	0.9	7 299	0.9	7 126	1.0	1 895	3 909	1 783	522	1 261
Schizophrenia	16 769	1.1	8 544	1.1	8 226	1.1	1 891	4 992	2 028	523	1 505
Epilepsy	7 854	0.5	4 234	0.5	3 621	0.5	1 837	2 258	1 067	161	907
Alcohol use disorders	23 738	1.6	21 154	2.7	2 584	0.4	790	4 245	4 830	1 839	2 991
Alzheimer and other dementias	11 158	0.7	4 312	0.5	6 847	0.9	440	1 665	2 209	1 359	849
Parkinson disease	1 710	0.1	854	0.1	856	0.1	72	267	336	263	74
Multiple sclerosis	1 527	0.1	656	0.1	871	0.1	114	357	244	118	126
Drug use disorders	8 370	0.5	6 586	0.8	1 784	0.2	938	1 259	2 433	1 101	1 333
Post-traumatic stress disorder	3 468	0.2	960	0.1	2 508	0.3	355	954	433	183	250
Obsessive-compulsive disorder	5 104	0.3	2 195	0.3	2 909	0.4	931	1 069	885	217	668
Panic disorder	6 991	0.5	2 374	0.3	4 617	0.6	860	1 967	884	276	608
Insomnia (primary)	3 623	0.2	1 562	0.2	2 060	0.3	336	1 038	660	266	394
Migraine	7 765	0.5	2 116	0.3	5 649	0.8	485	2 145	1 418	495	922
Sense organ disorders	**86 883**	**5.7**	**41 843**	**5.3**	**45 040**	**6.2**	**9 403**	**28 446**	**7 746**	**2 981**	**4 765**
Glaucoma	4 728	0.3	2 100	0.3	2 628	0.4	1 061	1 172	442	94	348
Cataracts	17 757	1.2	7 858	1.0	9 899	1.4	3 915	5 840	970	40	930
Refractive errors	27 745	1.8	13 769	1.7	13 977	1.9	1 394	9 310	2 360	932	1 428
Hearing loss, adult onset	27 356	1.8	14 073	1.8	13 283	1.8	2 207	9 218	2 797	1 383	1 414
Macular degeneration and other[h]	9 297	0.6	4 043	0.5	5 254	0.7	826	2 907	1 178	532	646

Cause[b]	Eastern Mediterranean			Europe			Western Pacific		
	Total	High income	Low and middle income	Total	High income	Low and middle income	Total	High income	Low and middle income
Population (millions)	520	31	489	883	407	476	1 738	204	1 534
	(000)	(000)	(000)	(000)	(000)	(000)	(000)	(000)	(000)
Total DALYs	141 993	4 379	137 614	151 461	49 331	102 130	264 772	22 305	242 466
Nutritional deficiencies	**4 289**	**82**	**4 207**	**1 893**	**285**	**1 608**	**4 920**	**237**	**4 683**
Protein-energy malnutrition	1 983	34	1 949	218	27	191	1 437	26	1 411
Iodine deficiency	710	0	710	687	2	684	163	0	163
Vitamin A deficiency	64	0	63	1	0	1	4	0	4
Iron-deficiency anaemia	1 280	47	1 233	933	251	682	3 266	207	3 060
II. Noncommunicable conditions	*58 551*	*2 779*	*55 772*	*116 097*	*43 484*	*72 613*	*182 370*	*18 675*	*163 696*
Malignant neoplasms	**4 239**	**174**	**4 064**	**17 086**	**8 273**	**8 813**	**24 853**	**3 636**	**21 217**
Mouth and oropharynx cancers	272	9	263	586	249	337	667	74	592
Oesophagus cancer	238	4	233	442	232	210	2 537	115	2 422
Stomach cancer	260	7	253	1 317	392	925	4 146	501	3 645
Colon and rectum cancer	229	12	217	1 895	994	901	1 704	472	1 232
Liver cancer	147	12	135	515	273	242	4 269	407	3 862
Pancreas cancer	58	4	54	735	387	347	656	201	454
Trachea, bronchus and lung cancers	345	10	335	3 264	1 627	1 637	4 426	579	3 848
Melanoma and other skin cancers	30	0	29	286	152	134	56	31	25
Breast cancer	442	17	425	1 738	908	830	1 351	238	1 113
Cervix uteri cancer	114	3	111	463	128	335	492	72	420
Corpus uteri cancer	26	1	25	347	128	219	108	44	65
Ovary cancer	90	3	87	486	222	263	293	74	219
Prostate cancer	56	3	54	550	364	187	153	80	72
Bladder cancer	210	4	205	435	235	200	256	51	204
Lymphomas and multiple myeloma	534	27	507	718	403	315	680	141	540
Leukaemia	519	27	492	745	306	438	1 496	119	1 376
Other neoplasms	**355**	**7**	**348**	**283**	**180**	**103**	**380**	**77**	**303**
Diabetes mellitus	**1 396**	**154**	**1 242**	**2 660**	**1 311**	**1 349**	**4 484**	**648**	**3 835**
Endocrine disorders	**851**	**102**	**749**	**1 266**	**718**	**549**	**1 823**	**234**	**1 589**
Neuropsychiatric disorders	**15 966**	**811**	**15 155**	**28 932**	**12 590**	**16 342**	**48 561**	**5 115**	**43 446**
Unipolar depressive disorders	5 197	281	4 916	8 446	3 754	4 692	15 186	1 336	13 850
Bipolar affective disorder	1 325	79	1 246	1 555	595	960	3 933	336	3 597
Schizophrenia	1 598	97	1 501	1 612	572	1 040	4 619	348	4 270
Epilepsy	647	29	618	624	245	378	1 407	95	1 312
Alcohol use disorders	272	15	257	5 000	1 554	3 446	8 565	772	7 793
Alzheimer and other dementias	362	17	345	3 072	2 070	1 002	3 388	924	2 465
Parkinson disease	100	3	97	476	296	180	457	131	326
Multiple sclerosis	118	7	111	302	154	148	389	40	349
Drug use disorders	1 672	6	1 667	1 369	708	661	674	68	605
Post-traumatic stress disorder	292	18	274	471	203	268	958	106	852
Obsessive-compulsive disorder	560	41	519	806	249	557	839	84	755
Panic disorder	654	37	617	817	310	507	1 798	167	1 631
Insomnia (primary)	208	7	201	633	341	292	741	150	591
Migraine	563	27	536	1 229	712	517	1 912	195	1 717
Sense organ disorders	**7 075**	**376**	**6 699**	**8 429**	**3 821**	**4 608**	**25 646**	**1 994**	**23 652**
Glaucoma	449	23	425	466	161	305	1 128	89	1 039
Cataracts	2 015	126	1 889	472	54	418	4 508	174	4 334
Refractive errors	1 705	64	1 641	2 370	1 191	1 179	10 578	542	10 035
Hearing loss, adult onset	2 161	128	2 034	3 926	1 827	2 099	7 005	843	6 162
Macular degeneration and other[h]	745	36	710	1 196	588	608	2 427	345	2 082

(Table A2 continued)

Cause[b]	Sex[c] Both sexes (000)	% total	Males (000)	% total	Females (000)	% total	Africa Low and middle income (000)	South East Asia Low and middle income (000)	The Americas Total (000)	High income (000)	Low and middle income (000)
Population (millions)	6 437		3 244		3 193		738	1 672	874	329	545
Total DALYs	1 523 259	100	796 133	100	727 126	100	376 525	442 979	143 233	45 116	98 116
Cardiovascular diseases	**151 377**	**9.9**	**82 894**	**10.4**	**68 483**	**9.4**	**14 243**	**42 061**	**15 217**	**6 291**	**8 926**
Rheumatic heart disease	5 188	0.3	2 301	0.3	2 887	0.4	315	2 494	140	31	109
Hypertensive heart disease	8 020	0.5	4 066	0.5	3 953	0.5	818	1 692	1 105	329	777
Ischaemic heart disease	62 587	4.1	37 271	4.7	25 316	3.5	3 513	21 583	6 523	3 050	3 474
Cerebrovascular disease	46 591	3.1	24 129	3.0	22 462	3.1	4 876	9 598	3 988	1 337	2 650
Inflammatory heart diseases[i]	6 236	0.4	3 689	0.5	2 547	0.4	1 148	1 469	842	360	482
Respiratory diseases	**59 039**	**3.9**	**33 215**	**4.2**	**25 824**	**3.6**	**7 169**	**16 270**	**7 758**	**2 966**	**4 792**
Chronic obstructive pulmonary disease	30 196	2.0	17 399	2.2	12 796	1.8	1 456	9 347	3 141	1 647	1 494
Asthma	16 317	1.1	8 856	1.1	7 461	1.0	2 991	4 476	2 629	756	1 873
Digestive diseases	**42 498**	**2.8**	**24 657**	**3.1**	**17 841**	**2.5**	**5 523**	**12 874**	**5 160**	**1 495**	**3 665**
Peptic ulcer disease	4 963	0.3	3 293	0.4	1 670	0.2	681	2 212	211	40	171
Cirrhosis of the liver	13 640	0.9	8 868	1.1	4 772	0.7	576	4 364	1 856	456	1 400
Appendicitis	418	0.0	259	0.0	160	0.0	75	118	65	13	52
Diseases of the genitourinary system	**14 754**	**1.0**	**8 735**	**1.1**	**6 019**	**0.8**	**2 179**	**4 518**	**1 698**	**499**	**1 199**
Nephritis and nephrosis	9 057	0.6	4 889	0.6	4 168	0.6	1 550	3 095	994	271	724
Benign prostatic hypertrophy	2 664	0.2	2 664	0.3	0	0.0	268	762	350	86	265
Skin diseases	**3 879**	**0.3**	**1 936**	**0.2**	**1 943**	**0.3**	**902**	**1 114**	**483**	**76**	**407**
Musculoskeletal diseases	**30 869**	**2.0**	**13 604**	**1.7**	**17 265**	**2.4**	**2 463**	**7 340**	**4 276**	**1 731**	**2 545**
Rheumatoid arthritis	5 050	0.3	1 446	0.2	3 604	0.5	308	1 068	989	326	663
Osteoarthritis	15 586	1.0	6 095	0.8	9 491	1.3	1 388	3 409	1 906	857	1 049
Congenital abnormalities	**25 280**	**1.7**	**12 853**	**1.6**	**12 427**	**1.7**	**5 797**	**7 649**	**2 942**	**665**	**2 277**
Oral diseases	**7 875**	**0.5**	**3 878**	**0.5**	**3 997**	**0.5**	**640**	**2 471**	**1 501**	**268**	**1 233**
Dental caries	4 882	0.3	2 476	0.3	2 406	0.3	438	1 417	1 030	171	859
Periodontal disease	320	0.0	160	0.0	160	0.0	38	122	39	13	26
Edentulism	2 555	0.2	1 191	0.1	1 364	0.2	126	901	419	81	338
III. Injuries	*187 614*	*12.3*	*123 366*	*15.5*	*64 249*	*8.8*	*29 658*	*62 818*	*19 805*	*4 493*	*15 311*
Unintentional	**138 564**	**9.1**	**87 130**	**10.9**	**51 434**	**7.1**	**20 229**	**51 243**	**10 998**	**3 017**	**7 981**
Road traffic accidents	41 223	2.7	29 240	3.7	11 983	1.6	7 151	11 003	4 582	1 332	3 250
Poisonings	7 447	0.5	4 893	0.6	2 554	0.4	1 145	1 840	579	500	79
Falls	17 157	1.1	10 447	1.3	6 710	0.9	992	6 414	1 205	382	823
Fires	11 271	0.7	4 534	0.6	6 738	0.9	2 016	6 599	247	85	163
Drownings	10 728	0.7	7 354	0.9	3 374	0.5	1 824	2 749	619	92	527
Other unintentional injuries	50 738	3.3	30 663	3.9	20 076	2.8	7 101	22 637	3 765	626	3 139
Intentional	**49 050**	**3.2**	**36 236**	**4.6**	**12 815**	**1.8**	**9 430**	**11 575**	**8 807**	**1 476**	**7 330**
Self-inflicted injuries	19 566	1.3	11 686	1.5	7 880	1.1	1 231	7 207	1 625	799	826
Violence	21 701	1.4	17 892	2.2	3 810	0.5	6 333	3 445	6 648	623	6 025
War and conflict	7 383	0.5	6 320	0.8	1 063	0.1	1 861	772	471	43	427

[a] See Annex Table C1 for a list of Member States by WHO region and income category.
[b] Estimates for specific causes may not sum to broader cause groupings due to omission of residual categories.
[c] World totals for males and females include residual populations living outside WHO Member States.
[d] For the Americas, Europe and Western Pacific regions, these figures include late effects of polio cases with onset prior to regional certification of polio eradication in 1994, 2000 and 2002, respectively.
[e] Does not include liver cancer and cirrhosis deaths resulting from chronic hepatitis virus infection.
[f] This category includes 'Causes arising in the perinatal period' as defined in the International Classification of Diseases, and does not include all deaths occurring in the perinatal period.
[g] Includes severe neonatal infections and other non-infectious causes arising in the perinatal period.
[h] Includes macular degeneration and other age-related causes of vision loss not correctable by provision of glasses or contact lenses, together with deaths due to other sense organ disorders.
[i] Includes myocarditis, pericarditis, endocarditis and cardiomyopathy.

Cause[b]	Eastern Mediterranean			Europe			Western Pacific		
	Total	High income	Low and middle income	Total	High income	Low and middle income	Total	High income	Low and middle income
Population (millions)	520	31	489	883	407	476	1 738	204	1 534
	(000)	*(000)*	*(000)*	*(000)*	*(000)*	*(000)*	*(000)*	*(000)*	*(000)*
Total DALYs	141 993	4 379	137 614	151 461	49 331	102 130	264 772	22 305	242 466
Cardiovascular diseases	**13 095**	**548**	**12 547**	**34 760**	**7 915**	**26 845**	**31 759**	**2 984**	**28 776**
Rheumatic heart disease	590	5	585	414	63	351	1 230	20	1 210
Hypertensive heart disease	939	90	849	1 139	294	844	2 303	77	2 225
Ischaemic heart disease	6 154	293	5 862	16 826	3 376	13 450	7 882	963	6 919
Cerebrovascular disease	2 695	53	2 641	9 531	2 037	7 494	15 843	1 311	14 533
Inflammatory heart diseases[i]	534	11	523	1 452	284	1 168	780	89	691
Respiratory diseases	**3 735**	**119**	**3 615**	**5 910**	**2 918**	**2 992**	**18 113**	**1 214**	**16 899**
Chronic obstructive pulmonary disease	1 406	40	1 366	2 961	1 475	1 486	11 852	479	11 373
Asthma	1 412	61	1 351	1 329	656	673	3 451	431	3 020
Digestive diseases	**3 439**	**91**	**3 348**	**6 945**	**2 190**	**4 755**	**8 491**	**899**	**7 592**
Peptic ulcer disease	295	4	291	478	110	367	1 082	37	1 045
Cirrhosis of the liver	1 158	15	1 144	3 099	817	2 282	2 567	356	2 211
Appendicitis	26	1	25	49	15	34	84	6	78
Diseases of the genitourinary system	**1 572**	**51**	**1 521**	**1 319**	**435**	**885**	**3 425**	**249**	**3 176**
Nephritis and nephrosis	1 033	34	999	676	189	487	1 693	127	1 566
Benign prostatic hypertrophy	210	15	195	274	122	153	794	77	718
Skin diseases	**346**	**18**	**328**	**331**	**89**	**242**	**693**	**41**	**652**
Musculoskeletal diseases	**1 878**	**116**	**1 762**	**5 435**	**2 172**	**3 263**	**9 418**	**1 184**	**8 234**
Rheumatoid arthritis	343	21	322	1 060	419	641	1 270	182	1 088
Osteoarthritis	800	47	753	3 140	1 170	1 970	4 915	686	4 229
Congenital abnormalities	**3 742**	**149**	**3 593**	**1 845**	**546**	**1 298**	**3 245**	**230**	**3 014**
Oral diseases	**865**	**63**	**802**	**896**	**328**	**569**	**1 480**	**170**	**1 310**
Dental caries	590	41	549	560	195	365	833	94	739
Periodontal disease	26	1	25	40	16	24	54	7	47
Edentulism	240	20	220	290	114	176	571	67	503
III. Injuries	*21 001*	*810*	*20 192*	*19 973*	*3 550*	*16 424*	*33 992*	*2 248*	*31 744*
Unintentional	**14 682**	**710**	**13 972**	**14 545**	**2 511**	**12 034**	**26 631**	**1 290**	**25 341**
Road traffic accidents	5 123	282	4 840	3 678	1 017	2 660	9 611	471	9 141
Poisonings	407	10	397	2 171	135	2 036	1 293	39	1 254
Falls	1 791	96	1 695	2 030	546	1 484	4 696	266	4 430
Fires	1 312	18	1 294	605	50	555	482	33	450
Drownings	933	52	881	796	76	719	3 788	83	3 705
Other unintentional injuries	5 117	252	4 865	5 265	686	4 579	6 760	399	6 361
Intentional	**6 319**	**99**	**6 220**	**5 428**	**1 039**	**4 389**	**7 362**	**958**	**6 403**
Self-inflicted injuries	1 092	45	1 047	3 092	880	2 213	5 303	881	4 421
Violence	1 391	45	1 346	1 970	144	1 826	1 850	74	1 776
War and conflict	3 764	5	3 759	360	15	344	108	2 107

Table A3: Deaths by cause and broad age group, countries grouped by income per capita,[a] 2004

Cause[b]	High income			Middle income			Low income		
	Total	0-14	15-59	Total	0-14	15-59	Total	0-14	15-59
Population (millions)	977	179	607	3 045	773	1 958	2 413	894	1 366
	(000)	*(000)*	*(000)*	*(000)*	*(000)*	*(000)*	*(000)*	*(000)*	*(000)*
Total deaths	8 144	103	1 245	24 349	2 341	7 275	26 251	9 439	8 129
Communicable, maternal, perinatal and nutritional conditions	*540*	*47*	*64*	*3 848*	*1 601*	*1 261*	*13 575*	*8 410*	*3 532*
Infectious and parasitic diseases	171	6	47	1 948	525	996	7 395	4 055	2 612
Tuberculosis	15	0	3	541	20	322	907	61	650
STDs excluding HIV	1	0	0	15	4	4	112	60	22
Syphilis	0	0	0	9	4	1	90	60	7
Chlamydia	0	0	0	1	0	1	8	0	7
Gonorrhoea	0	0	0	0	0	0	0	0	0
HIV/AIDS	21	0	19	509	52	444	1 509	249	1 224
Diarrhoeal diseases	14	3	1	343	268	32	1 806	1 535	129
Childhood-cluster diseases	1	0	0	66	57	7	780	768	10
Pertussis	0	0	0	11	11	0	243	243	0
Poliomyelitis[d]	1	0	0	0	0	0	0	0	0
Diphtheria	0	0	0	0	0	0	5	5	0
Measles	0	0	0	35	31	3	389	389	0
Tetanus	0	0	0	20	15	3	143	132	10
Meningitis	3	1	1	73	43	21	263	176	64
Hepatitis B[e]	7	0	3	42	2	28	56	9	36
Hepatitis C[e]	13	0	5	20	1	13	21	3	14
Malaria	0	0	0	32	27	4	857	817	36
Tropical-cluster diseases	0	0	0	21	2	10	131	43	74
Trypanosomiasis	0	0	0	3	1	1	50	21	27
Chagas disease	0	0	0	11	0	4	0	0	0
Schistosomiasis	0	0	0	5	0	4	36	2	25
Leishmaniasis	0	0	0	1	0	1	45	21	22
Lymphatic filariasis	0	0	0	0	0	0	0	0	0
Onchocerciasis	0	0	0	0	0	0	0	0	0
Leprosy	0	0	0	1	0	0	4	0	2
Dengue	0	0	0	7	6	1	11	10	0
Japanese encephalitis	0	0	0	3	2	0	8	7	1
Trachoma	0	0	0	0	0	0	0	0	0
Intestinal nematode infections	0	0	0	1	1	0	5	4	0
Ascariasis	0	0	0	0	0	0	2	2	0
Trichuriasis	0	0	0	0	0	0	2	2	0
Hookworm disease	0	0	0	0	0	0	0	0	0
Respiratory infections	311	4	14	955	284	163	2 990	1 770	366
Lower respiratory infections	307	4	14	925	274	156	2 943	1 746	358
Upper respiratory infections	4	0	0	30	10	6	43	22	6
Otitis media	0	0	0	1	0	1	4	2	2
Maternal conditions	2	0	2	75	0	75	449	2	447
Maternal haemorrhage	0	0	0	20	0	20	120	0	120
Maternal sepsis	0	0	0	7	0	7	55	0	54
Hypertensive disorders of pregnancy	0	0	0	13	0	13	49	2	47
Obstructed labour	0	0	0	3	0	3	31	0	31
Abortion	0	0	0	6	0	6	61	0	61
Perinatal conditions[f]	37	37	0	745	745	0	2 397	2 397	0
Prematurity and low birth weight	16	16	0	318	318	0	845	845	0
Birth asphyxia and birth trauma	7	7	0	194	194	0	655	655	0
Neonatal infections and other conditions[g]	14	14	0	233	233	0	897	897	0

Cause[b]	High income			Middle income			Low income		
	Total	0-14	15-59	Total	0-14	15-59	Total	0-14	15-59
Population (millions)	977	179	607	3 045	773	1 958	2 413	894	1 366
	(000)	(000)	(000)	(000)	(000)	(000)	(000)	(000)	(000)
Total deaths	8 144	103	1 245	24 349	2 341	7 275	26 251	9 439	8 129
Nutritional deficiencies	**19**	**0**	**1**	**124**	**46**	**28**	**344**	**186**	**107**
Protein-energy malnutrition	9	0	1	76	38	10	166	133	25
Iodine deficiency	0	0	0	0	0	0	5	4	0
Vitamin A deficiency	0	0	0	1	1	0	16	16	0
Iron-deficiency anaemia	8	0	0	38	5	15	107	22	70
II. Noncommunicable conditions	*7 096*	*39*	*903*	*17 547*	*347*	*4 023*	*10 358*	*580*	*3 106*
Malignant neoplasms	**2 163**	**5**	**394**	**3 698**	**38**	**1 268**	**1 560**	**43**	**563**
Mouth and oropharynx cancers	43	0	14	112	0	51	180	1	64
Oesophagus cancer	61	0	13	315	0	93	132	0	41
Stomach cancer	145	0	24	548	0	169	110	0	38
Colon and rectum cancer	266	0	38	300	0	82	73	0	27
Liver cancer	108	0	21	401	1	166	100	1	42
Pancreas cancer	122	0	19	114	0	33	29	0	10
Trachea, bronchus and lung cancers	478	0	83	694	0	205	151	0	45
Melanoma and other skin cancers	34	0	9	24	0	9	10	0	4
Breast cancer	162	0	48	232	0	116	125	0	59
Cervix uteri cancer	24	0	9	102	0	50	142	0	62
Corpus uteri cancer	21	0	3	26	0	8	8	0	2
Ovary cancer	48	0	12	58	0	25	38	0	15
Prostate cancer	122	0	4	112	0	8	73	0	6
Bladder cancer	63	0	5	85	0	16	39	0	6
Lymphomas and multiple myeloma	119	0	20	117	5	51	97	11	41
Leukaemia	78	2	15	134	18	69	64	13	34
Other neoplasms	**61**	**1**	**7**	**63**	**3**	**26**	**40**	**5**	**19**
Diabetes mellitus	**224**	**0**	**27**	**523**	**1**	**125**	**393**	**5**	**118**
Endocrine disorders	**76**	**3**	**16**	**132**	**23**	**43**	**94**	**22**	**32**
Neuropsychiatric disorders	**453**	**4**	**55**	**405**	**22**	**172**	**404**	**50**	**145**
Unipolar depressive disorders	3	0	0	1	0	1	10	0	8
Bipolar affective disorder	0	0	0	0	0	0	0	0	0
Schizophrenia	2	0	1	9	0	7	18	0	12
Epilepsy	11	1	5	53	8	38	78	28	37
Alcohol use disorders	23	0	15	47	0	36	18	0	13
Alzheimer and other dementias	277	0	2	101	1	9	113	1	2
Parkinson disease	51	0	1	43	0	4	15	0	0
Multiple sclerosis	8	0	4	7	0	4	2	0	1
Drug use disorders	10	0	10	37	0	36	44	0	43
Post-traumatic stress disorder	0	0	0	0	0	0	0	0	0
Obsessive-compulsive disorder	0	0	0	0	0	0	0	0	0
Panic disorder	0	0	0	0	0	0	0	0	0
Insomnia (primary)	0	0	0	0	0	0	0	0	0
Migraine	0	0	0	0	0	0	0	0	0
Sense organ disorders	**0**	**0**	**0**	**2**	**0**	**0**	**2**	**0**	**1**
Glaucoma	0	0	0	0	0	0	0	0	0
Cataracts	0	0	0	0	0	0	0	0	0
Refractive errors	0	0	0	0	0	0	0	0	0
Hearing loss, adult onset	0	0	0	0	0	0	0	0	0
Macular degeneration and other[h]	0	0	0	2	0	0	2	0	1

1

2

3

4

Annex A

Annex B

Annex C

References

(Table A3 continued)

Cause[b]	High income			Middle income			Low income		
	Total	0–14	15–59	Total	0–14	15–59	Total	0–14	15–59
Population (millions)	977	179	607	3 045	773	1 958	2 413	894	1 366
	(000)	(000)	(000)	(000)	(000)	(000)	(000)	(000)	(000)
Total deaths	8 144	103	1 245	24 349	2 341	7 275	26 251	9 439	8 129
Cardiovascular diseases	**3 027**	**3**	**268**	**8 896**	**38**	**1 565**	**5 142**	**82**	**1 314**
Rheumatic heart disease	18	0	2	131	3	57	149	17	72
Hypertensive heart disease	145	0	14	617	1	101	224	2	63
Ischaemic heart disease	1 331	0	134	3 395	2	632	2 468	8	649
Cerebrovascular disease	760	1	52	3 468	9	513	1 482	12	302
Inflammatory heart diseases[i]	78	1	15	233	5	60	129	12	44
Respiratory diseases	**476**	**1**	**30**	**2 231**	**24**	**259**	**1 328**	**37**	**385**
Chronic obstructive pulmonary disease	287	0	14	1 798	2	135	939	2	220
Asthma	21	0	4	120	4	55	146	7	91
Digestive diseases	**349**	**2**	**80**	**965**	**53**	**392**	**730**	**73**	**360**
Peptic ulcer disease	24	0	3	119	2	41	126	6	66
Cirrhosis of the liver	116	0	52	399	3	211	257	23	129
Appendicitis	1	0	0	10	1	4	11	1	4
Diseases of the genitourinary system	**173**	**0**	**12**	**401**	**9**	**129**	**353**	**21**	**135**
Nephritis and nephrosis	127	0	10	313	7	108	298	19	117
Benign prostatic hypertrophy	2	0	0	15	0	1	22	0	6
Skin diseases	**16**	**0**	**1**	**23**	**1**	**7**	**29**	**2**	**9**
Musculoskeletal diseases	**46**	**0**	**6**	**51**	**1**	**16**	**29**	**2**	**8**
Rheumatoid arthritis	9	0	1	11	0	3	6	0	2
Osteoarthritis	3	0	0	2	0	0	2	0	0
Congenital abnormalities	**31**	**20**	**7**	**156**	**134**	**18**	**253**	**237**	**14**
Oral diseases	**0**	**0**	**0**	**1**	**0**	**0**	**2**	**0**	**1**
Dental caries	0	0	0	0	0	0	0	0	0
Periodontal disease	0	0	0	0	0	0	0	0	0
Edentulism	0	0	0	0	0	0	0	0	0
III. Injuries	*509*	*17*	*278*	*2 954*	*393*	*1 990*	*2 318*	*449*	*1 491*
Unintentional	**343**	**14**	**158**	**1 922**	**292**	**1 244**	**1 640**	**399**	**939**
Road traffic accidents	116	6	80	674	53	512	485	108	311
Poisonings	31	0	27	173	9	134	142	23	82
Falls	76	1	13	199	11	97	149	23	52
Fires	9	1	4	62	10	35	240	62	151
Drownings	17	2	8	202	71	103	169	62	90
Other unintentional injuries	95	5	26	613	137	363	455	120	251
Intentional	**166**	**2**	**120**	**819**	**23**	**643**	**656**	**40**	**542**
Self-inflicted injuries	137	1	95	413	6	286	294	7	253
Violence	27	2	23	317	9	282	255	20	207
War and conflict	1	0	1	82	7	68	100	13	77

a See Annex Table C1 for a list of Member States by WHO region and income category.

b Estimates for specific causes may not sum to broader cause groupings due to omission of residual categories.

c World totals for males and females include residual populations living outside WHO Member States.

d For the Americas, Europe and Western Pacific regions, these figures include late effects of polio cases with onset prior to regional certification of polio eradication in 1994, 2000 and 2002, respectively.

e Does not include liver cancer and cirrhosis deaths resulting from chronic hepatitis virus infection.

f This category includes 'Causes arising in the perinatal period' as defined in the International Classification of Diseases, and does not include all deaths occurring in the perinatal period.

g Includes severe neonatal infections and other non-infectious causes arising in the perinatal period.

h Includes macular degeneration and other age-related causes of vision loss not correctable by provision of glasses or contact lenses, together with deaths due to other sense organ disorders.

i Includes myocarditis, pericarditis, endocarditis and cardiomyopathy.

Table A4: Burden of disease in DALYs by cause and broad age group, countries grouped by income per capita,[a] 2004

Cause[b]	High income			Middle income			Low income		
	Total	0-14	15-59	Total	0-14	15-59	Total	0-14	15-59
Population (millions)	977	179	607	3 045	773	1 958	2 413	894	1 366
	(000)	*(000)*	*(000)*	*(000)*	*(000)*	*(000)*	*(000)*	*(000)*	*(000)*
TOTAL DALYs	122 092	9 942	69 287	572 859	128 397	335 905	827 669	409 816	346 862
Communicable, maternal, perinatal and nutritional conditions	*7 340*	*2 688*	*3 131*	*127 572*	*71 185*	*50 202*	*468 811*	*332 459*	*125 391*
Infectious and parasitic diseases	**2 754**	**477**	**1 718**	**58 128**	**21 558**	**33 267**	**241 099**	**154 384**	**81 333**
Tuberculosis	185	12	112	11 661	828	9 246	22 356	2 537	18 185
STDs excluding HIV	215	8	205	2 327	319	1 970	7 877	2 986	4 698
Syphilis	7	3	4	301	158	126	2 535	2 046	340
Chlamydia	159	3	156	1 169	22	1 144	2 419	57	2 351
Gonorrhoea	46	2	44	799	136	661	2 703	852	1 851
HIV/AIDS	628	4	608	14 977	1 809	13 045	42 867	8 695	33 826
Diarrhoeal diseases	438	211	170	13 107	10 320	2 436	59 207	54 645	3 729
Childhood-cluster diseases	55	50	2	2 504	2 290	202	27 650	27 366	276
Pertussis	44	44	0	675	674	1	9 158	9 154	4
Poliomyelitis[d]	4	0	1	4	1	3	27	21	5
Diphtheria	0	0	0	11	10	1	163	159	3
Measles	3	3	0	1 238	1 116	123	13 601	13 598	3
Tetanus	4	3	0	576	490	75	4 701	4 433	260
Meningitis	108	57	39	2 412	1 744	600	8 905	6 984	1 770
Hepatitis B[e]	82	1	53	748	67	592	1 236	308	855
Hepatitis C[e]	153	0	99	325	23	254	476	122	326
Malaria	5	2	2	1 177	1 022	147	32 766	31 397	1 321
Tropical-cluster diseases	15	5	9	1 271	273	931	10 823	4 377	6 266
Trypanosomiasis	0	0	0	86	42	43	1 586	792	779
Chagas disease	2	0	2	423	0	375	3	0	3
Schistosomiasis	9	4	5	204	95	99	1 493	764	656
Leishmaniasis	4	2	2	110	44	64	1 861	926	905
Lymphatic filariasis	0	0	0	444	91	347	5 496	1 832	3 632
Onchocerciasis	0	0	0	4	1	3	383	63	291
Leprosy	0	0	0	34	7	21	160	53	98
Dengue	6	6	0	266	247	18	397	382	14
Japanese encephalitis	2	2	1	198	165	32	481	412	66
Trachoma	0	0	0	436	1	276	897	5	602
Intestinal nematode infections	24	13	10	1 293	862	401	2 694	2 352	323
Ascariasis	6	6	0	420	419	1	1 424	1 422	2
Trichuriasis	6	6	0	344	344	0	661	661	0
Hookworm disease	12	1	10	502	74	398	578	241	319
Respiratory infections	**1 374**	**250**	**315**	**17 565**	**11 433**	**3 830**	**78 807**	**64 480**	**9 368**
Lower respiratory infections	1 220	144	284	16 319	10 475	3 603	76 932	62 951	9 115
Upper respiratory infections	54	8	30	642	372	210	1 091	796	204
Otitis media	99	98	1	604	586	17	784	733	48
Maternal conditions	**667**	**2**	**665**	**9 227**	**100**	**9 127**	**29 022**	**429**	**28 593**
Maternal haemorrhage	6	0	6	592	0	591	3 838	0	3 838
Maternal sepsis	143	0	143	1 895	1	1 894	4 493	7	4 486
Hypertensive disorders of pregnancy	6	0	6	378	5	372	1 504	57	1 447
Obstructed labour	15	0	15	527	0	527	2 339	0	2 339
Abortion	31	2	29	1 515	90	1 425	5 875	343	5 532
Perinatal conditions[f]	**1 770**	**1 768**	**3**	**31 290**	**31 290**	**0**	**93 331**	**93 331**	**0**
Prematurity and low birth weight	739	739	0	11 459	11 459	0	32 099	32 099	0
Birth asphyxia and birth trauma	497	496	1	11 384	11 384	0	29 786	29 786	0
Neonatal infections and other conditions[g]	534	533	1	8 447	8 447	0	31 445	31 445	0

(Table A4 continued)

Cause[b]	High income			Middle income			Low income		
	Total	0-14	15-59	Total	0-14	15-59	Total	0-14	15-59
Population (millions)	977	179	607	3 045	773	1 958	2 413	894	1 366
	(000)	*(000)*	*(000)*	*(000)*	*(000)*	*(000)*	*(000)*	*(000)*	*(000)*
TOTAL DALYs	122 092	9 942	69 287	572 859	128 397	335 905	827 669	409 816	346 862
Nutritional deficiencies	**775**	**191**	**431**	**11 362**	**6 804**	**3 978**	**26 553**	**19 835**	**6 097**
Protein-energy malnutrition	128	97	11	4 032	3 676	237	13 294	12 653	598
Iodine deficiency	3	3	0	1 558	1 556	1	1 967	1 965	2
Vitamin A deficiency	0	0	0	41	40	1	587	585	2
Iron-deficiency anaemia	630	90	412	5 569	1 465	3 672	9 948	4 259	5 260
II. Noncommunicable conditions	*103 529*	*6 055*	*57 350*	*355 196*	*38 124*	*218 841*	*272 632*	*49 313*	*166 152*
Malignant neoplasms	**17 826**	**192**	**7 735**	**40 975**	**1 423**	**24 334**	**18 982**	**1 592**	**11 328**
Mouth and oropharynx cancers	432	1	251	1 374	14	949	1 983	32	1 196
Oesophagus cancer	488	0	210	2 963	1	1 539	1 317	5	728
Stomach cancer	1 027	0	415	5 294	8	3 001	1 167	7	728
Colon and rectum cancer	2 095	0	795	2 945	5	1 628	833	8	556
Liver cancer	845	5	352	4 625	36	3 041	1 240	50	815
Pancreas cancer	857	0	312	1 066	1	562	295	2	174
Trachea, bronchus and lung cancers	3 608	1	1 350	6 673	10	3 455	1 483	10	775
Melanoma and other skin cancers	316	1	184	269	4	178	121	4	78
Breast cancer	1 856	0	1 134	3 144	2	2 304	1 626	2	1 165
Cervix uteri cancer	330	0	234	1 486	1	1 109	1 901	1	1 318
Corpus uteri cancer	259	0	122	396	0	258	89	4	47
Ovary cancer	463	1	240	783	13	540	498	18	333
Prostate cancer	704	0	94	686	2	128	452	1	93
Bladder cancer	436	0	124	714	3	302	300	3	112
Lymphomas and multiple myeloma	900	11	376	1 729	198	1 144	1 653	406	970
Leukaemia	688	64	317	2 759	687	1 780	1 495	476	911
Other neoplasms	**366**	**25**	**136**	**865**	**114**	**552**	**721**	**179**	**449**
Diabetes mellitus	**3 623**	**11**	**2 033**	**10 081**	**94**	**6 606**	**5 991**	**237**	**3 818**
Endocrine disorders	**1 927**	**324**	**1 150**	**4 760**	**1 671**	**2 494**	**3 753**	**1 380**	**1 848**
Neuropsychiatric disorders	**31 558**	**2 173**	**23 232**	**94 822**	**13 483**	**74 405**	**72 824**	**14 937**	**54 342**
Unipolar depressive disorders	9 997	561	8 720	28 983	2 336	25 057	26 469	2 773	22 734
Bipolar affective disorder	1 543	56	1 484	7 041	328	6 708	5 836	338	5 496
Schizophrenia	1 553	253	1 289	8 429	884	7 499	6 782	494	6 237
Epilepsy	538	106	373	3 201	827	2 248	4 112	1 842	2 150
Alcohol use disorders	4 207	57	4 025	14 853	552	13 953	4 671	196	4 407
Alzheimer and other dementias	4 387	79	260	4 772	330	700	1 996	280	266
Parkinson disease	694	0	157	670	11	296	346	4	193
Multiple sclerosis	320	19	268	730	75	635	477	65	404
Drug use disorders	1 894	28	1 860	3 664	130	3 522	2 806	97	2 696
Post-traumatic stress disorder	512	6	500	1 663	24	1 627	1 292	30	1 257
Obsessive-compulsive disorder	597	16	575	2 484	221	2 223	2 020	396	1 603
Panic disorder	795	23	763	3 348	99	3 231	2 845	109	2 727
Insomnia (primary)	768	9	615	1 458	44	1 248	1 395	35	1 248
Migraine	1 437	375	1 063	3 512	1 162	2 350	2 813	1 827	985
Sense organ disorders	**9 235**	**312**	**5 191**	**41 604**	**2 642**	**27 083**	**36 010**	**1 539**	**25 046**
Glaucoma	371	2	194	2 517	29	1 540	1 837	65	1 294
Cataracts	406	7	259	8 813	87	5 560	8 527	86	6 163
Refractive errors	2 745	299	1 541	13 731	2 501	8 154	11 262	1 365	6 143
Hearing loss, adult onset	4 203	0	2 370	12 200	0	9 158	10 945	0	9 054
Macular degeneration and other[h]	1 510	3	826	4 343	24	2 670	3 439	22	2 392

Cause[b]	High income			Middle income			Low income		
	Total	0-14	15-59	Total	0-14	15-59	Total	0-14	15-59
Population (millions)	977	179	607	3 045	773	1 958	2 413	894	1 366
	(000)	(000)	(000)	(000)	(000)	(000)	(000)	(000)	(000)
TOTAL DALYs	122 092	9 942	69 287	572 859	128 397	335 905	827 669	409 816	346 862
Cardiovascular diseases	**17 853**	**121**	**6 827**	**76 204**	**1 610**	**35 086**	**57 258**	**3 404**	**30 188**
Rheumatic heart disease	120	2	43	2 050	126	1 413	3 016	658	1 975
Hypertensive heart disease	801	1	262	4 769	38	1 847	2 445	70	1 273
Ischaemic heart disease	7 739	3	2 779	28 866	66	13 500	25 958	290	13 913
Cerebrovascular disease	4 763	20	1 893	27 529	343	11 242	14 281	457	6 546
Inflammatory heart diseases[i]	748	32	397	2 806	183	1 663	2 678	479	1 672
Respiratory diseases	**7 266**	**943**	**3 808**	**29 044**	**3 911**	**14 135**	**22 706**	**4 335**	**12 154**
Chronic obstructive pulmonary disease	3 663	7	2 045	16 123	79	6 728	10 402	74	5 364
Asthma	1 919	805	1 004	6 897	2 711	3 778	7 494	2 878	4 286
Digestive diseases	**4 714**	**189**	**2 952**	**19 259**	**2 432**	**13 071**	**18 508**	**3 922**	**12 329**
Peptic ulcer disease	194	2	108	1 898	88	1 330	2 871	327	2 146
Cirrhosis of the liver	1 653	6	1 168	6 731	126	5 148	5 249	1 063	3 332
Appendicitis	35	6	23	191	33	131	192	42	116
Diseases of the genitourinary system	**1 248**	**31**	**505**	**7 008**	**499**	**4 851**	**6 491**	**1 050**	**4 175**
Nephritis and nephrosis	630	21	201	3 858	378	2 379	4 563	932	2 656
Benign prostatic hypertrophy	302	0	174	1 372	0	1 177	988	0	841
Skin diseases	**230**	**10**	**95**	**1 809**	**316**	**1 233**	**1 838**	**540**	**1 090**
Musculoskeletal diseases	**5 237**	**98**	**3 066**	**16 288**	**687**	**12 552**	**9 332**	**783**	**7 276**
Rheumatoid arthritis	955	43	647	2 655	213	2 069	1 437	181	1 089
Osteoarthritis	2 777	0	1 366	8 425	4	6 432	4 377	6	3 612
Congenital abnormalities	**1 606**	**1 419**	**162**	**8 530**	**7 971**	**537**	**15 134**	**14 679**	**445**
Oral diseases	**840**	**205**	**457**	**3 946**	**1 270**	**1 901**	**3 085**	**736**	**1 665**
Dental caries	507	204	249	2 459	1 257	1 055	1 913	717	1 022
Periodontal disease	38	0	36	121	0	111	160	1	151
Edentulism	287	0	168	1 319	0	709	948	0	452
III. Injuries	*11 222*	*1 199*	*8 806*	*90 092*	*19 088*	*66 863*	*86 226*	*28 045*	*55 318*
Unintentional	**7 595**	**1 050**	**5 616**	**65 905**	**17 704**	**45 126**	**65 015**	**25 781**	**36 890**
Road traffic accidents	3 127	300	2 633	21 382	3 306	17 252	16 697	5 871	10 343
Poisonings	693	11	660	3 687	352	3 117	3 064	842	1 939
Falls	1 297	198	752	8 640	2 573	5 352	7 215	3 523	3 162
Fires	187	50	114	2 196	754	1 339	8 886	3 759	4 951
Drownings	307	76	195	5 573	2 602	2 789	4 844	2 254	2 485
Other unintentional injuries	1 983	415	1 262	24 428	8 117	15 277	24 309	9 532	14 010
Intentional	**3 627**	**149**	**3 190**	**24 187**	**1 383**	**21 736**	**21 211**	**2 264**	**18 428**
Self-inflicted injuries	2 616	70	2 278	8 516	393	7 320	8 431	466	7 744
Violence	928	79	830	11 967	652	11 118	8 788	1 178	7 409
War and conflict	67	1	66	3 493	332	3 098	3 819	593	3 141

[a] See Annex Table C1 for a list of Member States by WHO region and income category.
[b] Estimates for specific causes may not sum to broader cause groupings due to omission of residual categories.
[c] World totals for males and females include residual populations living outside WHO Member States.
[d] For the Americas, Europe and Western Pacific regions, these figures include late effects of polio cases with onset prior to regional certification of polio eradication in 1994, 2000 and 2002, respectively.
[e] Does not include liver cancer and cirrhosis deaths resulting from chronic hepatitis virus infection.
[f] This category includes 'Causes arising in the perinatal period' as defined in the International Classification of Diseases, and does not include all deaths occurring in the perinatal period.
[g] Includes severe neonatal infections and other non-infectious causes arising in the perinatal period.
[h] Includes macular degeneration and other age-related causes of vision loss not correctable by provision of glasses or contact lenses, together with deaths due to other sense organ disorders.
[i] Includes myocarditis, pericarditis, endocarditis and cardiomyopathy.

1
2
3
4
Annex A
Annex B
Annex C
References

Table A5: Deaths by cause, sex and age group, countries grouped by income per capita,[a] 2004

Table A5a: Deaths (thousands) by age, sex, cause in the world, 2004

Cause[b]	World			Males			Females		
	Total[c]	Males	Females	0-14	15-59	60+	0-14	15-59	60+
Population (millions)	6 437	3 244	3 193	951	1 994	298	895	1 938	360
	(000)	*(000)*	*(000)*	*(000)*	*(000)*	*(000)*	*(000)*	*(000)*	*(000)*
TOTAL Deaths	58 772	31 082	27 690	6 171	9 991	14 920	5 716	6 666	15 308
Communicable, maternal, perinatal and nutritional conditions	*17 971*	*9 284*	*8 687*	*5 213*	*2 495*	*1 577*	*4 849*	*2 366*	*1 471*
Infectious and parasitic diseases	**9 519**	**5 198**	**4 321**	**2 379**	**2 108**	**711**	**2 209**	**1 549**	**562**
Tuberculosis	1 464	969	494	42	643	284	39	333	123
STDs excluding HIV	128	71	57	34	14	24	31	13	13
Syphilis	99	60	39	33	7	20	31	1	7
Chlamydia	9	0	9	0	0	0	0	7	1
Gonorrhoea	1	0	0	0	0	0	0	0	0
HIV/AIDS	2 040	1 027	1 013	153	845	29	149	843	21
Diarrhoeal diseases	2 163	1 127	1 037	938	96	92	868	66	103
Childhood-cluster diseases	847	458	390	445	11	2	382	6	2
Pertussis	254	129	125	129	0	0	125	0	0
Poliomyelitis[d]	1	1	1	0	0	0	0	0	0
Diphtheria	5	3	3	2	0	0	2	0	0
Measles	424	220	204	218	2	0	202	1	0
Tetanus	163	105	58	95	8	2	52	5	1
Meningitis	340	181	159	107	54	19	113	32	14
Hepatitis B[e]	105	74	31	5	51	17	5	15	10
Hepatitis C[e]	54	36	18	2	24	10	2	8	8
Malaria	889	456	433	434	19	2	410	20	3
Tropical-cluster diseases	152	94	58	27	54	13	18	30	9
Trypanosomiasis	52	33	19	14	18	1	8	10	1
Chagas disease	11	7	5	0	3	4	0	1	3
Schistosomiasis	41	26	15	1	18	7	1	11	4
Leishmaniasis	47	29	18	12	15	2	9	7	1
Lymphatic filariasis	0	0	0	0	0	0	0	0	0
Onchocerciasis	0	0	0	0	0	0	0	0	0
Leprosy	5	4	1	0	2	2	0	1	1
Dengue	18	9	9	8	1	0	8	1	0
Japanese encephalitis	11	5	6	4	1	0	5	1	0
Trachoma	0	0	0	0	0	0	0	0	0
Intestinal nematode infections	6	4	3	3	0	0	3	0	0
Ascariasis	2	1	1	1	0	0	1	0	0
Trichuriasis	2	1	1	1	0	0	1	0	0
Hookworm disease	0	0	0	0	0	0	0	0	0
Respiratory infections	**4 259**	**2 207**	**2 052**	**1 058**	**326**	**823**	**1 001**	**217**	**834**
Lower respiratory infections	4 177	2 163	2 014	1 040	316	806	985	212	818
Upper respiratory infections	77	41	36	16	8	16	16	4	16
Otitis media	5	3	2	1	1	0	1	1	0
Maternal conditions	**527**	**0**	**527**	**0**	**0**	**0**	**3**	**524**	**0**
Maternal haemorrhage	140	0	140	0	0	0	0	140	0
Maternal sepsis	62	0	62	0	0	0	0	62	0
Hypertensive disorders of pregnancy	62	0	62	0	0	0	2	60	0
Obstructed labour	34	0	34	0	0	0	0	34	0
Abortion	68	0	68	0	0	0	0	68	0
Perinatal conditions[f]	**3 180**	**1 657**	**1 523**	**1 657**	**0**	**0**	**1 523**	**0**	**0**
Prematurity and low birth weight	1 179	612	567	612	0	0	567	0	0
Birth asphyxia and birth trauma	857	446	411	446	0	0	411	0	0
Neonatal infections and other conditions[g]	1 144	599	546	599	0	0	545	0	0

Cause[b]	World			Males			Females		
	Total[c]	Males	Females	0-14	15-59	60+	0-14	15-59	60+
Population (millions)	6 437	3 244	3 193	951	1 994	298	895	1 938	360
	(000)	*(000)*	*(000)*	*(000)*	*(000)*	*(000)*	*(000)*	*(000)*	*(000)*
TOTAL Deaths	58 772	31 082	27 690	6 171	9 991	14 920	5 716	6 666	15 308
Nutritional deficiencies	**487**	**223**	**264**	**119**	**60**	**43**	**113**	**76**	**75**
Protein-energy malnutrition	251	127	124	88	21	18	84	16	24
Iodine deficiency	5	3	2	3	0	0	2	0	0
Vitamin A deficiency	17	9	8	9	0	0	8	0	0
Iron-deficiency anaemia	153	55	98	14	31	11	13	55	30
II. Noncommunicable conditions	*35 017*	*17 985*	*17 032*	*487*	*4 807*	*12 691*	*479*	*3 228*	*13 324*
Malignant neoplasms	**7 424**	**4 154**	**3 270**	**45**	**1 225**	**2 883**	**41**	**1 002**	**2 228**
Mouth and oropharynx cancers	335	239	96	1	100	139	1	30	65
Oesophagus cancer	508	331	177	0	100	231	0	47	130
Stomach cancer	803	499	304	0	150	348	0	80	224
Colon and rectum cancer	639	336	303	0	85	251	0	63	241
Liver cancer	610	418	192	1	172	244	1	57	134
Pancreas cancer	265	137	128	0	38	99	0	24	105
Trachea, bronchus and lung cancers	1 323	943	381	0	240	703	0	93	287
Melanoma and other skin cancers	68	37	31	0	13	24	0	9	22
Breast cancer	519	2	517	0	1	2	0	223	294
Cervix uteri cancer	268	0	268	0	0	0	0	121	147
Corpus uteri cancer	55	0	55	0	0	0	0	13	42
Ovary cancer	144	0	144	0	0	0	1	52	91
Prostate cancer	308	308	0	0	18	290	0	0	0
Bladder cancer	187	138	49	0	20	118	0	7	42
Lymphomas and multiple myeloma	332	191	142	10	74	107	6	37	98
Leukaemia	277	154	123	17	68	68	16	49	58
Other neoplasms	**163**	**83**	**80**	**4**	**28**	**50**	**5**	**25**	**51**
Diabetes mellitus	**1 141**	**508**	**633**	**3**	**141**	**364**	**4**	**130**	**499**
Endocrine disorders	**303**	**141**	**162**	**25**	**46**	**70**	**23**	**45**	**94**
Neuropsychiatric disorders	**1 263**	**647**	**616**	**41**	**258**	**348**	**36**	**114**	**466**
Unipolar depressive disorders	15	7	8	0	5	2	0	5	3
Bipolar affective disorder	1	0	1	0	0	0	0	0	0
Schizophrenia	30	15	14	0	11	4	0	8	6
Epilepsy	142	82	60	19	49	14	18	31	12
Alcohol use disorders	88	75	13	0	55	20	0	8	4
Alzheimer and other dementias	492	181	312	1	7	172	1	6	305
Parkinson disease	110	58	52	0	3	54	0	2	50
Multiple sclerosis	17	7	11	0	4	3	0	6	5
Drug use disorders	91	75	16	0	73	2	0	16	1
Post-traumatic stress disorder	0	0	0	0	0	0	0	0	0
Obsessive-compulsive disorder	0	0	0	0	0	0	0	0	0
Panic disorder	0	0	0	0	0	0	0	0	0
Insomnia (primary)	0	0	0	0	0	0	0	0	0
Migraine	0	0	0	0	0	0	0	0	0
Sense organ disorders	**4**	**2**	**2**	**0**	**1**	**1**	**0**	**1**	**1**
Glaucoma	0	0	0	0	0	0	0	0	0
Cataracts	0	0	0	0	0	0	0	0	0
Refractive errors	0	0	0	0	0	0	0	0	0
Hearing loss, adult onset	0	0	0	0	0	0	0	0	0
Macular degeneration and other[h]	4	2	2	0	1	1	0	1	1

1

2

3

4

Annex A

Annex B

Annex C

References

(Table A5a continued)

Cause[b]	World			Males			Females		
	Total[c]	Males	Females	0-14	15-59	60+	0-14	15-59	60+
Population (millions)	6 437	3 244	3 193	951	1 994	298	895	1 938	360
	(000)	*(000)*	*(000)*	*(000)*	*(000)*	*(000)*	*(000)*	*(000)*	*(000)*
TOTAL Deaths	58 772	31 082	27 690	6 171	9 991	14 920	5 716	6 666	15 308
Cardiovascular diseases	**17 073**	**8 338**	**8 735**	**61**	**1 974**	**6 303**	**62**	**1 175**	**7 499**
Rheumatic heart disease	298	127	171	9	61	57	12	69	90
Hypertensive heart disease	987	457	530	1	103	353	2	76	453
Ischaemic heart disease	7 198	3 827	3 371	6	982	2 839	4	434	2 933
Cerebrovascular disease	5 712	2 661	3 051	11	503	2 146	10	364	2 677
Inflammatory heart diseases[i]	440	229	211	9	78	141	9	42	161
Respiratory diseases	**4 036**	**2 155**	**1 881**	**32**	**391**	**1 731**	**30**	**282**	**1 568**
Chronic obstructive pulmonary disease	3 025	1 620	1 405	2	220	1 398	1	149	1 254
Asthma	287	151	136	6	79	66	6	71	60
Digestive diseases	**2 045**	**1 166**	**879**	**59**	**546**	**562**	**69**	**287**	**522**
Peptic ulcer disease	270	163	107	4	76	83	4	33	70
Cirrhosis of the liver	772	510	262	11	279	220	15	113	133
Appendicitis	22	13	9	1	6	6	1	3	6
Diseases of the genitourinary system	**928**	**493**	**435**	**16**	**155**	**322**	**15**	**122**	**298**
Nephritis and nephrosis	739	385	354	14	131	241	13	104	237
Benign prostatic hypertrophy	39	39	0	0	7	31	0	0	0
Skin diseases	**68**	**27**	**41**	**1**	**8**	**17**	**1**	**9**	**30**
Musculoskeletal diseases	**127**	**45**	**81**	**2**	**11**	**32**	**2**	**19**	**61**
Rheumatoid arthritis	26	8	18	0	2	6	0	4	15
Osteoarthritis	7	2	4	0	0	2	0	0	4
Congenital abnormalities	**440**	**225**	**215**	**198**	**22**	**5**	**193**	**18**	**5**
Oral diseases	**3**	**2**	**2**	**0**	**1**	**1**	**0**	**1**	**1**
Dental caries	0	0	0	0	0	0	0	0	0
Periodontal disease	0	0	0	0	0	0	0	0	0
Edentulism	0	0	0	0	0	0	0	0	0
III. Injuries	***5 784***	***3 812***	***1 972***	***472***	***2 688***	***652***	***388***	***1 071***	***512***
Unintentional	**3 906**	**2 520**	**1 386**	**390**	**1 665**	**465**	**315**	**676**	**394**
Road traffic accidents	1 275	944	331	101	709	134	65	195	70
Poisonings	346	222	124	19	172	32	14	72	38
Falls	424	260	164	20	122	118	14	40	110
Fires	310	120	190	33	70	18	41	121	29
Drownings	388	263	125	85	150	28	51	51	23
Other unintentional injuries	1 163	711	452	132	443	136	130	198	124
Intentional	**1 642**	**1 181**	**461**	**37**	**97v2**	**172**	**28**	**334**	**99**
Self-inflicted injuries	844	529	316	8	400	121	6	234	75
Violence	600	485	115	18	430	37	14	83	18
War and conflict	184	155	29	12	132	11	8	16	5

a   See Annex Table C1 for a list of Member States by WHO region and income category.

b   Estimates for specific causes may not sum to broader cause groupings due to omission of residual categories.

c   World totals for males and females include residual populations living outside WHO Member States.

d   For the Americas, Europe and Western Pacific regions, these figures include late effects of polio cases with onset prior to regional certification of polio eradication in 1994, 2000 and 2002, respectively.

e   Does not include liver cancer and cirrhosis deaths resulting from chronic hepatitis virus infection.

f   This category includes 'Causes arising in the perinatal period' as defined in the International Classification of Diseases, and does not include all deaths occurring in the perinatal period.

g   Includes severe neonatal infections and other non-infectious causes arising in the perinatal period.

h   Includes macular degeneration and other age-related causes of vision loss not correctable by provision of glasses or contact lenses, together with deaths due to other sense organ disorders.

i   Includes myocarditis, pericarditis, endocarditis and cardiomyopathy.

Table A5b: Deaths (thousands) by age, sex, cause in high-income countries, 2004

Cause[b]	High-income countries			Males			Females		
	Total[c]	Males	Females	0-14	15-59	60+	0-14	15-59	60+
Population (millions)	977	482	495	92	308	83	87	300	108
	(000)	(000)	(000)	(000)	(000)	(000)	(000)	(000)	(000)
TOTAL Deaths	8 144	4 106	4 038	57	820	3 229	45	425	3 568
Communicable, maternal, perinatal and nutritional conditions	*540*	*263*	*277*	*26*	*42*	*195*	*21*	*22*	*234*
Infectious and parasitic diseases	**171**	**89**	**81**	**3**	**32**	**54**	**3**	**15**	**63**
Tuberculosis	15	10	6	0	2	7	0	1	4
STDs excluding HIV	1	0	0	0	0	0	0	0	0
Syphilis	0	0	0	0	0	0	0	0	0
Chlamydia	0	0	0	0	0	0	0	0	0
Gonorrhoea	0	0	0	0	0	0	0	0	0
HIV/AIDS	21	16	5	0	14	1	0	5	0
Diarrhoeal diseases	14	5	9	1	0	4	1	0	7
Childhood-cluster diseases	1	0	0	0	0	0	0	0	0
Pertussis	0	0	0	0	0	0	0	0	0
Poliomyelitis[d]	1	0	0	0	0	0	0	0	0
Diphtheria	0	0	0	0	0	0	0	0	0
Measles	0	0	0	0	0	0	0	0	0
Tetanus	0	0	0	0	0	0	0	0	0
Meningitis	3	2	2	0	1	1	0	0	1
Hepatitis B[e]	7	4	3	0	2	2	0	1	2
Hepatitis C[e]	13	7	6	0	4	4	0	1	4
Malaria	0	0	0	0	0	0	0	0	0
Tropical-cluster diseases	0	0	0	0	0	0	0	0	0
Trypanosomiasis	0	0	0	0	0	0	0	0	0
Chagas disease	0	0	0	0	0	0	0	0	0
Schistosomiasis	0	0	0	0	0	0	0	0	0
Leishmaniasis	0	0	0	0	0	0	0	0	0
Lymphatic filariasis	0	0	0	0	0	0	0	0	0
Onchocerciasis	0	0	0	0	0	0	0	0	0
Leprosy	0	0	0	0	0	0	0	0	0
Dengue	0	0	0	0	0	0	0	0	0
Japanese encephalitis	0	0	0	0	0	0	0	0	0
Trachoma	0	0	0	0	0	0	0	0	0
Intestinal nematode infections	0	0	0	0	0	0	0	0	0
Ascariasis	0	0	0	0	0	0	0	0	0
Trichuriasis	0	0	0	0	0	0	0	0	0
Hookworm disease	0	0	0	0	0	0	0	0	0
Respiratory infections	**311**	**145**	**166**	**2**	**9**	**135**	**2**	**5**	**159**
Lower respiratory infections	307	143	164	2	9	133	2	5	157
Upper respiratory infections	4	2	2	0	0	2	0	0	2
Otitis media	0	0	0	0	0	0	0	0	0
Maternal conditions	**2**	**0**	**2**	**0**	**0**	**0**	**0**	**2**	**0**
Maternal haemorrhage	0	0	0	0	0	0	0	0	0
Maternal sepsis	0	0	0	0	0	0	0	0	0
Hypertensive disorders of pregnancy	0	0	0	0	0	0	0	0	0
Obstructed labour	0	0	0	0	0	0	0	0	0
Abortion	0	0	0	0	0	0	0	0	0
Perinatal conditions[f]	**37**	**21**	**16**	**21**	**0**	**0**	**16**	**0**	**0**
Prematurity and low birth weight	16	9	7	9	0	0	7	0	0
Birth asphyxia and birth trauma	7	4	3	4	0	0	3	0	0
Neonatal infections and other conditions[g]	14	8	6	8	0	0	6	0	0

(Table A5b continued)

Cause[b]	High-income countries			Males			Females		
	Total[c]	Males	Females	0-14	15-59	60+	0-14	15-59	60+
Population (millions)	977	482	495	92	308	83	87	300	108
	(000)	(000)	(000)	(000)	(000)	(000)	(000)	(000)	(000)
TOTAL Deaths	8 144	4 106	4 038	57	820	3 229	45	425	3 568
Nutritional deficiencies	**19**	**7**	**12**	**0**	**1**	**6**	**0**	**0**	**11**
Protein-energy malnutrition	9	3	5	0	0	3	0	0	5
Iodine deficiency	0	0	0	0	0	0	0	0	0
Vitamin A deficiency	0	0	0	0	0	0	0	0	0
Iron-deficiency anaemia	8	3	5	0	0	3	0	0	5
II. Noncommunicable conditions	*7 096*	*3 505*	*3 591*	*21*	*565*	*2 918*	*18*	*338*	*3 235*
Malignant neoplasms	**2 163**	**1 204**	**959**	**3**	**216**	**985**	**2**	**178**	**779**
Mouth and oropharynx cancers	43	32	11	0	12	20	0	3	9
Oesophagus cancer	61	47	14	0	11	36	0	2	12
Stomach cancer	145	89	56	0	15	74	0	8	48
Colon and rectum cancer	266	138	127	0	22	116	0	16	112
Liver cancer	108	73	35	0	17	56	0	4	31
Pancreas cancer	122	62	60	0	12	50	0	7	53
Trachea, bronchus and lung cancers	478	320	157	0	55	265	0	28	129
Melanoma and other skin cancers	34	20	14	0	6	14	0	3	10
Breast cancer	162	2	160	0	0	1	0	48	112
Cervix uteri cancer	24	0	24	0	0	0	0	9	15
Corpus uteri cancer	21	0	21	0	0	0	0	3	18
Ovary cancer	48	0	48	0	0	0	0	12	37
Prostate cancer	122	122	0	0	4	119	0	0	0
Bladder cancer	63	45	18	0	4	41	0	1	17
Lymphomas and multiple myeloma	119	62	56	0	12	50	0	7	49
Leukaemia	78	43	35	1	9	34	1	6	28
Other neoplasms	**61**	**30**	**30**	**0**	**4**	**26**	**0**	**3**	**27**
Diabetes mellitus	**224**	**103**	**121**	**0**	**18**	**86**	**0**	**10**	**111**
Endocrine disorders	**76**	**34**	**43**	**2**	**9**	**23**	**1**	**7**	**35**
Neuropsychiatric disorders	**453**	**183**	**270**	**2**	**37**	**144**	**2**	**18**	**251**
Unipolar depressive disorders	3	1	2	0	0	1	0	0	2
Bipolar affective disorder	0	0	0	0	0	0	0	0	0
Schizophrenia	2	1	1	0	0	1	0	0	1
Epilepsy	11	6	5	0	4	2	0	2	3
Alcohol use disorders	23	18	5	0	12	7	0	3	2
Alzheimer and other dementias	277	83	194	0	1	82	0	1	193
Parkinson disease	51	28	24	0	0	27	0	0	24
Multiple sclerosis	8	3	5	0	1	1	0	2	3
Drug use disorders	10	8	2	0	7	0	0	2	0
Post-traumatic stress disorder	0	0	0	0	0	0	0	0	0
Obsessive-compulsive disorder	0	0	0	0	0	0	0	0	0
Panic disorder	0	0	0	0	0	0	0	0	0
Insomnia (primary)	0	0	0	0	0	0	0	0	0
Migraine	0	0	0	0	0	0	0	0	0
Sense organ disorders	**0**	**0**	**0**	**0**	**0**	**0**	**0**	**0**	**0**
Glaucoma	0	0	0	0	0	0	0	0	0
Cataracts	0	0	0	0	0	0	0	0	0
Refractive errors	0	0	0	0	0	0	0	0	0
Hearing loss, adult onset	0	0	0	0	0	0	0	0	0
Macular degeneration and other[h]	0	0	0	0	0	0	0	0	0

Cause[b]	High-income countries			Males			Females		
	Total[c]	Males	Females	0-14	15-59	60+	0-14	15-59	60+
Population (millions)	977	482	495	92	308	83	87	300	108
	(000)	*(000)*	*(000)*	*(000)*	*(000)*	*(000)*	*(000)*	*(000)*	*(000)*
TOTAL Deaths	8 144	4 106	4 038	57	820	3 229	45	425	3 568
Cardiovascular diseases	**3 027**	**1 398**	**1 628**	**2**	**193**	**1 204**	**1**	**75**	**1 552**
Rheumatic heart disease	18	6	12	0	1	5	0	1	11
Hypertensive heart disease	145	55	89	0	10	46	0	5	84
Ischaemic heart disease	1 331	698	634	0	107	591	0	28	606
Cerebrovascular disease	760	312	448	0	31	281	0	20	427
Inflammatory heart diseases[i]	78	44	34	0	11	32	0	4	30
Respiratory diseases	**476**	**258**	**218**	**1**	**17**	**240**	**1**	**12**	**205**
Chronic obstructive pulmonary disease	287	162	125	0	8	154	0	6	119
Asthma	21	9	12	0	2	7	0	2	10
Digestive diseases	**349**	**181**	**167**	**1**	**57**	**123**	**1**	**22**	**144**
Peptic ulcer disease	24	11	13	0	2	9	0	1	12
Cirrhosis of the liver	116	79	37	0	39	40	0	13	24
Appendicitis	1	1	1	0	0	1	0	0	1
Diseases of the genitourinary system	**173**	**78**	**95**	**0**	**7**	**70**	**0**	**5**	**89**
Nephritis and nephrosis	127	60	67	0	6	53	0	4	63
Benign prostatic hypertrophy	2	2	0	0	0	2	0	0	0
Skin diseases	**16**	**5**	**11**	**0**	**1**	**5**	**0**	**1**	**10**
Musculoskeletal diseases	**46**	**14**	**32**	**0**	**2**	**12**	**0**	**4**	**29**
Rheumatoid arthritis	9	2	7	0	0	2	0	0	6
Osteoarthritis	3	1	2	0	0	1	0	0	2
Congenital abnormalities	**31**	**16**	**15**	**10**	**4**	**2**	**9**	**3**	**2**
Oral diseases	**0**	**0**	**0**	**0**	**0**	**0**	**0**	**0**	**0**
Dental caries	0	0	0	0	0	0	0	0	0
Periodontal disease	0	0	0	0	0	0	0	0	0
Edentulism	0	0	0	0	0	0	0	0	0
III. Injuries	*509*	*339*	*171*	*11*	*212*	*116*	*6*	*65*	*99*
Unintentional	**343**	**214**	**128**	**9**	**120**	**85**	**5**	**37**	**86**
Road traffic accidents	116	83	32	4	61	18	2	19	11
Poisonings	31	21	10	0	19	2	0	8	2
Falls	76	38	37	0	10	28	0	2	35
Fires	9	5	3	0	2	2	0	1	2
Drownings	17	12	5	1	7	4	1	1	3
Other unintentional injuries	95	55	40	3	21	31	2	5	33
Intentional	**166**	**124**	**42**	**1**	**92**	**31**	**1**	**28**	**13**
Self-inflicted injuries	137	102	35	0	73	29	0	23	12
Violence	27	20	7	1	18	1	1	5	1
War and conflict	1	1	0	0	1	0	0	0	0

1

2

3

4

Annex A

Annex B

Annex C

References

a See Annex Table C1 for a list of Member States by WHO region and income category.

b Estimates for specific causes may not sum to broader cause groupings due to omission of residual categories.

c World totals for males and females include residual populations living outside WHO Member States.

d For the Americas, Europe and Western Pacific regions, these figures include late effects of polio cases with onset prior to regional certification of polio eradication in 1994, 2000 and 2002, respectively.

e Does not include liver cancer and cirrhosis deaths resulting from chronic hepatitis virus infection.

f This category includes 'Causes arising in the perinatal period' as defined in the International Classification of Diseases, and does not include all deaths occurring in the perinatal period.

g Includes severe neonatal infections and other non-infectious causes arising in the perinatal period.

h Includes macular degeneration and other age-related causes of vision loss not correctable by provision of glasses or contact lenses, together with deaths due to other sense organ disorders.

i Includes myocarditis, pericarditis, endocarditis and cardiomyopathy.

Table A5c: Deaths (thousands) by age, sex, cause in middle-income countries, 2004

Cause[b]	Middle-income countries			Males			Females		
	Total[c]	Males	Females	0-14	15-59	60+	0-14	15-59	60+
Population (millions)	3 045	1 531	1 513	400	989	142	372	969	172
	(000)	*(000)*	*(000)*	*(000)*	*(000)*	*(000)*	*(000)*	*(000)*	*(000)*
TOTAL Deaths	24 349	13 150	11 199	1 235	4 681	7 234	1 106	2 594	7 499
Communicable, maternal, perinatal and nutritional conditions	*3 848*	*2 100*	*1 748*	*837*	*742*	*521*	*764*	*520*	*464*
Infectious and parasitic diseases	**1 948**	**1 148**	**800**	**274**	**619**	**254**	**251**	**377**	**173**
Tuberculosis	541	372	170	10	220	142	10	102	58
STDs excluding HIV	15	8	8	2	2	3	2	3	3
Syphilis	9	5	4	2	1	2	2	0	2
Chlamydia	1	0	1	0	0	0	0	1	0
Gonorrhoea	0	0	0	0	0	0	0	0	0
HIV/AIDS	509	280	229	27	247	7	26	197	6
Diarrhoeal diseases	343	178	165	139	19	20	129	13	23
Childhood-cluster diseases	66	37	28	32	5	1	25	2	1
Pertussis	11	6	5	6	0	0	5	0	0
Poliomyelitis[d]	0	0	0	0	0	0	0	0	0
Diphtheria	0	0	0	0	0	0	0	0	0
Measles	35	18	16	16	2	0	15	1	0
Tetanus	20	13	7	10	3	1	5	1	1
Meningitis	73	38	35	22	12	5	21	9	4
Hepatitis B[e]	42	32	11	1	23	7	1	5	5
Hepatitis C[e]	20	14	5	0	10	4	0	2	3
Malaria	32	17	15	14	2	0	13	2	0
Tropical-cluster diseases	21	12	8	1	7	5	1	4	4
Trypanosomiasis	3	2	1	1	1	0	0	1	0
Chagas disease	11	6	5	0	3	4	0	1	3
Schistosomiasis	5	3	2	0	2	1	0	1	0
Leishmaniasis	1	1	1	0	1	0	0	0	0
Lymphatic filariasis	0	0	0	0	0	0	0	0	0
Onchocerciasis	0	0	0	0	0	0	0	0	0
Leprosy	1	1	0	0	0	1	0	0	0
Dengue	7	4	4	3	0	0	3	0	0
Japanese encephalitis	3	1	2	1	0	0	1	0	0
Trachoma	0	0	0	0	0	0	0	0	0
Intestinal nematode infections	1	1	1	1	0	0	1	0	0
Ascariasis	0	0	0	0	0	0	0	0	0
Trichuriasis	0	0	0	0	0	0	0	0	0
Hookworm disease	0	0	0	0	0	0	0	0	0
Respiratory infections	**955**	**505**	**450**	**147**	**111**	**248**	**137**	**52**	**261**
Lower respiratory infections	925	489	435	142	106	242	132	50	253
Upper respiratory infections	30	16	14	5	5	6	5	2	7
Otitis media	1	1	0	0	0	0	0	0	0
Maternal conditions	**75**	**0**	**75**	**0**	**0**	**0**	**0**	**75**	**0**
Maternal haemorrhage	20	0	20	0	0	0	0	20	0
Maternal sepsis	7	0	7	0	0	0	0	7	0
Hypertensive disorders of pregnancy	13	0	13	0	0	0	0	13	0
Obstructed labour	3	0	3	0	0	0	0	3	0
Abortion	6	0	6	0	0	0	0	6	0
Perinatal conditions[f]	**745**	**391**	**354**	**391**	**0**	**0**	**354**	**0**	**0**
Prematurity and low birth weight	318	167	151	167	0	0	151	0	0
Birth asphyxia and birth trauma	194	101	93	101	0	0	93	0	0
Neonatal infections and other conditions[g]	233	123	110	123	0	0	110	0	0

Cause[b]	Middle-income countries			Males			Females		
	Total[c]	Males	Females	0-14	15-59	60+	0-14	15-59	60+
Population (millions)	3 045	1 531	1 513	400	989	142	372	969	172
	(000)	*(000)*	*(000)*	*(000)*	*(000)*	*(000)*	*(000)*	*(000)*	*(000)*
TOTAL Deaths	24 349	13 150	11 199	1 235	4 681	7 234	1 106	2 594	7 499
Nutritional deficiencies	**124**	**55**	**69**	**25**	**11**	**19**	**22**	**16**	**31**
Protein-energy malnutrition	76	39	37	21	7	12	18	4	15
Iodine deficiency	0	0	0	0	0	0	0	0	0
Vitamin A deficiency	1	1	1	1	0	0	0	0	0
Iron-deficiency anaemia	38	13	25	3	4	6	2	11	12
II. Noncommunicable conditions	*17 547*	*9 047*	*8 500*	*181*	*2 482*	*6 384*	*166*	*1 541*	*6 793*
Malignant neoplasms	**3 698**	**2 142**	**1 556**	**21**	**735**	**1 386**	**18**	**533**	**1 005**
Mouth and oropharynx cancers	112	84	28	0	42	42	0	10	18
Oesophagus cancer	315	209	105	0	66	143	0	27	79
Stomach cancer	548	347	201	0	113	234	0	56	145
Colon and rectum cancer	300	156	144	0	47	110	0	36	108
Liver cancer	401	276	125	0	126	150	1	40	84
Pancreas cancer	114	60	54	0	21	39	0	12	43
Trachea, bronchus and lung cancers	694	502	192	0	150	352	0	55	137
Melanoma and other skin cancers	24	12	12	0	5	7	0	4	8
Breast cancer	232	1	231	0	0	0	0	116	116
Cervix uteri cancer	102	0	102	0	0	0	0	50	52
Corpus uteri cancer	26	0	26	0	0	0	0	8	18
Ovary cancer	58	0	58	0	0	0	0	25	33
Prostate cancer	112	112	0	0	8	104	0	0	0
Bladder cancer	85	64	20	0	12	52	0	4	16
Lymphomas and multiple myeloma	117	69	48	3	35	32	2	17	29
Leukaemia	134	75	59	10	40	25	9	29	22
Other neoplasms	**63**	**33**	**30**	**2**	**14**	**17**	**2**	**13**	**16**
Diabetes mellitus	**523**	**217**	**306**	**1**	**61**	**156**	**1**	**64**	**240**
Endocrine disorders	**132**	**62**	**70**	**12**	**21**	**29**	**11**	**22**	**37**
Neuropsychiatric disorders	**405**	**230**	**175**	**13**	**121**	**96**	**10**	**51**	**114**
Unipolar depressive disorders	1	1	1	0	0	0	0	0	0
Bipolar affective disorder	0	0	0	0	0	0	0	0	0
Schizophrenia	9	5	5	0	4	1	0	3	2
Epilepsy	53	33	20	4	24	4	3	14	3
Alcohol use disorders	47	41	6	0	31	10	0	5	1
Alzheimer and other dementias	101	40	61	1	5	34	1	4	56
Parkinson disease	43	21	22	0	2	18	0	1	21
Multiple sclerosis	7	3	4	0	2	1	0	3	2
Drug use disorders	37	31	7	0	30	1	0	6	0
Post-traumatic stress disorder	0	0	0	0	0	0	0	0	0
Obsessive-compulsive disorder	0	0	0	0	0	0	0	0	0
Panic disorder	0	0	0	0	0	0	0	0	0
Insomnia (primary)	0	0	0	0	0	0	0	0	0
Migraine	0	0	0	0	0	0	0	0	0
Sense organ disorders	**2**	**1**	**1**	**0**	**0**	**1**	**0**	**0**	**1**
Glaucoma	0	0	0	0	0	0	0	0	0
Cataracts	0	0	0	0	0	0	0	0	0
Refractive errors	0	0	0	0	0	0	0	0	0
Hearing loss, adult onset	0	0	0	0	0	0	0	0	0
Macular degeneration and other[h]	2	1	1	0	0	1	0	0	1

(Table A5c continued)

Cause[b]	Middle-income countries			Males			Females		
	Total[c]	Males	Females	0-14	15-59	60+	0-14	15-59	60+
Population (millions)	3 045	1 531	1 513	400	989	142	372	969	172
	(000)	*(000)*	*(000)*	*(000)*	*(000)*	*(000)*	*(000)*	*(000)*	*(000)*
TOTAL Deaths	24 349	13 150	11 199	1 235	4 681	7 234	1 106	2 594	7 499
Cardiovascular diseases	**8 896**	**4 303**	**4 593**	**20**	**1 009**	**3 274**	**18**	**556**	**4 019**
Rheumatic heart disease	131	49	81	1	23	24	2	33	47
Hypertensive heart disease	617	299	318	1	60	238	0	40	277
Ischaemic heart disease	3 395	1 738	1 657	1	456	1 281	1	177	1 480
Cerebrovascular disease	3 468	1 629	1 839	5	303	1 322	4	210	1 624
Inflammatory heart diseases[i]	233	122	111	3	43	76	2	17	91
Respiratory diseases	**2 231**	**1 158**	**1 073**	**13**	**157**	**989**	**11**	**102**	**960**
Chronic obstructive pulmonary disease	1 798	925	873	1	82	842	1	53	819
Asthma	120	66	54	2	30	33	2	25	27
Digestive diseases	**965**	**580**	**385**	**27**	**275**	**278**	**26**	**117**	**241**
Peptic ulcer disease	119	72	47	1	28	43	1	12	34
Cirrhosis of the liver	399	270	129	1	154	114	1	57	71
Appendicitis	10	6	4	0	3	2	0	1	2
Diseases of the genitourinary system	**401**	**210**	**191**	**5**	**69**	**137**	**4**	**61**	**126**
Nephritis and nephrosis	313	160	154	4	58	98	3	50	100
Benign prostatic hypertrophy	15	15	0	0	1	14	0	0	0
Skin diseases	**23**	**10**	**13**	**0**	**3**	**6**	**0**	**3**	**10**
Musculoskeletal diseases	**51**	**18**	**33**	**1**	**6**	**12**	**1**	**11**	**22**
Rheumatoid arthritis	11	4	8	0	1	3	0	2	6
Osteoarthritis	2	1	1	0	0	1	0	0	1
Congenital abnormalities	**156**	**82**	**74**	**69**	**11**	**2**	**64**	**8**	**2**
Oral diseases	**1**	**1**	**0**	**0**	**0**	**0**	**0**	**0**	**0**
Dental caries	0	0	0	0	0	0	0	0	0
Periodontal disease	0	0	0	0	0	0	0	0	0
Edentulism	0	0	0	0	0	0	0	0	0
III. Injuries	***2 954***	***2 003***	***952***	***217***	***1 457***	***329***	***177***	***533***	***242***
Unintentional	**1 922**	**1 308**	**614**	**164**	**922**	**222**	**127**	**322**	**165**
Road traffic accidents	674	504	170	33	398	72	19	114	37
Poisonings	173	121	52	5	100	17	5	34	12
Falls	199	129	70	6	75	48	4	22	44
Fires	62	33	29	5	20	8	5	15	8
Drownings	202	137	65	46	76	15	25	27	13
Other unintentional injuries	613	384	229	69	253	62	68	110	51
Intentional	**819**	**594**	**225**	**13**	**488**	**93**	**10**	**156**	**59**
Self-inflicted injuries	413	247	165	4	173	70	2	113	50
Violence	317	267	50	5	245	17	4	38	8
War and conflict	82	74	8	4	64	6	3	4	1

a   See Annex Table C1 for a list of Member States by WHO region and income category.
b   Estimates for specific causes may not sum to broader cause groupings due to omission of residual categories.
c   World totals for males and females include residual populations living outside WHO Member States.
d   For the Americas, Europe and Western Pacific regions, these figures include late effects of polio cases with onset prior to regional certification of polio eradication in 1994, 2000 and 2002, respectively.
e   Does not include liver cancer and cirrhosis deaths resulting from chronic hepatitis virus infection.
f   This category includes 'Causes arising in the perinatal period' as defined in the International Classification of Diseases, and does not include all deaths occurring in the perinatal period.
g   Includes severe neonatal infections and other non-infectious causes arising in the perinatal period.
h   Includes macular degeneration and other age-related causes of vision loss not correctable by provision of glasses or contact lenses, together with deaths due to other sense organ disorders.
i   Includes myocarditis, pericarditis, endocarditis and cardiomyopathy.

Table A5d: Deaths (thousands) by age, sex, cause in low-income countries, 2004

Cause[b]	Low-income countries			Males			Females		
	Total[c]	Males	Females	0-14	15-59	60+	0-14	15-59	60+
Population (millions)	2 413	1 229	1 184	459	697	73	435	668	81
	(000)	*(000)*	*(000)*	*(000)*	*(000)*	*(000)*	*(000)*	*(000)*	*(000)*
TOTAL Deaths	26 251	13 812	12 439	4 877	4 485	4 450	4 562	3 644	4 233
Communicable, maternal, perinatal and nutritional conditions	*13 575*	*6 918*	*6 657*	*4 348*	*1 709*	*860*	*4 062*	*1 823*	*772*
Infectious and parasitic diseases	**7 395**	**3 958**	**3 437**	**2 101**	**1 455**	**402**	**1 954**	**1 156**	**326**
Tuberculosis	907	588	319	32	421	135	29	230	61
STDs excluding HIV	112	63	49	31	12	20	29	10	10
Syphilis	90	55	35	31	6	18	29	1	6
Chlamydia	8	0	8	0	0	0	0	7	1
Gonorrhoea	0	0	0	0	0	0	0	0	0
HIV/AIDS	1 509	730	778	126	583	21	123	641	15
Diarrhoeal diseases	1 806	943	863	797	77	69	737	53	73
Childhood-cluster diseases	780	419	361	413	6	1	356	4	1
Pertussis	243	124	120	124	0	0	120	0	0
Poliomyelitis[d]	0	0	0	0	0	0	0	0	0
Diphtheria	5	2	2	2	0	0	2	0	0
Measles	389	201	187	201	0	0	187	0	0
Tetanus	143	92	51	86	6	1	46	4	1
Meningitis	263	140	123	85	41	14	91	23	9
Hepatitis B[e]	56	38	18	4	26	7	4	10	4
Hepatitis C[e]	21	15	7	2	10	3	2	4	1
Malaria	857	439	418	420	17	2	397	18	2
Tropical-cluster diseases	131	82	49	26	48	9	18	26	5
Trypanosomiasis	50	31	18	13	17	1	8	10	1
Chagas disease	0	0	0	0	0	0	0	0	0
Schistosomiasis	36	22	13	1	15	6	1	9	3
Leishmaniasis	45	28	17	12	15	2	9	7	1
Lymphatic filariasis	0	0	0	0	0	0	0	0	0
Onchocerciasis	0	0	0	0	0	0	0	0	0
Leprosy	4	3	1	0	2	1	0	0	1
Dengue	11	5	5	5	0	0	5	0	0
Japanese encephalitis	8	4	4	3	0	0	4	0	0
Trachoma	0	0	0	0	0	0	0	0	0
Intestinal nematode infections	5	3	2	3	0	0	2	0	0
Ascariasis	2	1	1	1	0	0	1	0	0
Trichuriasis	2	1	1	1	0	0	1	0	0
Hookworm disease	0	0	0	0	0	0	0	0	0
Respiratory infections	**2 990**	**1 555**	**1 435**	**908**	**206**	**440**	**862**	**160**	**414**
Lower respiratory infections	2 943	1 529	1 414	896	202	432	850	156	407
Upper respiratory infections	43	23	20	11	4	8	10	3	6
Otitis media	4	2	2	1	1	0	1	1	0
Maternal conditions	**449**	**0**	**449**	**0**	**0**	**0**	**2**	**447**	**0**
Maternal haemorrhage	120	0	120	0	0	0	0	120	0
Maternal sepsis	55	0	55	0	0	0	0	54	0
Hypertensive disorders of pregnancy	49	0	49	0	0	0	2	47	0
Obstructed labour	31	0	31	0	0	0	0	31	0
Abortion	61	0	61	0	0	0	0	61	0
Perinatal conditions[f]	**2 397**	**1 244**	**1 153**	**1 244**	**0**	**0**	**1 153**	**0**	**0**
Prematurity and low birth weight	845	436	408	436	0	0	408	0	0
Birth asphyxia and birth trauma	655	341	315	341	0	0	315	0	0
Neonatal infections and other conditions[g]	897	468	429	468	0	0	429	0	0

(Table A5d continued)

Cause[b]	Low-income countries			Males			Females		
	Total[c]	Males	Females	0-14	15-59	60+	0-14	15-59	60+
Population (millions)	2 413	1 229	1 184	459	697	73	435	668	81
	(000)	*(000)*	*(000)*	*(000)*	*(000)*	*(000)*	*(000)*	*(000)*	*(000)*
TOTAL Deaths	26 251	13 812	12 439	4 877	4 485	4 450	4 562	3 644	4 233
Nutritional deficiencies	**344**	**160**	**183**	**95**	**48**	**18**	**91**	**59**	**33**
Protein-energy malnutrition	166	84	81	67	14	4	66	12	3
Iodine deficiency	5	3	2	3	0	0	2	0	0
Vitamin A deficiency	16	9	7	8	0	0	7	0	0
Iron-deficiency anaemia	107	40	67	11	27	2	11	43	13
II. Noncommunicable conditions	*10 358*	*5 425*	*4 933*	*285*	*1 758*	*3 383*	*295*	*1 348*	*3 290*
Malignant neoplasms	**1 560**	**806**	**754**	**22**	**273**	**511**	**21**	**290**	**443**
Mouth and oropharynx cancers	180	124	57	0	47	77	0	18	39
Oesophagus cancer	132	75	58	0	23	52	0	18	39
Stomach cancer	110	63	47	0	22	41	0	16	31
Colon and rectum cancer	73	41	32	0	16	25	0	11	21
Liver cancer	100	68	32	1	29	39	1	13	18
Pancreas cancer	29	15	14	0	5	10	0	5	9
Trachea, bronchus and lung cancers	151	120	31	0	34	85	0	10	21
Melanoma and other skin cancers	10	5	5	0	2	3	0	2	3
Breast cancer	125	0	125	0	0	0	0	59	66
Cervix uteri cancer	142	0	142	0	0	0	0	62	80
Corpus uteri cancer	8	0	8	0	0	0	0	2	6
Ovary cancer	38	0	38	0	0	0	0	15	22
Prostate cancer	73	73	0	0	6	67	0	0	0
Bladder cancer	39	29	10	0	4	24	0	2	9
Lymphomas and multiple myeloma	97	59	38	7	27	25	4	14	20
Leukaemia	64	35	29	6	19	9	7	14	8
Other neoplasms	**40**	**20**	**20**	**2**	**10**	**8**	**3**	**9**	**8**
Diabetes mellitus	**393**	**187**	**206**	**2**	**63**	**122**	**3**	**56**	**147**
Endocrine disorders	**94**	**45**	**49**	**12**	**16**	**18**	**10**	**16**	**22**
Neuropsychiatric disorders	**404**	**233**	**171**	**26**	**99**	**108**	**24**	**46**	**101**
Unipolar depressive disorders	10	5	5	0	4	1	0	4	1
Bipolar affective disorder	0	0	0	0	0	0	0	0	0
Schizophrenia	18	10	8	0	7	2	0	5	4
Epilepsy	78	43	35	14	22	7	14	15	6
Alcohol use disorders	18	16	2	0	12	4	0	1	1
Alzheimer and other dementias	113	57	56	0	1	56	0	1	55
Parkinson disease	15	9	6	0	0	9	0	0	6
Multiple sclerosis	2	1	1	0	0	0	0	0	0
Drug use disorders	44	36	8	0	35	1	0	7	0
Post-traumatic stress disorder	0	0	0	0	0	0	0	0	0
Obsessive-compulsive disorder	0	0	0	0	0	0	0	0	0
Panic disorder	0	0	0	0	0	0	0	0	0
Insomnia (primary)	0	0	0	0	0	0	0	0	0
Migraine	0	0	0	0	0	0	0	0	0
Sense organ disorders	**2**	**1**	**1**	**0**	**0**	**1**	**0**	**0**	**1**
Glaucoma	0	0	0	0	0	0	0	0	0
Cataracts	0	0	0	0	0	0	0	0	0
Refractive errors	0	0	0	0	0	0	0	0	0
Hearing loss, adult onset	0	0	0	0	0	0	0	0	0
Macular degeneration and other[h]	2	1	1	0	0	1	0	0	1

Cause[b]	Low-income countries			Males			Females		
	Total[c]	Males	Females	0-14	15-59	60+	0-14	15-59	60+
Population (millions)	2 413	1 229	1 184	459	697	73	435	668	81
	(000)	*(000)*	*(000)*	*(000)*	*(000)*	*(000)*	*(000)*	*(000)*	*(000)*
TOTAL Deaths	26 251	13 812	12 439	4 877	4 485	4 450	4 562	3 644	4 233
Cardiovascular diseases	**5 142**	**2 633**	**2 510**	**40**	**771**	**1 822**	**42**	**543**	**1 924**
Rheumatic heart disease	149	72	77	7	37	28	10	35	32
Hypertensive heart disease	224	102	122	1	33	69	1	30	91
Ischaemic heart disease	2 468	1 389	1 079	5	419	965	3	230	846
Cerebrovascular disease	1 482	719	764	6	169	544	6	133	625
Inflammatory heart diseases[i]	129	63	66	6	24	33	6	20	40
Respiratory diseases	**1 328**	**738**	**589**	**19**	**217**	**503**	**18**	**168**	**403**
Chronic obstructive pulmonary disease	939	533	406	1	130	402	1	90	315
Asthma	146	77	70	4	47	26	4	44	22
Digestive diseases	**730**	**404**	**326**	**31**	**213**	**160**	**42**	**148**	**136**
Peptic ulcer disease	126	79	47	3	46	30	3	20	25
Cirrhosis of the liver	257	161	96	9	86	66	14	44	38
Appendicitis	11	6	4	1	3	3	0	1	3
Diseases of the genitourinary system	**353**	**205**	**148**	**11**	**80**	**114**	**10**	**56**	**82**
Nephritis and nephrosis	298	165	133	10	67	88	9	49	74
Benign prostatic hypertrophy	22	22	0	0	6	16	0	0	0
Skin diseases	**29**	**12**	**17**	**1**	**4**	**7**	**1**	**5**	**11**
Musculoskeletal diseases	**29**	**13**	**16**	**1**	**3**	**9**	**1**	**4**	**11**
Rheumatoid arthritis	6	2	4	0	1	2	0	1	3
Osteoarthritis	2	1	1	0	0	1	0	0	1
Congenital abnormalities	**253**	**127**	**126**	**118**	**8**	**1**	**119**	**7**	**1**
Oral diseases	**2**	**1**	**1**	**0**	**1**	**0**	**0**	**1**	**0**
Dental caries	0	0	0	0	0	0	0	0	0
Periodontal disease	0	0	0	0	0	0	0	0	0
Edentulism	0	0	0	0	0	0	0	0	0
III. Injuries	***2 318***	***1 469***	***849***	***244***	***1 018***	***207***	***205***	***473***	***171***
Unintentional	**1 640**	**997**	**643**	**216**	**622**	**158**	**183**	**317**	**143**
Road traffic accidents	485	356	128	64	249	43	44	63	22
Poisonings	142	80	62	14	53	13	9	29	24
Falls	149	92	57	13	37	42	10	16	31
Fires	240	82	157	27	47	8	35	104	18
Drownings	169	114	55	38	68	9	25	23	8
Other unintentional injuries	455	272	183	60	169	43	61	82	40
Intentional	**656**	**462**	**195**	**23**	**391**	**48**	**18**	**151**	**26**
Self-inflicted injuries	294	179	115	4	154	22	3	99	13
Violence	255	198	58	11	168	19	9	40	9
War and conflict	100	79	20	7	66	6	5	11	4

1
2
3
4

Annex A

Annex B

Annex C

References

a See Annex Table C1 for a list of Member States by WHO region and income category.

b Estimates for specific causes may not sum to broader cause groupings due to omission of residual categories.

c World totals for males and females include residual populations living outside WHO Member States.

d For the Americas, Europe and Western Pacific regions, these figures include late effects of polio cases with onset prior to regional certification of polio eradication in 1994, 2000 and 2002, respectively.

e Does not include liver cancer and cirrhosis deaths resulting from chronic hepatitis virus infection.

f This category includes 'Causes arising in the perinatal period' as defined in the International Classification of Diseases, and does not include all deaths occurring in the perinatal period.

g Includes severe neonatal infections and other non-infectious causes arising in the perinatal period.

h Includes macular degeneration and other age-related causes of vision loss not correctable by provision of glasses or contact lenses, together with deaths due to other sense organ disorders.

i Includes myocarditis, pericarditis, endocarditis and cardiomyopathy.

Table A6: Burden of disease in DALYs by cause, sex and age group, countries grouped by income per capita,ᵃ 2004

Table A6a: DALYs (thousands) by age, sex, cause in the world, 2004

Causeᵇ	World			Males			Females		
	Totalᶜ	Males	Females	0-14	15-59	60+	0-14	15-59	60+
Population (millions)	6 437	3 244	3 193	951	1 994	298	895	1 938	360
	(000)	*(000)*	*(000)*	*(000)*	*(000)*	*(000)*	*(000)*	*(000)*	*(000)*
TOTAL DALYs	1 523 259	796 133	727 126	283 314	403 131	109 688	265 052	349 256	112 817
Communicable, maternal, perinatal and nutritional conditions	*603 993*	*294 075*	*309 918*	*209 259*	*75 063*	*9 753*	*197 231*	*103 763*	*8 924*
Infectious and parasitic diseases	**302 144**	**159 741**	**142 403**	**91 646**	**63 028**	**5 067**	**84 859**	**53 361**	**4 182**
Tuberculosis	34 217	21 658	12 558	1 723	17 683	2 252	1 655	9 873	1 031
STDs excluding HIV	10 425	3 558	6 866	1 675	1 743	141	1 639	5 136	92
Syphilis	2 846	1 531	1 316	1 145	264	121	1 062	208	46
Chlamydia	3 748	320	3 428	9	311	0	72	3 341	14
Gonorrhoea	3 550	1 554	1 996	502	1 052	1	489	1 505	2
HIV/AIDS	58 513	28 569	29 944	5 322	22 975	272	5 191	24 539	214
Diarrhoeal diseases	72 777	37 905	34 872	33 808	3 505	592	31 390	2 832	650
Childhood-cluster diseases	30 226	16 221	14 005	15 912	295	13	13 811	184	10
Pertussis	9 882	5 009	4 873	5 007	2	0	4 870	3	0
Poliomyelitisᵈ	34	19	15	11	7	1	11	3	1
Diphtheria	174	86	88	83	3	0	86	1	0
Measles	14 853	7 699	7 154	7 624	75	0	7 102	52	0
Tetanus	5 283	3 409	1 875	3 188	209	12	1 741	126	8
Meningitis	11 426	5 891	5 536	4 314	1 451	126	4 472	959	104
Hepatitis Bᵉ	2 068	1 437	630	192	1 125	121	184	376	70
Hepatitis Cᵉ	955	653	302	73	507	73	72	172	58
Malaria	33 976	17 340	16 636	16 595	719	26	15 851	754	31
Tropical-cluster diseases	12 113	8 264	3 850	3 075	5 050	138	1 582	2 159	109
Trypanosomiasis	1 673	1 041	631	515	518	9	320	305	5
Chagas disease	430	231	199	0	205	27	0	176	22
Schistosomiasis	1 707	1 021	686	503	467	51	360	292	34
Leishmaniasis	1 974	1 227	748	565	644	17	407	327	14
Lymphatic filariasis	5 941	4 521	1 420	1 459	3 045	17	463	935	22
Onchocerciasis	389	223	166	33	172	18	31	123	12
Leprosy	194	116	78	32	74	11	28	45	4
Dengue	670	336	334	320	15	1	316	17	1
Japanese encephalitis	681	330	351	279	49	2	300	49	2
Trachoma	1 334	338	997	2	233	102	4	647	346
Intestinal nematode infections	4 013	2 052	1 961	1 654	373	24	1 574	361	26
Ascariasis	1 851	943	908	942	2	0	906	1	0
Trichuriasis	1 012	525	487	525	0	0	487	0	0
Hookworm disease	1 092	551	541	160	369	23	157	359	25
Respiratory infections	**97 786**	**51 266**	**46 520**	**39 303**	**7 819**	**4 144**	**36 890**	**5 702**	**3 929**
Lower respiratory infections	94 511	49 542	44 969	37 967	7 523	4 052	35 633	5 487	3 850
Upper respiratory infections	1 787	952	835	601	262	89	574	183	78
Otitis media	1 488	772	716	735	34	3	682	32	2
Maternal conditions	**38 936**	**0**	**38 936**	**0**	**0**	**0**	**531**	**38 404**	**0**
Maternal haemorrhage	4 439	0	4 439	0	0	0	1	4 438	0
Maternal sepsis	6 535	0	6 535	0	0	0	8	6 527	0
Hypertensive disorders of pregnancy	1 888	0	1 888	0	0	0	62	1 827	0
Obstructed labour	2 882	0	2 882	0	0	0	0	2 882	0
Abortion	7 424	0	7 424	0	0	0	436	6 989	0
Perinatal conditionsᶠ	**126 423**	**64 633**	**61 791**	**64 631**	**2**	**0**	**61 789**	**1**	**0**
Prematurity and low birth weight	44 307	22 624	21 683	22 624	0	0	21 682	0	0
Birth asphyxia and birth trauma	41 684	21 051	20 633	21 050	1	0	20 632	1	0
Neonatal infections and other conditionsᵍ	40 433	20 957	19 476	20 957	1	0	19 475	1	0

Cause[b]	World			Males			Females		
	Total[c]	Males	Females	0-14	15-59	60+	0-14	15-59	60+
Population (millions)	6 437	3 244	3 193	951	1 994	298	895	1 938	360
	(000)	*(000)*	*(000)*	*(000)*	*(000)*	*(000)*	*(000)*	*(000)*	*(000)*
TOTAL DALYs	1 523 259	796 133	727 126	283 314	403 131	109 688	265 052	349 256	112 817
Nutritional deficiencies	**38 703**	**18 436**	**20 268**	**13 679**	**4 215**	**542**	**13 161**	**6 294**	**813**
Protein-energy malnutrition	17 462	8 925	8 536	8 365	481	80	8 067	366	103
Iodine deficiency	3 529	1 789	1 740	1 787	1	0	1 737	2	1
Vitamin A deficiency	629	339	291	336	2	0	289	2	0
Iron-deficiency anaemia	16 152	6 918	9 234	2 973	3 555	390	2 843	5 792	599
II. Noncommunicable conditions	*731 652*	*378 693*	*352 959*	*47 526*	*235 848*	*95 318*	*46 003*	*206 670*	*100 286*
Malignant neoplasms	**77 812**	**41 893**	**35 919**	**1 682**	**22 708**	**17 503**	**1 527**	**20 705**	**13 687**
Mouth and oropharynx cancers	3 790	2 790	999	24	1 830	936	24	565	410
Oesophagus cancer	4 768	3 121	1 647	4	1 646	1 472	3	832	813
Stomach cancer	7 491	4 683	2 808	11	2 598	2 074	4	1 547	1 257
Colon and rectum cancer	5 874	3 207	2 666	9	1 680	1 518	4	1 301	1 362
Liver cancer	6 712	4 726	1 986	47	3 096	1 584	44	1 114	828
Pancreas cancer	2 219	1 228	992	3	637	588	1	412	579
Trachea, bronchus and lung cancers	11 766	8 312	3 454	11	3 937	4 364	11	1 643	1 800
Melanoma and other skin cancers	706	389	317	4	248	138	5	193	119
Breast cancer	6 629	18	6 611	0	9	9	4	4 595	2 011
Cervix uteri cancer	3 719	0	3 719	0	0	0	2	2 663	1 054
Corpus uteri cancer	745	0	745	0	0	0	4	428	313
Ovary cancer	1 745	0	1 745	0	0	0	32	1 113	600
Prostate cancer	1 843	1 843	0	3	315	1 525	0	0	0
Bladder cancer	1 451	1 079	372	4	394	681	2	144	226
Lymphomas and multiple myeloma	4 284	2 660	1 624	380	1 660	621	236	831	557
Leukaemia	4 944	2 805	2 139	638	1 781	386	590	1 228	321
Other neoplasms	**1 953**	**1 016**	**937**	**151**	**612**	**253**	**166**	**525**	**245**
Diabetes mellitus	**19 705**	**9 046**	**10 659**	**161**	**6 055**	**2 830**	**181**	**6 408**	**4 071**
Endocrine disorders	**10 446**	**4 793**	**5 653**	**1 801**	**2 351**	**642**	**1 576**	**3 144**	**933**
Neuropsychiatric disorders	**199 280**	**98 328**	**100 952**	**15 521**	**76 342**	**6 465**	**15 086**	**75 693**	**10 172**
Unipolar depressive disorders	65 472	24 392	41 080	2 787	20 594	1 011	2 885	35 938	2 257
Bipolar affective disorder	14 425	7 299	7 126	394	6 901	4	328	6 792	6
Schizophrenia	16 769	8 544	8 226	1 279	7 223	42	352	7 807	67
Epilepsy	7 854	4 234	3 621	1 439	2 640	155	1 338	2 134	149
Alcohol use disorders	23 738	21 154	2 584	694	19 995	465	111	2 397	75
Alzheimer and other dementias	11 158	4 312	6 847	355	591	3 366	334	635	5 878
Parkinson disease	1 710	854	856	8	337	509	7	309	540
Multiple sclerosis	1 527	656	871	70	563	22	90	743	38
Drug use disorders	8 370	6 586	1 784	169	6 393	24	86	1 690	8
Post-traumatic stress disorder	3 468	960	2 508	34	921	5	26	2 464	19
Obsessive-compulsive disorder	5 104	2 195	2 909	211	1 959	25	422	2 445	42
Panic disorder	6 991	2 374	4 617	116	2 247	11	115	4 476	26
Insomnia (primary)	3 623	1 562	2 060	45	1 362	155	44	1 749	267
Migraine	7 765	2 116	5 649	888	1 228	0	2 477	3 172	0
Sense organ disorders	**86 883**	**41 843**	**45 040**	**2 375**	**28 404**	**11 064**	**2 119**	**28 938**	**13 983**
Glaucoma	4 728	2 100	2 628	74	1 399	628	22	1 631	974
Cataracts	17 757	7 858	9 899	106	5 498	2 254	75	6 492	3 331
Refractive errors	27 745	13 769	13 977	2 164	7 981	3 624	2 002	7 862	4 113
Hearing loss, adult onset	27 356	14 073	13 283	0	10 851	3 223	0	9 738	3 545
Macular degeneration and other[h]	9 297	4 043	5 254	30	2 677	1 336	20	3 214	2 020

(Table A6a continued)

Cause[b]	World			Males			Females		
	Total[c]	Males	Females	0-14	15-59	60+	0-14	15-59	60+
Population (millions)	6 437	3 244	3 193	951	1 994	298	895	1 938	360
	(000)	(000)	(000)	(000)	(000)	(000)	(000)	(000)	(000)
TOTAL DALYs	1 523 259	796 133	727 126	283 314	403 131	109 688	265 052	349 256	112 817
Cardiovascular diseases	151 377	82 894	68 483	2 546	44 066	36 283	2 591	28 065	37 827
Rheumatic heart disease	5 188	2 301	2 887	342	1 610	350	443	1 823	621
Hypertensive heart disease	8 020	4 066	3 953	54	1 934	2 079	56	1 450	2 447
Ischaemic heart disease	62 587	37 271	25 316	213	20 373	16 685	145	9 831	15 340
Cerebrovascular disease	46 591	24 129	22 462	423	11 227	12 479	398	8 462	13 602
Inflammatory heart diseases[i]	6 236	3 689	2 547	357	2 421	911	336	1 313	897
Respiratory diseases	59 039	33 215	25 824	4 644	17 706	10 865	4 549	12 402	8 872
Chronic obstructive pulmonary disease	30 196	17 399	12 796	93	8 480	8 826	67	5 661	7 068
Asthma	16 317	8 856	7 461	3 128	5 302	426	3 269	3 769	424
Digestive diseases	42 498	24 657	17 841	3 278	17 354	4 025	3 267	11 011	3 563
Peptic ulcer disease	4 963	3 293	1 670	268	2 480	546	148	1 105	417
Cirrhosis of the liver	13 640	8 868	4 772	522	6 641	1 706	673	3 012	1 087
Appendicitis	418	259	160	50	176	33	31	95	34
Diseases of the genitourinary system	14 754	8 735	6 019	831	5 888	2 016	749	3 648	1 622
Nephritis and nephrosis	9 057	4 889	4 168	695	2 944	1 249	636	2 295	1 237
Benign prostatic hypertrophy	2 664	2 664	0	0	2 193	471	0	0	0
Skin diseases	3 879	1 936	1 943	510	1 202	224	357	1 219	368
Musculoskeletal diseases	30 869	13 604	17 265	701	10 514	2 390	868	12 389	4 007
Rheumatoid arthritis	5 050	1 446	3 604	127	1 066	253	311	2 741	552
Osteoarthritis	15 586	6 095	9 491	4	4 559	1 531	6	6 854	2 631
Congenital abnormalities	25 280	12 853	12 427	12 187	638	28	11 892	507	29
Oral diseases	7 875	3 878	3 997	1 138	2 010	730	1 074	2 015	907
Dental caries	4 882	2 476	2 406	1 122	1 180	174	1 057	1 148	201
Periodontal disease	320	160	160	0	150	9	2	147	11
Edentulism	2 555	1 191	1 364	0	651	540	0	679	685
III. Injuries	*187 614*	*123 366*	*64 249*	*26 529*	*92 220*	*4 617*	*21 819*	*38 823*	*3 607*
Unintentional	138 564	87 130	51 434	24 340	59 345	3 445	20 211	28 318	2 905
Road traffic accidents	41 223	29 240	11 983	5 308	22 974	958	4 174	7 266	542
Poisonings	7 447	4 893	2 554	678	3 979	236	528	1 739	287
Falls	17 157	10 447	6 710	3 312	6 336	799	2 984	2 933	793
Fires	11 271	4 534	6 738	2 051	2 367	116	2 514	4 038	185
Drownings	10 728	7 354	3 374	3 094	4 079	181	1 839	1 392	143
Other unintentional injuries	50 738	30 663	20 076	9 898	19 610	1 155	8 171	10 951	954
Intentional	49 050	36 236	12 815	2 189	32 874	1 172	1 609	10 505	701
Self-inflicted injuries	19 566	11 686	7 880	432	10 471	783	498	6 874	508
Violence	21 701	17 892	3 810	1 213	16 403	276	696	2 971	142
War and conflict	7 383	6 320	1 063	524	5 694	102	401	616	47

[a] See Annex Table C1 for a list of Member States by WHO region and income category.
[b] Estimates for specific causes may not sum to broader cause groupings due to omission of residual categories.
[c] World totals for males and females include residual populations living outside WHO Member States.
[d] For the Americas, Europe and Western Pacific regions, these figures include late effects of polio cases with onset prior to regional certification of polio eradication in 1994, 2000 and 2002, respectively.
[e] Does not include liver cancer and cirrhosis deaths resulting from chronic hepatitis virus infection.
[f] This category includes 'Causes arising in the perinatal period' as defined in the International Classification of Diseases, and does not include all deaths occurring in the perinatal period.
[g] Includes severe neonatal infections and other non-infectious causes arising in the perinatal period.
[h] Includes macular degeneration and other age-related causes of vision loss not correctable by provision of glasses or contact lenses, together with deaths due to other sense organ disorders.
[i] Includes myocarditis, pericarditis, endocarditis and cardiomyopathy.

Table A6b: DALYs (thousands) by age, sex, cause in high-income countries, 2004

Cause[b]	High-income countries			Males			Females		
	Total[c]	Males	Females	0–14	15–59	60+	0–14	15–59	60+
Population (millions)	977	482	495	92	308	83	87	300	108
	(000)	*(000)*	*(000)*	*(000)*	*(000)*	*(000)*	*(000)*	*(000)*	*(000)*
TOTAL DALYs	122 092	64 189	57 902	5 277	37 789	21 124	4 665	31 499	21 739
Communicable, maternal, perinatal and nutritional conditions	*7 340*	*3 482*	*3 858*	*1 423*	*1 288*	*770*	*1 265*	*1 843*	*750*
Infectious and parasitic diseases	**2 754**	**1 500**	**1 254**	**237**	**984**	**279**	**240**	**734**	**280**
Tuberculosis	185	120	65	6	74	40	6	38	21
STDs excluding HIV	215	35	180	3	32	0	5	174	2
Syphilis	7	4	3	1	2	0	1	2	0
Chlamydia	159	13	145	0	13	0	2	143	0
Gonorrhoea	46	17	29	1	16	0	1	28	0
HIV/AIDS	628	466	162	2	452	11	2	155	5
Diarrhoeal diseases	438	213	225	102	88	24	109	82	33
Childhood-cluster diseases	55	28	27	25	1	1	25	1	2
Pertussis	44	22	22	22	0	0	22	0	0
Poliomyelitis[d]	4	2	2	0	1	1	0	0	1
Diphtheria	0	0	0	0	0	0	0	0	0
Measles	3	2	2	1	0	0	2	0	0
Tetanus	4	2	1	2	0	0	1	0	0
Meningitis	108	56	52	29	22	5	28	18	6
Hepatitis B[e]	82	57	26	0	41	15	0	12	13
Hepatitis C[e]	153	98	56	0	72	26	0	26	29
Malaria	5	3	2	2	1	0	1	1	0
Tropical-cluster diseases	15	9	6	3	6	0	2	3	0
Trypanosomiasis	0	0	0	0	0	0	0	0	0
Chagas disease	2	1	1	0	1	0	0	1	0
Schistosomiasis	9	5	3	2	3	0	2	2	0
Leishmaniasis	4	2	2	1	1	0	1	1	0
Lymphatic filariasis	0	0	0	0	0	0	0	0	0
Onchocerciasis	0	0	0	0	0	0	0	0	0
Leprosy	0	0	0	0	0	0	0	0	0
Dengue	6	3	3	3	0	0	2	0	0
Japanese encephalitis	2	1	1	1	0	0	1	0	0
Trachoma	0	0	0	0	0	0	0	0	0
Intestinal nematode infections	24	12	12	7	5	1	6	5	1
Ascariasis	6	3	3	3	0	0	3	0	0
Trichuriasis	6	3	3	3	0	0	3	0	0
Hookworm disease	12	6	6	0	5	0	0	5	1
Respiratory infections	**1 374**	**742**	**632**	**123**	**194**	**425**	**127**	**121**	**383**
Lower respiratory infections	1 220	663	557	69	178	417	76	106	375
Upper respiratory infections	54	28	27	4	16	8	4	15	8
Otitis media	99	51	48	50	0	0	48	0	0
Maternal conditions	**667**	**0**	**667**	**0**	**0**	**0**	**2**	**665**	**0**
Maternal haemorrhage	6	0	6	0	0	0	0	6	0
Maternal sepsis	143	0	143	0	0	0	0	143	0
Hypertensive disorders of pregnancy	6	0	6	0	0	0	0	6	0
Obstructed labour	15	0	15	0	0	0	0	15	0
Abortion	31	0	31	0	0	0	2	29	0
Perinatal conditions[f]	**1 770**	**968**	**803**	**966**	**1**	**0**	**801**	**1**	**0**
Prematurity and low birth weight	739	406	333	406	0	0	333	0	0
Birth asphyxia and birth trauma	497	264	234	263	1	0	233	0	0
Neonatal infections and other conditions[g]	534	298	236	297	1	0	235	1	0

(Table A6b continued)

Cause[b]	High-income countries			Males			Females		
	Total[c]	Males	Females	0-14	15-59	60+	0-14	15-59	60+
Population (millions)	977	482	495	92	308	83	87	300	108
	(000)	*(000)*	*(000)*	*(000)*	*(000)*	*(000)*	*(000)*	*(000)*	*(000)*
TOTAL DALYs	122 092	64 189	57 902	5 277	37 789	21 124	4 665	31 499	21 739
Nutritional deficiencies	**775**	**272**	**504**	**97**	**109**	**66**	**95**	**322**	**87**
Protein-energy malnutrition	128	65	64	49	6	9	48	4	12
Iodine deficiency	3	2	2	1	0	0	1	0	0
Vitamin A deficiency	0	0	0	0	0	0	0	0	0
Iron-deficiency anaemia	630	200	430	45	100	55	45	312	73
II. Noncommunicable conditions	*103 529*	*52 701*	*50 829*	*3 109*	*29 932*	*19 659*	*2 945*	*27 417*	*20 466*
Malignant neoplasms	**17 826**	**9 604**	**8 222**	**107**	**3 886**	**5 611**	**86**	**3 849**	**4 287**
Mouth and oropharynx cancers	432	336	96	1	201	134	0	49	46
Oesophagus cancer	488	394	94	0	177	218	0	33	61
Stomach cancer	1 027	652	375	0	256	396	0	159	216
Colon and rectum cancer	2 095	1 155	940	0	445	709	0	350	590
Liver cancer	845	614	231	2	282	330	2	70	159
Pancreas cancer	857	474	383	0	194	281	0	119	264
Trachea, bronchus and lung cancers	3 608	2 388	1 220	1	874	1 513	1	475	744
Melanoma and other skin cancers	316	192	124	0	111	81	0	73	50
Breast cancer	1 856	11	1 845	0	5	6	0	1 129	716
Cervix uteri cancer	330	0	330	0	0	0	0	234	95
Corpus uteri cancer	259	0	259	0	0	0	0	122	137
Ovary cancer	463	0	463	0	0	0	1	240	222
Prostate cancer	704	704	0	0	94	609	0	0	0
Bladder cancer	436	330	106	0	98	232	0	26	79
Lymphomas and multiple myeloma	900	508	392	7	233	268	4	142	246
Leukaemia	688	396	292	36	186	173	28	130	134
Other neoplasms	**366**	**196**	**170**	**12**	**77**	**107**	**13**	**59**	**99**
Diabetes mellitus	**3 623**	**1 772**	**1 851**	**6**	**1 064**	**703**	**5**	**969**	**876**
Endocrine disorders	**1 927**	**860**	**1 067**	**177**	**490**	**193**	**148**	**660**	**260**
Neuropsychiatric disorders	**31 558**	**14 785**	**16 773**	**1 131**	**11 365**	**2 289**	**1 042**	**11 868**	**3 864**
Unipolar depressive disorders	9 997	3 525	6 472	273	3 010	242	288	5 711	474
Bipolar affective disorder	1 543	783	760	31	751	1	25	733	2
Schizophrenia	1 553	823	730	169	649	5	84	639	7
Epilepsy	538	296	242	56	212	28	50	161	30
Alcohol use disorders	4 207	3 372	835	45	3 225	101	12	800	24
Alzheimer and other dementias	4 387	1 515	2 872	40	121	1 354	39	139	2 694
Parkinson disease	694	364	331	0	89	274	0	68	263
Multiple sclerosis	320	139	181	10	118	11	10	149	22
Drug use disorders	1 894	1 427	468	17	1 405	4	11	455	2
Post-traumatic stress disorder	512	137	376	3	132	2	3	367	5
Obsessive-compulsive disorder	597	249	348	7	239	4	9	336	3
Panic disorder	795	269	526	12	254	3	10	508	7
Insomnia (primary)	768	334	434	5	273	56	4	342	88
Migraine	1 437	368	1 070	147	221	0	228	842	0
Sense organ disorders	**9 235**	**4 442**	**4 792**	**157**	**2 586**	**1 699**	**155**	**2 604**	**2 033**
Glaucoma	371	153	218	0	84	68	2	109	107
Cataracts	406	187	219	3	129	55	5	130	84
Refractive errors	2 745	1 327	1 418	153	777	397	146	764	508
Hearing loss, adult onset	4 203	2 164	2 038	0	1 271	893	0	1 099	940
Macular degeneration and other[h]	1 510	611	899	1	325	285	3	502	395

Cause[b]	High-income countries			Males			Females		
	Total[c]	Males	Females	0-14	15-59	60+	0-14	15-59	60+
Population (millions)	977	482	495	92	308	83	87	300	108
	(000)	(000)	(000)	(000)	(000)	(000)	(000)	(000)	(000)
TOTAL DALYs	122 092	64 189	57 902	5 277	37 789	21 124	4 665	31 499	21 739
Cardiovascular diseases	**17 853**	**10 272**	**7 581**	**64**	**4 576**	**5 632**	**57**	**2 251**	**5 274**
Rheumatic heart disease	120	44	76	1	19	24	1	24	52
Hypertensive heart disease	801	396	406	0	172	223	0	90	315
Ischaemic heart disease	7 739	4 996	2 743	1	2 164	2 830	1	615	2 126
Cerebrovascular disease	4 763	2 403	2 360	11	1 048	1 344	9	845	1 506
Inflammatory heart diseases[i]	748	481	267	17	278	186	15	119	133
Respiratory diseases	**7 266**	**3 874**	**3 392**	**457**	**2 014**	**1 402**	**485**	**1 794**	**1 113**
Chronic obstructive pulmonary disease	3 663	1 912	1 750	5	990	917	2	1 055	693
Asthma	1 919	1 021	898	377	604	40	428	400	70
Digestive diseases	**4 714**	**2 684**	**2 030**	**102**	**1 788**	**793**	**87**	**1 165**	**779**
Peptic ulcer disease	194	107	86	1	63	43	1	45	41
Cirrhosis of the liver	1 653	1 160	493	5	851	305	1	317	175
Appendicitis	35	21	14	3	14	3	2	9	3
Diseases of the genitourinary system	**1 248**	**750**	**498**	**14**	**341**	**396**	**18**	**165**	**316**
Nephritis and nephrosis	630	326	304	9	115	201	12	86	207
Benign prostatic hypertrophy	302	302	0	0	174	128	0	0	0
Skin diseases	**230**	**96**	**134**	**5**	**45**	**46**	**5**	**50**	**79**
Musculoskeletal diseases	**5 237**	**2 116**	**3 121**	**35**	**1 378**	**702**	**63**	**1 688**	**1 370**
Rheumatoid arthritis	955	268	688	9	173	85	34	474	179
Osteoarthritis	2 777	1 107	1 670	0	630	477	0	735	934
Congenital abnormalities	**1 606**	**839**	**767**	**737**	**91**	**11**	**683**	**71**	**13**
Oral diseases	**840**	**411**	**429**	**105**	**231**	**75**	**100**	**226**	**103**
Dental caries	507	257	251	104	128	24	99	121	30
Periodontal disease	38	19	19	0	18	1	0	18	1
Edentulism	287	132	155	0	83	49	0	85	70
III. Injuries	***11 222***	***8 007***	***3 215***	***744***	***6 568***	***694***	***455***	***2 238***	***523***
Unintentional	**7 595**	**5 264**	**2 331**	**654**	**4 113**	**497**	**396**	**1 503**	**432**
Road traffic accidents	3 127	2 262	865	180	1 964	118	120	669	75
Poisonings	693	479	214	7	460	11	4	200	11
Falls	1 297	838	459	123	556	159	75	196	188
Fires	187	118	69	29	76	13	22	38	10
Drownings	307	242	65	53	166	23	22	29	14
Other unintentional injuries	1 983	1 325	658	262	891	173	153	371	134
Intentional	**3 627**	**2 743**	**884**	**91**	**2 455**	**197**	**59**	**736**	**90**
Self-inflicted injuries	2 616	1 946	670	44	1 717	185	26	562	82
Violence	928	717	211	46	659	12	32	171	8
War and conflict	67	64	2	0	64	0	0	2	0

[a] See Annex Table C1 for a list of Member States by WHO region and income category.

[b] Estimates for specific causes may not sum to broader cause groupings due to omission of residual categories.

[c] World totals for males and females include residual populations living outside WHO Member States.

[d] For the Americas, Europe and Western Pacific regions, these figures include late effects of polio cases with onset prior to regional certification of polio eradication in 1994, 2000 and 2002, respectively.

[e] Does not include liver cancer and cirrhosis deaths resulting from chronic hepatitis virus infection.

[f] This category includes 'Causes arising in the perinatal period' as defined in the International Classification of Diseases, and does not include all deaths occurring in the perinatal period.

[g] Includes severe neonatal infections and other non-infectious causes arising in the perinatal period.

[h] Includes macular degeneration and other age-related causes of vision loss not correctable by provision of glasses or contact lenses, together with deaths due to other sense organ disorders.

[i] Includes myocarditis, pericarditis, endocarditis and cardiomyopathy.

1
2
3
4
Annex A
Annex B
Annex C
References

Table A6c: DALYs (thousands) by age, sex, cause in middle-income countries, 2004

Cause[b]	Middle-income countries			Males			Females		
	Total[c]	Males	Females	0-14	15-59	60+	0-14	15-59	60+
Population (millions)	3 045	1 531	1 513	400	989	142	372	969	172
	(000)	*(000)*	*(000)*	*(000)*	*(000)*	*(000)*	*(000)*	*(000)*	*(000)*
TOTAL DALYs	572 859	313 409	259 450	67 138	192 506	53 765	61 259	143 399	54 792
Communicable, maternal, perinatal and nutritional conditions	*127 572*	*63 208*	*64 364*	*36 742*	*23 084*	*3 383*	*34 443*	*27 118*	*2 803*
Infectious and parasitic diseases	**58 128**	**32 029**	**26 099**	**11 197**	**18 905**	**1 927**	**10 362**	**14 362**	**1 376**
Tuberculosis	11 661	7 692	3 969	411	6 176	1 105	417	3 070	482
STDs excluding HIV	2 327	610	1 717	157	436	17	162	1 534	21
Syphilis	301	160	141	85	65	10	72	61	8
Chlamydia	1 169	97	1 072	2	95	0	20	1 050	3
Gonorrhoea	799	331	468	68	262	0	68	398	2
HIV/AIDS	14 977	8 043	6 935	916	7 062	64	892	5 983	59
Diarrhoeal diseases	13 107	6 817	6 290	5 348	1 298	171	4 971	1 139	180
Childhood-cluster diseases	2 504	1 393	1 112	1 251	135	7	1 039	68	4
Pertussis	675	345	329	345	0	0	329	1	0
Poliomyelitis[d]	4	3	1	0	2	0	0	1	0
Diphtheria	11	6	5	5	0	0	4	1	0
Measles	1 238	654	584	581	73	0	535	50	0
Tetanus	576	385	192	319	59	7	171	16	4
Meningitis	2 412	1 259	1 153	896	329	34	847	271	34
Hepatitis B[e]	748	574	174	35	482	58	32	110	32
Hepatitis C[e]	325	246	78	12	207	28	11	47	19
Malaria	1 177	598	579	519	75	4	503	72	4
Tropical-cluster diseases	1 271	796	475	177	582	38	97	349	29
Trypanosomiasis	86	53	32	26	27	0	16	16	0
Chagas disease	423	228	195	0	202	26	0	174	22
Schistosomiasis	204	121	83	54	61	7	41	38	4
Leishmaniasis	110	73	37	27	45	1	17	20	1
Lymphatic filariasis	444	319	125	69	246	3	22	101	3
Onchocerciasis	4	2	2	0	2	0	1	1	0
Leprosy	34	20	14	4	11	5	4	9	1
Dengue	266	134	133	125	8	0	122	10	1
Japanese encephalitis	198	95	103	78	16	1	86	16	1
Trachoma	436	106	330	0	69	37	1	207	122
Intestinal nematode infections	1 293	661	632	442	204	14	420	196	16
Ascariasis	420	215	205	214	1	0	204	0	0
Trichuriasis	344	178	167	177	0	0	167	0	0
Hookworm disease	502	254	247	38	202	14	36	196	15
Respiratory infections	**17 565**	**9 612**	**7 953**	**5 915**	**2 485**	**1 211**	**5 518**	**1 344**	**1 091**
Lower respiratory infections	16 319	8 947	7 372	5 429	2 340	1 178	5 046	1 263	1 064
Upper respiratory infections	642	351	291	182	137	32	190	74	27
Otitis media	604	313	291	303	9	1	282	8	0
Maternal conditions	**9 227**	**0**	**9 227**	**0**	**0**	**0**	**100**	**9 127**	**0**
Maternal haemorrhage	592	0	592	0	0	0	0	591	0
Maternal sepsis	1 895	0	1 895	0	0	0	1	1 894	0
Hypertensive disorders of pregnancy	378	0	378	0	0	0	5	372	0
Obstructed labour	527	0	527	0	0	0	0	527	0
Abortion	1 515	0	1 515	0	0	0	90	1 425	0
Perinatal conditions[f]	**31 290**	**16 147**	**15 143**	**16 147**	**0**	**0**	**15 143**	**0**	**0**
Prematurity and low birth weight	11 459	5 948	5 511	5 948	0	0	5 511	0	0
Birth asphyxia and birth trauma	11 384	5 777	5 607	5 777	0	0	5 607	0	0
Neonatal infections and other conditions[g]	8 447	4 422	4 025	4 422	0	0	4 025	0	0

Cause[b]	Middle-income countries			Males			Females		
	Total[c]	Males	Females	0-14	15-59	60+	0-14	15-59	60+
Population (millions)	3 045	1 531	1 513	400	989	142	372	969	172
	(000)	*(000)*	*(000)*	*(000)*	*(000)*	*(000)*	*(000)*	*(000)*	*(000)*
TOTAL DALYs	572 859	313 409	259 450	67 138	192 506	53 765	61 259	143 399	54 792
Nutritional deficiencies	**11 362**	**5 421**	**5 941**	**3 483**	**1 693**	**245**	**3 321**	**2 284**	**336**
Protein-energy malnutrition	4 032	2 112	1 920	1 910	150	52	1 766	88	66
Iodine deficiency	1 558	770	789	769	0	0	787	1	1
Vitamin A deficiency	41	22	19	21	1	0	18	0	0
Iron-deficiency anaemia	5 569	2 454	3 115	748	1 522	184	717	2 150	248
II. Noncommunicable conditions	*355 196*	*188 117*	*167 078*	*19 744*	*120 408*	*47 966*	*18 380*	*98 433*	*50 264*
Malignant neoplasms	**40 975**	**22 963**	**18 013**	**764**	**13 464**	**8 735**	**659**	**10 871**	**6 483**
Mouth and oropharynx cancers	1 374	1 064	310	8	760	295	6	189	116
Oesophagus cancer	2 963	1 999	964	1	1 075	923	1	464	500
Stomach cancer	5 294	3 370	1 925	6	1 931	1 432	2	1 069	853
Colon and rectum cancer	2 945	1 576	1 369	4	908	665	1	720	647
Liver cancer	4 625	3 292	1 333	17	2 273	1 002	18	769	546
Pancreas cancer	1 066	601	465	1	354	246	0	208	257
Trachea, bronchus and lung cancers	6 673	4 777	1 896	6	2 478	2 293	4	977	914
Melanoma and other skin cancers	269	138	131	1	96	40	3	82	46
Breast cancer	3 144	7	3 137	0	4	3	2	2 300	835
Cervix uteri cancer	1 486	0	1 486	0	0	0	1	1 109	376
Corpus uteri cancer	396	0	396	0	0	0	0	258	138
Ovary cancer	783	0	783	0	0	0	13	540	230
Prostate cancer	686	686	0	2	128	556	0	0	0
Bladder cancer	714	535	179	2	221	313	1	81	97
Lymphomas and multiple myeloma	1 729	1 101	628	126	774	201	72	370	186
Leukaemia	2 759	1 584	1 175	367	1 061	156	320	719	137
Other neoplasms	**865**	**452**	**413**	**57**	**293**	**102**	**56**	**259**	**98**
Diabetes mellitus	**10 081**	**4 367**	**5 713**	**43**	**3 023**	**1 301**	**51**	**3 583**	**2 079**
Endocrine disorders	**4 760**	**2 147**	**2 614**	**853**	**1 038**	**256**	**818**	**1 456**	**340**
Neuropsychiatric disorders	**94 822**	**48 686**	**46 137**	**7 104**	**38 818**	**2 724**	**6 340**	**35 586**	**4 210**
Unipolar depressive disorders	28 983	10 785	18 198	1 121	9 205	460	1 215	15 852	1 130
Bipolar affective disorder	7 041	3 511	3 530	161	3 348	2	167	3 360	3
Schizophrenia	8 429	4 323	4 106	688	3 616	19	195	3 883	27
Epilepsy	3 201	1 775	1 425	449	1 264	63	378	984	63
Alcohol use disorders	14 853	13 517	1 335	515	12 691	311	37	1 262	36
Alzheimer and other dementias	4 772	1 921	2 851	170	341	1 410	160	359	2 332
Parkinson disease	670	326	343	6	158	162	5	138	200
Multiple sclerosis	730	306	424	31	268	7	45	366	13
Drug use disorders	3 664	2 856	808	85	2 762	10	46	760	3
Post-traumatic stress disorder	1 663	470	1 193	14	454	2	10	1 173	10
Obsessive-compulsive disorder	2 484	1 082	1 402	95	971	16	125	1 252	24
Panic disorder	3 348	1 126	2 222	48	1 073	5	51	2 158	13
Insomnia (primary)	1 458	537	921	24	460	53	20	788	114
Migraine	3 512	928	2 585	327	600	0	835	1 749	0
Sense organ disorders	**41 604**	**20 288**	**21 316**	**1 379**	**13 715**	**5 195**	**1 264**	**13 368**	**6 684**
Glaucoma	2 517	1 124	1 393	15	736	372	14	804	575
Cataracts	8 813	3 953	4 860	41	2 637	1 274	46	2 922	1 892
Refractive errors	13 731	6 861	6 870	1 307	4 107	1 447	1 194	4 047	1 628
Hearing loss, adult onset	12 200	6 404	5 795	0	4 955	1 450	0	4 203	1 592
Macular degeneration and other[h]	4 343	1 946	2 398	16	1 279	651	9	1 391	998

(Table A6c continued)

Cause[b]	Middle-income countries			Males			Females		
	Total[c]	Males	Females	0-14	15-59	60+	0-14	15-59	60+
Population (millions)	3 045	1 531	1 513	400	989	142	372	969	172
	(000)	(000)	(000)	(000)	(000)	(000)	(000)	(000)	(000)
TOTAL DALYs	572 859	313 409	259 450	67 138	192 506	53 765	61 259	143 399	54 792
Cardiovascular diseases	**76 204**	**42 151**	**34 053**	**814**	**22 230**	**19 107**	**796**	**12 856**	**20 401**
Rheumatic heart disease	2 050	812	1 238	57	600	154	68	813	356
Hypertensive heart disease	4 769	2 496	2 273	21	1 095	1 380	17	752	1 504
Ischaemic heart disease	28 866	17 179	11 687	36	9 501	7 641	29	3 998	7 659
Cerebrovascular disease	27 529	14 467	13 062	187	6 561	7 720	156	4 681	8 225
Inflammatory heart diseases[i]	2 806	1 759	1 047	99	1 181	479	83	482	481
Respiratory diseases	**29 044**	**16 936**	**12 109**	**1 968**	**8 972**	**5 995**	**1 943**	**5 163**	**5 002**
Chronic obstructive pulmonary disease	16 123	9 586	6 536	42	4 447	5 098	37	2 281	4 218
Asthma	6 897	3 800	3 097	1 291	2 294	216	1 420	1 484	193
Digestive diseases	**19 259**	**11 836**	**7 423**	**1 251**	**8 553**	**2 032**	**1 181**	**4 518**	**1 724**
Peptic ulcer disease	1 898	1 252	646	52	921	279	36	409	201
Cirrhosis of the liver	6 731	4 625	2 106	67	3 681	877	59	1 467	581
Appendicitis	191	116	76	19	84	13	15	48	13
Diseases of the genitourinary system	**7 008**	**4 049**	**2 959**	**251**	**2 906**	**891**	**248**	**1 945**	**767**
Nephritis and nephrosis	3 858	2 019	1 839	187	1 296	536	191	1 083	565
Benign prostatic hypertrophy	1 372	1 372	0	0	1 177	196	0	0	0
Skin diseases	**1 809**	**841**	**967**	**168**	**573**	**100**	**147**	**660**	**160**
Musculoskeletal diseases	**16 288**	**7 054**	**9 234**	**296**	**5 580**	**1 177**	**391**	**6 972**	**1 871**
Rheumatoid arthritis	2 655	718	1 937	56	552	111	157	1 517	262
Osteoarthritis	8 425	3 234	5 191	2	2 464	768	2	3 968	1 220
Congenital abnormalities	**8 530**	**4 418**	**4 112**	**4 099**	**307**	**12**	**3 872**	**230**	**10**
Oral diseases	**3 946**	**1 930**	**2 016**	**656**	**935**	**339**	**614**	**967**	**435**
Dental caries	2 459	1 243	1 216	649	528	66	608	527	81
Periodontal disease	121	60	61	0	55	5	0	55	6
Edentulism	1 319	607	712	0	342	265	0	368	345
III. Injuries	*90 092*	*62 083*	*28 009*	*10 653*	*49 014*	*2 416*	*8 435*	*17 848*	*1 725*
Unintentional	**65 905**	**43 401**	**22 504**	**9 832**	**31 806**	**1 763**	**7 873**	**13 320**	**1 312**
Road traffic accidents	21 382	15 328	6 053	1 847	12 950	531	1 459	4 301	293
Poisonings	3 687	2 572	1 115	169	2 276	127	183	842	91
Falls	8 640	5 396	3 244	1 312	3 716	367	1 261	1 636	347
Fires	2 196	1 121	1 074	370	702	49	384	637	53
Drownings	5 573	3 856	1 717	1 673	2 079	104	929	710	78
Other unintentional injuries	24 428	15 127	9 301	4 460	10 083	584	3 657	5 194	450
Intentional	**24 187**	**18 682**	**5 504**	**821**	**17 208**	**653**	**562**	**4 528**	**413**
Self-inflicted injuries	8 516	5 040	3 476	193	4 385	461	200	2 935	341
Violence	11 967	10 292	1 675	432	9 722	139	220	1 396	58
War and conflict	3 493	3 166	327	192	2 924	50	140	174	13

[a] See Annex Table C1 for a list of Member States by WHO region and income category.
[b] Estimates for specific causes may not sum to broader cause groupings due to omission of residual categories.
[c] World totals for males and females include residual populations living outside WHO Member States.
[d] For the Americas, Europe and Western Pacific regions, these figures include late effects of polio cases with onset prior to regional certification of polio eradication in 1994, 2000 and 2002, respectively.
[e] Does not include liver cancer and cirrhosis deaths resulting from chronic hepatitis virus infection.
[f] This category includes 'Causes arising in the perinatal period' as defined in the International Classification of Diseases, and does not include all deaths occurring in the perinatal period.
[g] Includes severe neonatal infections and other non-infectious causes arising in the perinatal period.
[h] Includes macular degeneration and other age-related causes of vision loss not correctable by provision of glasses or contact lenses, together with deaths due to other sense organ disorders.
[i] Includes myocarditis, pericarditis, endocarditis and cardiomyopathy.

Table A6d: DALYs (thousands) by age, sex, cause in low-income countries, 2004

Cause[b]	Low-income countries			Males			Females		
	Total[c]	Males	Females	0-14	15-59	60+	0-14	15-59	60+
Population (millions)	2 413	1 229	1 184	459	697	73	435	668	81
	(000)	(000)	(000)	(000)	(000)	(000)	(000)	(000)	(000)
TOTAL DALYs	827 669	418 206	409 463	210 789	172 662	34 754	199 027	174 199	36 236
Communicable, maternal, perinatal and nutritional conditions	*468 811*	*227 259*	*241 552*	*171 013*	*50 652*	*5 595*	*161 446*	*74 740*	*5 366*
Infectious and parasitic diseases	241 099	126 131	114 968	80 170	43 104	2 858	74 214	38 229	2 524
Tuberculosis	22 356	13 837	8 520	1 306	11 424	1 107	1 231	6 761	528
STDs excluding HIV	7 877	2 912	4 965	1 515	1 274	123	1 471	3 424	69
Syphilis	2 535	1 366	1 169	1 058	196	111	988	144	38
Chlamydia	2 419	210	2 209	7	203	0	50	2 148	11
Gonorrhoea	2 703	1 205	1 498	433	772	0	419	1 078	0
HIV/AIDS	42 867	20 042	22 825	4 401	15 445	196	4 294	18 382	149
Diarrhoeal diseases	59 207	30 862	28 345	28 346	2 119	396	26 299	1 610	437
Childhood-cluster diseases	27 650	14 793	12 857	14 628	160	5	12 738	116	4
Pertussis	9 158	4 639	4 519	4 637	2	0	4 517	2	0
Poliomyelitis[d]	27	15	12	11	4	0	11	1	0
Diphtheria	163	80	82	78	2	0	82	1	0
Measles	13 601	7 038	6 563	7 037	1	0	6 561	2	0
Tetanus	4 701	3 021	1 680	2 866	150	4	1 567	109	4
Meningitis	8 905	4 575	4 330	3 387	1 100	87	3 596	670	64
Hepatitis B[e]	1 236	806	430	157	602	48	151	254	25
Hepatitis C[e]	476	308	168	61	228	19	61	98	9
Malaria	32 766	16 725	16 041	16 062	641	21	15 335	680	27
Tropical-cluster diseases	10 823	7 456	3 367	2 895	4 461	100	1 482	1 805	79
Trypanosomiasis	1 586	987	598	488	490	9	304	289	5
Chagas disease	3	2	2	0	1	0	0	1	0
Schistosomiasis	1 493	893	600	446	403	44	317	253	29
Leishmaniasis	1 861	1 152	709	537	599	16	389	306	13
Lymphatic filariasis	5 496	4 202	1 295	1 390	2 798	13	442	834	19
Onchocerciasis	383	220	163	33	170	18	30	121	12
Leprosy	160	96	64	28	62	6	25	36	3
Dengue	397	199	198	191	7	1	191	7	1
Japanese encephalitis	481	234	247	200	33	1	213	33	1
Trachoma	897	231	666	2	164	66	3	438	224
Intestinal nematode infections	2 694	1 378	1 316	1 205	164	9	1 147	160	10
Ascariasis	1 424	725	700	724	1	0	699	1	0
Trichuriasis	661	344	317	344	0	0	317	0	0
Hookworm disease	578	291	287	121	161	8	120	158	9
Respiratory infections	78 807	40 891	37 915	33 249	5 137	2 506	31 231	4 231	2 453
Lower respiratory infections	76 932	39 911	37 021	32 453	5 002	2 456	30 498	4 113	2 410
Upper respiratory infections	1 091	573	517	415	110	49	381	94	42
Otitis media	784	407	377	381	25	1	352	24	1
Maternal conditions	29 022	0	29 022	0	0	0	429	28 593	0
Maternal haemorrhage	3 838	0	3 838	0	0	0	0	3 838	0
Maternal sepsis	4 493	0	4 493	0	0	0	7	4 486	0
Hypertensive disorders of pregnancy	1 504	0	1 504	0	0	0	57	1 447	0
Obstructed labour	2 339	0	2 339	0	0	0	0	2 339	0
Abortion	5 875	0	5 875	0	0	0	343	5 532	0
Perinatal conditions[f]	93 331	47 500	45 831	47 500	0	0	45 831	0	0
Prematurity and low birth weight	32 099	16 265	15 834	16 265	0	0	15 834	0	0
Birth asphyxia and birth trauma	29 786	15 001	14 785	15 001	0	0	14 785	0	0
Neonatal infections and other conditions[g]	31 445	16 234	15 212	16 234	0	0	15 212	0	0

(Table A6d continued)

Cause[b]	Low-income countries			Males			Females		
	Total[c]	Males	Females	0-14	15-59	60+	0-14	15-59	60+
Population (millions)	2 413	1 229	1 184	459	697	73	435	668	81
	(000)	(000)	(000)	(000)	(000)	(000)	(000)	(000)	(000)
TOTAL DALYs	827 669	418 206	409 463	210 789	172 662	34 754	199 027	174 199	36 236
Nutritional deficiencies	**26 553**	**12 737**	**13 816**	**10 095**	**2 411**	**231**	**9 740**	**3 686**	**389**
Protein-energy malnutrition	13 294	6 745	6 549	6 402	324	19	6 251	274	24
Iodine deficiency	1 967	1 017	950	1 016	1	0	949	1	0
Vitamin A deficiency	587	316	271	315	1	0	270	1	0
Iron-deficiency anaemia	9 948	4 262	5 686	2 179	1 933	151	2 080	3 327	278
II. Noncommunicable conditions	*272 632*	*137 727*	*134 906*	*24 654*	*85 417*	*27 655*	*24 659*	*80 735*	*29 512*
Malignant neoplasms	**18 982**	**9 313**	**9 669**	**810**	**5 351**	**3 152**	**782**	**5 976**	**2 911**
Mouth and oropharynx cancers	1 983	1 390	593	15	869	507	17	327	249
Oesophagus cancer	1 317	727	590	3	393	331	2	335	252
Stomach cancer	1 167	660	507	5	410	245	2	318	187
Colon and rectum cancer	833	476	357	6	326	144	2	230	125
Liver cancer	1 240	819	421	27	541	252	23	275	123
Pancreas cancer	295	152	144	2	89	61	0	86	58
Trachea, bronchus and lung cancers	1 483	1 145	338	4	584	557	6	191	141
Melanoma and other skin cancers	121	59	62	2	41	16	2	37	23
Breast cancer	1 626	0	1 626	0	0	0	2	1 164	459
Cervix uteri cancer	1 901	0	1 901	0	0	0	1	1 318	582
Corpus uteri cancer	89	0	89	0	0	0	4	47	38
Ovary cancer	498	0	498	0	0	0	18	333	148
Prostate cancer	452	452	0	1	93	359	0	0	0
Bladder cancer	300	213	88	2	74	137	1	37	49
Lymphomas and multiple myeloma	1 653	1 050	603	247	651	152	159	319	125
Leukaemia	1 495	824	671	234	533	57	242	378	50
Other neoplasms	**721**	**367**	**354**	**82**	**241**	**44**	**97**	**208**	**49**
Diabetes mellitus	**5 991**	**2 902**	**3 090**	**112**	**1 965**	**824**	**124**	**1 853**	**1 113**
Endocrine disorders	**3 753**	**1 784**	**1 969**	**770**	**821**	**193**	**609**	**1 027**	**333**
Neuropsychiatric disorders	**72 824**	**34 821**	**38 003**	**7 240**	**26 131**	**1 450**	**7 697**	**28 210**	**2 095**
Unipolar depressive disorders	26 469	10 073	16 396	1 392	8 372	309	1 381	14 362	652
Bipolar affective disorder	5 836	3 003	2 834	202	2 800	1	136	2 696	1
Schizophrenia	6 782	3 395	3 386	421	2 955	19	72	3 282	32
Epilepsy	4 112	2 160	1 952	933	1 163	64	909	987	56
Alcohol use disorders	4 671	4 259	413	134	4 073	52	63	334	15
Alzheimer and other dementias	1 996	875	1 121	144	130	601	135	136	850
Parkinson disease	346	164	182	3	90	71	2	103	77
Multiple sclerosis	477	210	266	30	177	4	35	227	4
Drug use disorders	2 806	2 299	507	67	2 222	10	30	474	3
Post-traumatic stress disorder	1 292	353	939	18	335	1	13	922	4
Obsessive-compulsive disorder	2 020	863	1 157	109	748	6	287	855	15
Panic disorder	2 845	977	1 868	55	919	3	54	1 808	6
Insomnia (primary)	1 395	691	704	15	629	46	20	619	65
Migraine	2 813	820	1 993	413	406	0	1 414	579	0
Sense organ disorders	**36 010**	**17 097**	**18 914**	**839**	**12 092**	**4 166**	**700**	**12 954**	**5 259**
Glaucoma	1 837	822	1 014	59	577	187	6	717	291
Cataracts	8 527	3 713	4 814	62	2 727	924	24	3 436	1 354
Refractive errors	11 262	5 577	5 686	704	3 095	1 778	662	3 049	1 975
Hearing loss, adult onset	10 945	5 500	5 445	0	4 621	878	0	4 433	1 012
Macular degeneration and other[h]	3 439	1 484	1 955	14	1 071	399	8	1 320	627

Cause[b]	Low-income countries			Males			Females		
	Total[c]	Males	Females	0-14	15-59	60+	0-14	15-59	60+
Population (millions)	2 413	1 229	1 184	459	697	73	435	668	81
	(000)	(000)	(000)	(000)	(000)	(000)	(000)	(000)	(000)
TOTAL DALYs	827 669	418 206	409 463	210 789	172 662	34 754	199 027	174 199	36 236
Cardiovascular diseases	**57 258**	**30 439**	**26 819**	**1 666**	**17 242**	**11 530**	**1 737**	**12 946**	**12 136**
Rheumatic heart disease	3 016	1 445	1 572	284	990	171	374	985	213
Hypertensive heart disease	2 445	1 172	1 272	32	666	475	38	607	626
Ischaemic heart disease	25 958	15 082	10 876	175	8 700	6 207	114	5 214	5 548
Cerebrovascular disease	14 281	7 251	7 030	226	3 614	3 411	232	2 932	3 866
Inflammatory heart diseases[i]	2 678	1 447	1 231	241	961	245	238	711	282
Respiratory diseases	**22 706**	**12 393**	**10 313**	**2 217**	**6 713**	**3 463**	**2 118**	**5 441**	**2 754**
Chronic obstructive pulmonary disease	10 402	5 896	4 506	46	3 040	2 809	27	2 324	2 156
Asthma	7 494	4 031	3 463	1 458	2 402	170	1 419	1 884	160
Digestive diseases	**18 508**	**10 127**	**8 381**	**1 924**	**7 005**	**1 198**	**1 998**	**5 323**	**1 059**
Peptic ulcer disease	2 871	1 933	937	215	1 495	223	111	651	175
Cirrhosis of the liver	5 249	3 079	2 171	450	2 106	523	613	1 226	331
Appendicitis	192	122	70	28	78	16	14	38	17
Diseases of the genitourinary system	**6 491**	**3 932**	**2 559**	**566**	**2 638**	**728**	**484**	**1 537**	**538**
Nephritis and nephrosis	4 563	2 541	2 022	499	1 531	511	434	1 125	464
Benign prostatic hypertrophy	988	988	0	0	841	147	0	0	0
Skin diseases	**1 838**	**998**	**840**	**337**	**582**	**79**	**204**	**507**	**129**
Musculoskeletal diseases	**9 332**	**4 430**	**4 903**	**369**	**3 551**	**509**	**414**	**3 724**	**764**
Rheumatoid arthritis	1 437	460	978	62	341	57	119	749	110
Osteoarthritis	4 377	1 751	2 627	2	1 464	286	4	2 148	475
Congenital abnormalities	**15 134**	**7 590**	**7 543**	**7 346**	**240**	**4**	**7 333**	**205**	**5**
Oral diseases	**3 085**	**1 535**	**1 550**	**376**	**843**	**315**	**360**	**822**	**368**
Dental caries	1 913	975	938	368	523	83	349	499	90
Periodontal disease	160	81	80	0	77	4	1	74	4
Edentulism	948	451	496	0	226	225	0	226	270
III. Injuries	***86 226***	***53 220***	***33 006***	***15 122***	***36 593***	***1 504***	***12 923***	***18 725***	***1 358***
Unintentional	**65 015**	**38 431**	**26 584**	**13 845**	**23 403**	**1 183**	**11 936**	**13 488**	**1 160**
Road traffic accidents	16 697	11 637	5 060	3 278	8 051	308	2 593	2 292	174
Poisonings	3 064	1 841	1 223	501	1 243	97	341	697	186
Falls	7 215	4 210	3 005	1 876	2 062	272	1 647	1 100	258
Fires	8 886	3 293	5 593	1 651	1 588	54	2 108	3 363	122
Drownings	4 844	3 253	1 591	1 367	1 832	54	887	653	51
Other unintentional injuries	24 309	14 197	10 111	5 172	8 627	398	4 359	5 383	369
Intentional	**21 211**	**14 789**	**6 422**	**1 277**	**13 191**	**321**	**987**	**5 237**	**198**
Self-inflicted injuries	8 431	4 698	3 733	194	4 367	137	272	3 377	84
Violence	8 788	6 867	1 922	734	6 007	125	444	1 402	76
War and conflict	3 819	3 085	734	332	2 702	51	261	439	34

[a] See Annex Table C1 for a list of Member States by WHO region and income category.
[b] Estimates for specific causes may not sum to broader cause groupings due to omission of residual categories.
[c] World totals for males and females include residual populations living outside WHO Member States.
[d] For the Americas, Europe and Western Pacific regions, these figures include late effects of polio cases with onset prior to regional certification of polio eradication in 1994, 2000 and 2002, respectively.
[e] Does not include liver cancer and cirrhosis deaths resulting from chronic hepatitis virus infection.
[f] This category includes 'Causes arising in the perinatal period' as defined in the International Classification of Diseases, and does not include all deaths occurring in the perinatal period.
[g] Includes severe neonatal infections and other non-infectious causes arising in the perinatal period.
[h] Includes macular degeneration and other age-related causes of vision loss not correctable by provision of glasses or contact lenses, together with deaths due to other sense organ disorders.
[i] Includes myocarditis, pericarditis, endocarditis and cardiomyopathy.

Annex B

Data sources and methods

B1.	Population and all-cause mortality estimates for 2004	98
B2.	Estimation of deaths by cause	98
B3.	Causes of death for children aged under five years	103
B4.	YLD revisions	106
B5.	Cause-specific revisions and updates	106
B6.	Prevalence of long-term disability	116
B7.	Projections of mortality and burden of disease	117
B8.	Uncertainty of estimates and projections	117

This update of the Global Burden of Disease (GBD) Study for the year 2004 uses the same general methods as previous revisions carried out by the World Health Organization (WHO) for 2001 and 2002 *(11)*. Country groupings and regions used in this report are defined in Tables C1 and C2 (Annex C). GBD 2004 estimates are also available for other regional groupings on the WHO web site.[a] Table C3 (Annex C) lists the GBD cause categories and their definitions in terms of the *International classification of diseases, tenth revision* (ICD-10). The GBD cause categories are grouped into three broad cause groups: Group I (communicable, maternal, perinatal and nutritional conditions), Group II (noncommunicable diseases) and Group III (injuries). General methods and data sources for the GBD estimates have been documented elsewhere *(11)*; this part of the report documents the specific revisions for the 2004 estimates.

Apart from the incorporation of new epidemiological data for specific causes, the GBD 2004 has incorporated:

- more recent death registration data for many countries;
- new African mortality data using verbal autopsy methods to assign cause of death;
- improvements in methods used for the estimation of causes of child deaths in countries without good death registration data.

For these reasons, and also because of revisions to the United Nations population estimates, the GBD estimates for 2004 are not directly comparable with the previous GBD 2002 estimates.

B1. Population and all-cause mortality estimates for 2004

Life tables for the 192 WHO Member States in 2004 were published in the *World health report 2006 (25)*, with data and methods described in the Statistical Annex Notes. Age- and sex-specific all-cause mortality rates from these life tables were further adjusted for revisions in estimates of human immunodeficiency virus (HIV) mortality and deaths due to conflict and natural disasters. These cause-specific revisions and updates are outlined in Section B5. Total deaths by age and sex were estimated for each Member State by applying these death rates to the estimated 2004 de facto resident populations prepared by the United Nations Population Division in its 2006 revision *(13)*. Total deaths in the neonatal period (the first four weeks of life) for 2004 were estimated country by country using methods documented elsewhere in collaboration with the Department of Making Pregnancy Safer *(26)*.

For China, recorded age-specific death rates for ages over five years from the 2000 census were adjusted for estimated underreporting of 11.3% for males and 18.1% for females *(27)*, projected forward to 2004 assuming an annual rate of mortality decline of 1.5%, based on the estimated rates of mortality for the two intercensal periods, 1982–1990 and 1990–2000. The projection of child mortality rate takes into account other sources of data such as the Child Mortality Surveillance System *(28)*.

For India, the all-cause mortality envelope was derived from a time series analysis of age-specific death rates from the sample registration system for years 1990–2002, after correction for underregistration (88% completeness) *(29)*. Child and adult mortality rates were then projected to 2004 using a regression model that gave more weight to recent years of observation. The child mortality rate was projected independently taking into account other sources such as the Demographic and Health Survey 2005/2006 *(30)*.

B2. Estimation of deaths by cause

Death registration data containing usable information on cause-of-death distributions were available for 112 countries; the majority of these countries were in the high-income group, Latin America and the Caribbean, and Europe and Central Asia. The data sources and methods for estimation of mortality are outlined in Table C4 (Annex C). Population-based epidemiological studies, disease registers and notifications systems also contributed to the estimation of mortality due to 21 specific communicable causes of death, including HIV/AIDS (acquired immune

---

[a] http://www.who.int/evidence/bod

deficiency syndrome), malaria, tuberculosis (TB), childhood immunizable diseases, schistosomiasis, trypanosomiasis and Chagas disease (see Section B5 below).

Cause-of-death statistics are reported to WHO on an annual basis by country, year, cause, age and sex. The number of countries reporting data using ICD-10 has continued to increase. For the GBD 2002 estimates, a total of 72 countries had complete data (defined as coverage of 85% and more), but only 35 countries were reporting data coded to the third or fourth character of ICD-10. For the GBD 2004 estimates, in the same group of 72 countries, there are now 55 countries reporting data to the third or fourth character of ICD-10. This increase of 20 countries reporting data at the detailed level of ICD-10 enhances the comparability of the 2004 estimates. However, 10 countries with complete data still report to WHO using the ninth revision of ICD (ICD-9).

GBD correction algorithms (11) were also applied to resolve problems of miscoding for cardiovascular diseases (mainly involving redistribution of deaths coded to heart failure or ill-defined heart disease), cancer (involving redistribution of deaths coded to secondary sites or ill-defined primary sites) and injuries (involving redistribution of deaths coded as due to events of undetermined intent).

Coding of natural causes of death for neonates varies a great deal among countries. Some countries code these deaths to the 'P chapter' (i.e. codes that refer to conditions originating in the perinatal period) while others use a combination of P codes and other codes as well. In some instances the age of death is not always taken into account. Some conditions, such as septicaemia and pneumonia, have specific codes within P00–P96 which should be used for neonates (0–27 days). For countries with vital registration data, we have recoded all the deaths aged 0–27 days from natural causes that were initially coded outside the 'P chapter' to codes in the 'P chapter' whenever possible. In a number of countries, neonatal septicaemia (P36) is frequently assigned to A40 and A41 (septicaemia). In this case we have recoded them back to P36, thus identifying more deaths due to causes originating in the perinatal period.

Cause of death for countries with complete or incomplete vital registration data

Since the GBD 2002 analyses, the number of countries with complete data (coverage of 85% or more) has remained stable at 76. Vital registration data were used to estimate deaths by cause for 78 countries, including two very small countries where coverage was lower than 85%. Where the latest available year was earlier than 2004, death registration data from 1980 up to the latest available year were analysed as a basis for projecting recent trends for specific causes, and these trend estimates were used to project the cause distribution for 2004 from the latest available year. When estimating cause-of-death distributions for very small countries, an average of the three last years of data were used to minimize stochastic variation. Adjustments for deaths due to HIV, drug use disorders, war and natural disasters were based on other sources of information as described in Section B6 below.

For 34 countries with less than 85% coverage, cause-of-death modelling (CodMod) was used to adjust the proportions of deaths occurring in Groups I, II and III by age and sex as described elsewhere (11). The regional distribution of the 112 countries for which complete or incomplete vital registration data were used is shown in Table B1.

Cause of death for countries without usable vital registration data

To estimate deaths by cause for the remaining 78 countries without usable death registration data, CodMod was applied at country level for estimating the proportion of deaths in Groups I, II and III by age and sex, based on all-cause mortality levels (excluding HIV, war and natural disasters), gross national income per capita and region. The statistical model for cause-of-death composition was estimated using a substantially larger data set (1613 country-years) than that used for the 1990 GBD study (11, 31).

Detailed proportional cause distributions within Groups I, II and III were based on death registration data from within each region (see Table C4, Annex C, for more details). Specific causes were further adjusted on the basis of epidemiological evidence from registries, verbal autopsy studies, disease surveillance systems and analyses from WHO technical programmes. The evidence used for the revision of specific causes is described in Section B5.

For all regions except the WHO African Region, the choice of death registration data for the estimation of within-group cause distributions was consistent with that used for the GBD 2002. For countries in the WHO African Region, the GBD 2002 used cause-of-death distributions based on 1996 death registration data from rural provinces of South Africa, and grouped countries into two mortality strata labelled D and E (6). For the 2004 update, the regional pattern was based on a greater range of information on cause-of-death distributions in Africa. These included the South African 2004 vital registration data, the Zimbabwe National Burden of Disease Study 1997 (32), INDEPTH verbal autopsy data from seven sites in Africa for 1999–2002 (33), data from Antananarivo in Madagascar for 1976–1995 (34), and Mozambique Maputo Central Hospital Mortuary data for 1993–2004 (35).

For Groups I, II and III, the proportional distributions of total deaths (excluding HIV and war) for urban populations were based on averages of the Madagascar urban death registration data, South African death registration data for 2004, the Zimbabwean 1997 estimates and CodMod predictions for 2004. As all the African INDEPTH sites were rural, the INDEPTH data were taken as representative of rural populations. The Group II fraction of deaths in the African INDEPTH data flattened out above age 50 years, and was lower than in all other African data sources. We thus used an average of INDEPTH and South African data for rural provinces, giving less weight to the INDEPTH data with increasing age for rural populations. For countries in the D mortality stratum, 44% of the population were assumed to be urban, and 29% for the E mortality stratum.

Proportional cause distributions for Groups I, II and III for individual African countries were adjusted away from regional average distributions using CodMod together with country-specific inputs on mortality levels and income per capita. Figure B1 compares the final resulting African regional cause distributions for Groups II and III for 2004 with those for the GBD 2002.

Table B1: Methods and data for cause-of-death estimation for 2004, by WHO region

Data/method	Number of Member States						
	Africa	The Americas	Eastern Mediter- ranean	Europe	South- East Asia	Western Pacific	World
Vital registration data with coverage of 85% or more	3	21	2	39	1	12	78
Vital registration data with cover- age of <85% – use of CodMod	–	12	7	11	1	3	34
Sample registration system	–	–	–	–	1	1	2
CodMod, regional pattern of causes of death, and cause- specific estimates[a]	43	2	12	2	8	11	78
Total Member States	46	35	21	52	11	27	192

CodMod, cause-of-death model.

[a] Epidemiological estimates obtained from studies, WHO technical programmes and UNAIDS for the following conditions: AIDS, TB, diphtheria, measles, pertussis, poliomyelitis, tetanus, dengue, malaria, schistosomiasis, trypanosomiasis, Japanese encephalitis, Chagas, maternal conditions (including abortion), cancers, drug use disorders, rheumatoid arthritis and war.

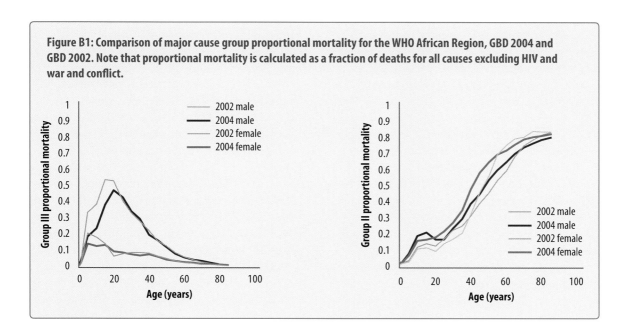

Figure B1: Comparison of major cause group proportional mortality for the WHO African Region, GBD 2004 and GBD 2002. Note that proportional mortality is calculated as a fraction of deaths for all causes excluding HIV and war and conflict.

Data sources and methods for some specific countries

China

Cause-specific mortality data for China continued to be available from two sources – the sample vital registration system (VR) monitored by the Ministry of Health, and the Disease Surveillance Points system (DSP) monitored by the Chinese Center for Disease Control and Prevention. The following table gives a brief summary of the characteristics of the most recently available data from these systems.

Both data sets were assessed for suitability in estimating 2004 cause-specific mortality for China at the national level. According to Chinese authorities, the sampling distribution of sites in the DSP was more nationally representative than the VR (36), but they advised that DSP data for 2004 were not yet finalized, with further adjustments to cause attributions pending. We therefore based the update of the broad

Table B2: Distribution of deaths by stratum[a] from the Chinese sample vital registration system (VR) and the Disease Surveillance Points system (DSP)

Source	TOTAL	URBAN	Urban 1	Urban 2	RURAL	Rural 1	Rural 2	Rural 3	Rural 4
VR 2005 data									
Population (millions)	57.27	36.35	17.87	18.47	20.92	NA	NA	NA	NA
Deaths	310 826	200 360	99 742	100 618	110 466	NA	NA	NA	NA
Death rate/100 000	543	551	558	545	528	NA	NA	NA	NA
DSP 2004 data									
Population (millions)	9.29	2.29	1.90	0.39	7.00	1.95	2.81	1.83	0.40
Deaths	46 101	11 109	9 290	1 819	34 992	10 023	13 487	9 635	1 847
Death rate/100 000	496	484	489	463	500	515	479	526	457

NA, data not available.

a   See Mathers et al (11) for definitions of strata. Urban 1 stratum contains large cities, urban 2 stratum small- and medium-size cities. The rural strata are based on socioeconomic status, with rural 1 containing the highest status areas and rural 4 the lowest.

cause-of-death patterns (Groups I, II and III) for 2004 on earlier DSP data for 1997–1999, as for the GBD 2002 estimates. CodMod was used to adjust for changes in mortality rates and income levels from 2002 to 2004. For the within-group cause-specific estimates, we used specific proportionate mortality distributions from the VR 2005 data weighted as follows: 40% urban and 60% rural. Supplementary information from WHO technical programmes and the Joint United Nations Programme on HIV/AIDS (UNAIDS) was also used in estimating specific causes of death.

India

For the GBD 2002 estimates for India, cause patterns of mortality were based on the Medical Certificate of Cause of Death Database (MCCD) for urban India (1996), the Annual Survey of Causes of Death (SCD) for rural areas of India for 1996–1998 (11) and information from WHO technical programmes and UNAIDS. Verbal autopsy methods used in the sample registration system for assigning cause of death have been substantially revised as part of the Million Deaths Study (37). Preliminary data for a nationally representative sample of 62 553 deaths in 2001–2003 were assessed for use in the GBD 2004. However, as validation studies and analysis of the verbal autopsy-assigned cause-of-death information were not yet completed, these data were not used for the GBD 2004 revision.

Instead, the GBD 2002 cause distributions for India were adjusted to the 2004 all-cause envelope, and the resulting cause-specific estimates were further adjusted with information for 2004 from WHO technical programmes and UNAIDS on maternal, perinatal and childhood cluster conditions, as well as epidemiological estimates for TB, HIV, illicit drug dependence and problem use, rheumatoid arthritis and war deaths (see below). It should be noted that WHO and UNAIDS have substantially reduced estimates of HIV deaths for India compared to previous estimates used for the GBD 2002.

The Islamic Republic of Iran

The latest death registration data available for the Islamic Republic of Iran were for the period 21 March 2004 to 20 March 2005, as per the Iranian calendar. The registration system operated by the

Deputy of Health Programme (Ministry of Health and Medical Education) captured deaths from 29 out of 30 provinces, with an estimated coverage of around 65% of all deaths occurring in the country. Tehran Province, which is the most populous province (population 12 million), was the only province not covered by the death registration system (38). Coverage has substantially improved compared to earlier years. In 1999, the system was capturing deaths in only four provinces with coverage of 5% of all deaths in the entire country. In 2001, the system further expanded by recording deaths in 18 provinces and one district with coverage of nearly 40% of all deaths in the country.

The 2004 data were coded to a condensed list of 318 cause categories, using the ICD-10 classification system. As coverage was partial, CodMod was used to predict the proportionate mortality distributions for Groups I, II and III, and specific cause mortality distributions adjusted within these groups. Supplementary information from WHO technical programmes and UNAIDS was also used in estimating specific causes of death.

Mexico

Cause-specific mortality for Mexico was estimated using death registration data for 2004, assessed to be nearly 100% complete. As well as the standard redistributions for ill-defined cause codes, further corrections for miscertification of deaths due to diabetes and cardiovascular diseases were carried out based on in-depth analyses undertaken by the Harvard Initiative for Global Health (39).

South Africa

The completeness of the 2004 death registration data for South Africa was assessed to lie in the range of 75–89%. Approximately 13 000 deaths were reported to be due to HIV/AIDS, although UNAIDS has estimated that HIV/AIDS was responsible for 290 000 deaths in 2003 and 320 000 deaths in 2005 (40). Comparison of age-specific death rates for individual causes in 2004 with the corresponding death rates for 1993 and 1996 (when there were far fewer HIV deaths – around 11 000 and 45 000, respectively) showed clear evidence of miscoding of HIV deaths into other causes. This was particularly evident for diarrhoea and gastroenteritis of presumed infectious origin, respiratory TB and herpes zoster, causes which the national statistical office had also found to be often associated with HIV/AIDS *(41)*. In addition, deaths classified as ill-defined showed spurious peaks in the same adult age groups as for deaths from HIV/AIDS. AIDS-defining diseases such as Kaposi sarcoma were also examined. Averaged age distributions for cause-specific mortality rates for 1993 and 1996 were used to remove the embedded misdiagnosed HIV/AIDS deaths in the 2004 data, in order to obtain HIV/AIDS-free sex-age-cause distribution patterns. A total of 224 000 deaths were reassigned from other causes to HIV/AIDS, resulting in an estimated national total for HIV/AIDS deaths of 292 000 in 2004, close to the UNAIDS estimate of 295 000, derived independently from prevalence data.

The HIV/AIDS-free sex-age-cause distribution patterns thus obtained were then proportionately adjusted to the WHO estimated number of deaths by sex and age for South Africa in 2004. Supplementary information from WHO technical programmes for some specific diseases and causes was also used to adjust final estimates by cause. Nearly 70% of all injury deaths in the 2004 death registration data were classified as due to events of undetermined intent, and less than 10% of all injury deaths were classified as caused by homicides. We used separate estimates of the external cause distribution for injury deaths based on data from the National Injury Mortality Surveillance System prepared for the revised South African Burden of Disease study *(42)*.

Thailand

Death registration data were available for the year 2002, with an estimated coverage of about 85%. However, the proportion of ill-defined conditions was nearly 50%, since many deaths in Thailand occur at home, and the cause of death is reported by lay people. In order to improve the usability of the death registration data, the Thai Ministry of Health conducted a re-test survey on a sample of about 33 000 deaths, using verbal autopsy methods, to ascertain the true cause of death *(43)*. This included a sample of 12 000 deaths with ill-defined causes. The reallocation algorithm for ill-defined causes from the verbal autopsy study was used to correct the high proportion of ill-defined deaths from the

death registration data. Deaths from septicaemia and pneumonia (approximately 27 000 in total in the 2002 data) were also reallocated based on the outcomes of the verbal autopsy study. The resultant cause-specific proportionate mortality was inflated to the national mortality envelope derived from the life table analysis. Supplementary information from WHO technical programmes and UNAIDS was also used in estimating specific causes of death.

Turkey

Death registration data for 2003 were only available for urban areas of Turkey, with an estimated national coverage of 45%. Causes of death were coded using the condensed list of the ICD eighth revision. Instead of using these data, we used a detailed analysis of causes of death for the year 2000, from a national burden of disease study conducted by the national authorities in Turkey *(44)*. Proportional distributions for Groups I, II and III in 2004 were derived using CodMod. Supplementary information from WHO technical programmes and UNAIDS was also used in estimating specific causes of death.

B3. Causes of death for children aged under five years

In the *World health report 2005*, WHO published estimates of deaths of children aged under five years by cause for the years 2000–2003 that drew on extensive analyses carried out by the WHO Child Health Epidemiology Reference Group as well as cause-specific estimates from WHO technical programmes and UNAIDS *(45)*. For the GBD 2004, cause-specific and multicause models for causes of child deaths under five years *(46, 47)* and for neonatal deaths *(48, 49)* were rerun with updated inputs for the year 2004. Outputs were adjusted and mapped to GBD cause categories as described below. Together with cause-specific inputs from WHO technical programmes and UNAIDS, the resulting cause-specific inputs were adjusted country by country to fit neonatal, infant and child under-five death envelopes.

For 76 countries with death registration data covering 85% or more of deaths, deaths by cause were estimated using the most recent death registration data, after adjusting for deaths coded to ill-defined categories (see above). For the other 116 countries, available mortality data together with CodMod (see above) were used to estimate the broad cause-of-death patterns (Groups I, II and III) for infant deaths (under one year) and child deaths at ages one to four years.

Neonatal deaths

Total estimated deaths in the neonatal period were distributed to specific causes using a model developed by the Child Health Epidemiology Reference Group (CHERG) for countries without usable death registration data *(48, 49)*. The CHERG neonatal working group undertook an extensive exercise to derive global estimates for seven programme-relevant causes of neonatal death, including preterm birth, asphyxia, severe infection, neonatal tetanus, diarrhoea, congenital malformation and other causes, based on 56 studies of neonatal deaths from 29 countries that met inclusion criteria. Multinomial models developed to estimate simultaneously the distribution of these seven causes of death by country were rerun for 2004 using updated input data for covariates, and then mapped to GBD cause categories.

The GBD 2002 residual cause category "Other conditions" for the cause group "Conditions arising in the perinatal period" includes a number of infectious disease categories as well as some non-infection causes. For the GBD 2004, this cause category has been renamed "Neonatal infections and other conditions" (arising in the perinatal period). Under ICD rules, some deaths due to neonatal infections should be coded to specific infectious causes (e.g. meningitis, syphilis) and others to codes within the perinatal conditions chapter (e.g. neonatal sepsis). Clinically, it may be difficult to distinguish pneumonia, sepsis and other causes of neonatal infection. The cause category "Severe infection" was mapped to GBD cause categories based on an analysis of available death registration data and expert advice on the evidence from neonatal mortality studies, as summarized in Table B3.

The GBD cause category "Neonatal infections and other conditions" also includes other non-infectious causes arising in the perinatal period (such as deaths resulting from maternal factors such as maternal hypertension and surgery, umbilical and

other neonatal haemorrhage, haemolytic disease, neonatal jaundice, hypothermia). Mapping of the CHERG "Other neonatal category" to GBD categories resulted in 21% of the "Neonatal infections and other conditions" deaths being due to non-infectious causes, reasonably consistent with the low end of the proportions in death registration data.

The GBD cause category "Prematurity and low birth weight" (formerly labelled "Low birth weight" in the GBD 2001 and 2002) includes the CHERG neonatal category "Preterm birth" as well as deaths of infants born at term but small for gestational age. Based on expert advice, together with an analysis of available death registration data, term but small-for-gestational age deaths were assumed to be 0.4% of total neonatal deaths, and this fraction was added to the CHERG estimate for deaths of preterm infants.

The CHERG neonatal category "Congenital abnormalities" includes the GBD cause "Congenital anomalies" plus other Group II causes which comprise genetic conditions (e.g. inherited neurological and metabolic conditions and miscoded congenital heart conditions). Non-genetic Group II conditions include cancers, endocrine and skin conditions. In mapping the CHERG neonatal congenital category to GBD cause groups, it was assumed that 90% of the deaths in the CHERG group were in the GBD congenital cause group, based on an analysis of previous mortality estimates for GBD Group II conditions in infants.

Outputs from the CHERG neonatal model were used for all causes except neonatal tetanus. Outputs for neonatal tetanus deaths were compared country by country with estimates prepared by the WHO Department of Immunization, Vaccines and Biologicals (see Section B5). Final estimates from these models were reasonably consistent and the estimates prepared by this department were used for the GBD 2004.

Postneonatal deaths

Table B4 summarizes the data inputs and assumptions used for preparing estimates of postneonatal deaths by cause (ages one month to under five years) for the 116 countries without usable death registration data for child deaths. There were 63 countries where the resulting sum of the cause fractions for Group I

Table B3: Mapping of severe neonatal infection deaths to GBD cause categories

Cause	Data inputs and assumptions
Neonatal infections and other conditions	Estimates for severe neonatal infection deaths from the CHERG neonatal model, after subtraction of the proportions of deaths listed below
Meningitis	A proportion of severe infection deaths ranging from around 10% in high-income countries down to 5% in low-income countries, based on a regression model using GDP per capita
Syphilis	A proportion of severe infection deaths ranging from around 0 in high-income countries up to 3% in low-income countries, based on a regression model using GDP per capita
Acute respiratory infections	Around one third of severe infection deaths were considered attributable to pneumonia, but on advice from CHERG these deaths were left in the "Neonatal infections and other conditions" group and not shifted to the "Acute lower respiratory infections" cause group
Other infectious causes	A proportion of severe infection deaths ranging from around 7% in high-income countries down to 1% in low-income countries, based on a regression model using GDP per capita

CHERG, Child Health Epidemiology Reference Group; GDP, gross domestic product.

Table B4: Data inputs and assumptions for estimation of postneonatal deaths by cause

Cause	Data inputs and assumptions
Tuberculosis	Country-specific estimates prepared by the Stop TB programme (see Section B5)
HIV/AIDS	Country-specific estimates prepared by UNAIDS and WHO (see Section B5)
Diarrhoeal diseases	Single cause model developed by CHERG (see Section B5)
Pertussis, diphtheria, polio, measles and postneonatal tetanus	Country-specific estimates prepared by IVB Department (see Section B5)
Meningitis	Country-specific estimates prepared by IVB Department (see Section B5)
Malaria	Single cause model developed by CHERG for African countries, various sources for other countries (see Section B5)
Prematurity and low birth weight	2% of infant deaths due to this cause were assumed to fall in the postneonatal period
Congenital anomalies	12.5% of infant deaths due to congenital anomalies were assumed to fall in the postneonatal period
Other causes	Specific cause distributions within the "other causes" CHERG category were assumed to follow GBD 2002 cause distributions updated for revisions in the Group I, II and III proportions for child deaths

causes exceeded the CodMod-derived Group I fraction. For these 63 countries, the estimated cause-specific child deaths exceeded the child death envelopes by 9% or 937 000 deaths. For these countries, deaths for all Group I causes except HIV were adjusted pro-rata to match the CodMod-derived Group I fraction. HIV/AIDS deaths were excluded, as they have been treated as outside the mortality envelopes for countries with high HIV death rates. Adjustment of estimated cause-specific deaths to fit the under-five envelopes differentially affected specific causes. For example, the total estimated malaria deaths before adjustment were 932 000 and after adjustment 812 000, a 12% reduction.

B4. YLD revisions

Years lost due to disability (YLD) estimates were revised for a number of causes where updated estimates for incidence or prevalence for national or regional populations were available (see Section B5 for details). For other causes, YLD estimates from the GBD 2002 were projected forwards to 2004 using one of the four methods outlined below. Except as noted in Section B5, disability weights used for YLD calculations are the same as those used in previous versions of the GBD for years 2000 to 2002 and tabulated in Annex Table A6 of Mathers et al. *(11)*.

Constant YLD rates

For disease and injury causes where mortality is not responsible for a significant proportion of the total burden, or where there is insufficient evidence to predict variations in YLD rates from variations in mortality rates, YLD rates per 1000 population by age and sex for 2002 were applied to the 2004 population estimates to estimate YLD for 2004. Causes for which constant YLD rates were assumed included sexually transmitted diseases excluding HIV infections, diarrhoeal diseases, trypanosomiasis, leishmaniasis, Japanese encephalitis, intestinal nematode infections, upper respiratory infections, otitis media, obstructed labour, vitamin A deficiency, bipolar affective disorder, schizophrenia, epilepsy, Alzheimer and other dementias, multiple sclerosis, post-traumatic stress disorder, obsessive-compulsive disorder, panic disorder, insomnia (primary), migraine, appendicitis, benign prostatic hypertrophy, skin diseases, musculoskeletal diseases, cleft lip and palate, Down syndrome, dental caries and periodontal disease.

Declining YLD rates

Age-sex-specific YLD rates for leprosy were assumed to have declined by 4% from 2002 to 2004.

YLD/YLL ratios

For disease and injury causes where mortality was responsible for a significant proportion of the total burden, regional estimates of YLD/YLL ratios by age and sex for 2002 were used together with 2004 YLL to estimate 2004 YLD. The causes for which this ratio method were used included meningitis, hepatitis B and C, lower respiratory infections, endocrine disorders, rheumatic heart disease, hypertensive heart disease, inflammatory heart disease, chronic obstructive pulmonary disease, peptic ulcer disease, cirrhosis of the liver, and nephritis/nephrosis.

Group cause YLD/YLL ratios

For certain causes, regional age-sex-specific YLD/YLL ratios for the overall cause group were used for estimating YLD for 2004. These causes included maternal haemorrhage and sepsis, hypertensive disorders of pregnancy, causes arising in the perinatal period, congenital malformations excluding cleft lip and palate and Down syndrome, and all the injury causes apart from war and conflict.

B5. Cause-specific revisions and updates

Tuberculosis

Estimates of incidence, average case duration for treated and untreated cases, and deaths due to TB (excluding HIV-infected individuals) for all countries in 2004 formed the basis of estimates of TB prevalence in 2004 *(50)*. For countries with VR data for TB deaths, incidence estimates have been revised to be consistent with estimated deaths.

HIV/AIDS

Country-specific estimates of HIV/AIDS mortality are revised annually by UNAIDS and WHO to take into account new data and improved methods *(12)*. For the most recent round of estimates released in November 2007, advances in methodology applied to an increased range of country data have resulted in substantial changes in estimates of incidence, prevalence and mortality for HIV. The estimated global prevalence of HIV infections for 2004 was revised to 32 million, a reduction of 16% compared to the estimate of 38 million for 2004 prepared in 2006. Similarly, the estimated global deaths due to HIV were revised from 2.7 million to 2.0 million for 2004. The single biggest reason for this reduction was the intensive exercise to assess India's HIV epidemic, which resulted in a major revision to that country's estimates, with almost a halving of estimated prevalence to 2.5 million. Around 70% of the reduction in HIV infection estimates are due to changes in India and five African countries: Angola, Kenya, Mozambique, Nigeria and Zimbabwe.

For countries with death registration data, HIV/AIDS mortality estimates were generally based on the most recently available vital registration data except where there was evidence of miscoding of HIV/AIDS deaths. In such cases, a time series analysis of causes where there was likely miscoding of HIV/AIDS deaths was carried out to identify and re-assign miscoded HIV/AIDS deaths. For other countries, estimates were based on UNAIDS and WHO estimated HIV/AIDS mortality for 2004, or in some cases where that was not available, on estimated prevalence of HIV infections and AIDS in 2004 multiplied by the average subregional mortality to prevalence ratio.

For the 2004 incremental update, the disease model for estimating YLD for HIV was updated to include three sequelae: HIV cases (not progressed to AIDS), AIDS cases not receiving antiretroviral therapy and AIDS cases receiving antiretroviral therapy. Average durations for these three sequelae were revised in line with the most recent UNAIDS estimates of survival with and without antiretroviral therapy (20). The disability weight for AIDS cases receiving antiretroviral therapy was set to be the same as that for HIV cases, apart from the terminal stage assumed to be have the same duration and disability weight as AIDS cases not receiving antiretroviral therapy.

Diarrhoeal diseases

For countries with usable death registration data, deaths due to diarrhoeal diseases were estimated directly from these data. For other countries, a regression model was used to estimate proportional mortality from diarrhoea for children aged under five years (51). The final regression model for the GBD 2004 included the logit of the proportional mortality from diarrhoeal diseases in children aged 0–4 years as a dependent variable and total under-five mortality rates, mid-year of study and WHO regions as explanatory variables. The regression data were drawn from more than 60 community-based studies since 1980 with study durations of multiples of 12 months. This model was validated and supplemented with vital statistics from developing countries where coverage was high. Estimates of child deaths due to diarrhoeal disease for 2004 from this model were assumed to include the neonatal diarrhoea deaths estimated using the CHERG neonatal model.

Vaccine-preventable childhood diseases

Pertussis

Pertussis cases and deaths were based on a natural history model using vaccine coverage and age-specific case fatality rates from community-based studies (52). Updated estimates for 2004 were prepared by the WHO Department of Immunization, Vaccines and Biologicals using WHO–United Nations Children's Fund (UNICEF) estimates for vaccine coverage in 2004, interpolated for missing data (53, 54).

Polio

Incidence estimates for polio were based on reported cases in 2004 (55) with adjustments for underreporting. Mortality estimates were derived from incidence estimates assuming a 10% case fatality rate.

Diphtheria

Updated incidence estimates for 2004 were prepared by the WHO Department of Immunization, Vaccines and Biologicals using WHO–UNICEF estimates for vaccine coverage in 2004, interpolated for missing data (53). A case fatality rate of 10% was assumed for diphtheria in countries without high vital events coverage (56).

Measles

Measles incidence and mortality for 2004 were estimated using a revised natural history model whose inputs included routine vaccine coverage (53), supplementary immunization activities, reported measles cases, estimates of notification efficiency and estimates of age-specific case fatality rates (57). Estimated case fatality rates were validated by comparison with a single cause proportional mortality model based on 28 studies in 16 countries.

Tetanus

Estimates of neonatal tetanus deaths from the CHERG neonatal model (see Section B3) were compared country by country with estimates of neonatal tetanus deaths for 2004 prepared by the WHO Department of Immunization, Vaccines and Biologicals using surveillance and vaccination coverage data (58, 59). Assumptions and inputs for both sets of estimates were revised to take account of most recent available data on numbers of susceptible births (not protected by vaccination of the mother) and from elimination status surveys. Final estimates were reasonably consistent and WHO Department of Immunization, Vaccines and Biologicals estimates for neonatal and postneonatal tetanus incidence and mortality were used for the GBD 2004.

Meningitis

Haemophilus influenzae type B (HiB) meningitis incidence, together with incidence for meningitis due to *Streptococcus pneumoniae* and *Neisseria meningitidis* were estimated by the Department of Immunization, Vaccines and Biologicals using an incidence-based model whose inputs included vaccine coverage and estimates of age-specific case fatality rates (60, 61). These models estimated meningitis incidence and mortality in the 1–59 month age group. Neonatal meningitis deaths were separately estimated, as described in Section B3. For ages 5 years and over, GBD 2002 estimates were applied to 2004 populations.

Malaria

Revised incidence estimates for episodes of illness due to all forms of malaria, and the proportions due to *Plasmodium falciparum*, were based on estimates prepared by the Roll Back Malaria Partnership in 2004 and 2005 (62–64). These incidence estimates were adjusted as follows. First, case reports data from national health information systems were updated to 2004. Second, the risk-based estimates were compared to national case reports and adjusted downwards where necessary to be consistent with a minimum reporting completeness of 2% rather than the 1% used in the Roll Back Malaria estimates. This reduced estimated cases for certain large countries in South-East Asia to levels more consistent with country studies and advice. Third, for other countries outside Africa with reporting completeness greater than 2%, incidence estimates were reduced by 10% to account for reductions in endemicity levels associated with increased urbanisation (65). Fourth, incidence and mortality estimates for 2004 were compared country by country with estimates for 2006 prepared for the Global Malaria Report 2008, and adjusted for countries where improved 2006 estimates were available based on an analysis of health facility and survey data (66). Finally, implied case fatality rates were calculated using the mortality estimates (described below) and for a few countries where case fatality rates were zero or very high, adjustments made to mortality or incidence estimates – these were mostly countries with low levels of malaria. Global and regional estimates of the total number of malaria cases in 2004 are shown in Table B5.

Revised mortality estimates for children aged under five years in sub-Saharan Africa were based on the analysis by Rowe et al. (67). Cause fractions for malaria and other major child causes of death were adjusted to fit postneonatal child death envelopes for 2004 country-by country as described in Section B2. Countries with larger numbers of malaria deaths tended to be those where cause-specific fractions required greater adjustment, so the input estimates for malaria deaths (804 600 for sub-Saharan Africa) were adjusted to 724 400. This is quite similar to the implied figure of 744 000 estimated by Breman et al. in the Disease Control Priorities project (68). For countries outside sub-Saharan Africa, child mortality due to malaria was based on either recent death registration data, or on the GBD 2002 estimates adjusted for consistency with postneonatal child death envelopes and for plausibility of implied case fatality rates.

The GBD 2002 applied an assumption that 90% of malaria deaths were children aged under five years in all regions of the world, based on some information

Table B5: Estimated malaria cases (episodes of illness) by WHO region, 2004

	Africa	The Americas	Eastern Mediter- ranean	Europe	South- East Asia	Western Pacific	World
Total cases (millions)	203.9	2.9	8.6	0.0	23.3	2.7	241.3
P. falciparum cases (millions)	190.7	0.7	6.8	0.0	13.4	1.5	213.2

on age distribution in endemic areas of Africa. However, in areas with low intensity transmission, fewer children develop immunity and the proportion of deaths at older ages is higher. Breman et al. *(68)* quoted estimates prepared by Snow et al. *(69)* that the age distribution in Africa was 65% for ages under five years, 19% for ages 5–14 years, and 16% for ages over 15 years. Recent verbal autopsy data from the INDEPTH network for malaria (excluding fever of unknown origin) also gave around 62% of deaths for children aged under five years, but only 7% for those aged 5–14 years *(33)*.

For the 2004 estimates of malaria mortality, the relationship between malaria mortality rates at ages 5–19 years and 20–39 years and child malaria mortality rates for ages 0–4 years was estimated using a model of age-specific malaria mortality by transmission intensity *(70)*. The revised death rates for malaria at ages five years and over result in an estimated 10% of malaria deaths at ages five years and over in the African region, and 13% globally. For the lower transmission areas outside Africa, the death rates are lower for children and higher for adults. At very low transmission, the death rates are similar across all ages, but slightly higher for younger children and older adults. The resulting global age distribution of malaria deaths is very similar to that in the original GBD study for 1990 *(3)*. Estimated total malaria deaths for 2004 were 0.89 million, of which 771 000 were in children aged under five years. These estimates are lower than those in the GBD 2002 (1.27 million deaths, of which 1.15 million deaths were of children aged under five years).

Other tropical diseases

Human African trypanosomiasis (sleeping sickness)

The GBD 2002 disease model for human African trypanosomiasis (HAT) did not distinguish the two forms of HAT (infection with *Trypanosoma brucei gambiense* or *Trypanosoma brucei rhodesiense*) and assumed an average five-year duration with close to 100% case fatality. For GBD 2004 calculations, separate estimates were made for incidence of cases of infection with *T.b. gambiense* and *T.b. rhodesiense.* An average duration of five years was assumed for *T.b. gambiense* and one year for *T.b. rhodesiense*, so giving a lower prevalence than 2002 estimates. For the mortality estimates, 85% of cases were assumed to be untreated with 100% case fatality, and 15% treated with 5% case fatality.

WHO programme data on populations at risk and levels of endemicity in African countries, the form of HAT present in each country, and numbers of reported cases of disease were used to develop estimates of the incidence of the two forms of HAT for 2004. Completeness of reporting of cases was assumed to be around 33% for *T.b. gambiense* and 5% for *T.b. rhodesiense (71)*. The resulting total incidence of HAT in 2004 is estimated at 60 300, consistent with recent WHO estimates of global incidence in the range 50 000–70 000 *(72)*.

Chagas disease

Updated Chagas disease incidence and prevalence estimates for 2005 were provided by the Pan American Health Organization *(73)*. These estimates were supplemented with and validated against vital statistics from Latin American countries where coverage was high. Over 9000 deaths due to Chagas disease were recorded in death registration data for the region and the implied annual case fatality rate for prevalent cases in countries with good registration data was 0.18%. For a number of countries where the number of deaths in the death registration data for 2004 was much lower than that implied by the prevalence and case fatality estimates, a conservative estimate of numbers of Chagas disease deaths was based on an average of the number estimated from the prevalence estimates and the death registration number.

Schistosomiasis

The GBD 1990 estimated 1.5 million DALYs and 8000 deaths due to schistosoma infections. Schistosomiasis cases were treated as a single sequela, with an average disability weight of 0.006 (74). The GBD 2002 used the same disease model with updated prevalence estimates to estimate that 1.7 million DALYs and 15 371 deaths were due to schistosomiasis in 2002.

There are five different types of schistosoma species: *Schistosoma haematobium* (the most prevalent and widespread species in Africa and the Middle East), *S. mansoni* (found in Africa and the only species seen in Latin America), *S. japonicum* (restricted to the Pacific region including China and the Philippines), *S. mekongi* (found in limited areas of the Lao People's Democratic Republic and Cambodia) and *S. intercalatum* (found in 10 countries in the rainforest belt of Africa). For the 2004 revision, the incidence and prevalence of cases of infection were separately estimated by country for *S. mansoni, S. haematobium* and *S. japonicum* plus *S. mekongi*. Severe renal damage (*S. haematobium*) and severe liver damage (other forms) were also modelled, assuming the incidence of these sequelae was the same as the estimated numbers of deaths, and the disability weights were the same as those for end-stage renal disease. Cancer outcomes were not included as sequelae for schistosomiasis, but are included with overall cancer burden estimates. A separate calculation would be required to estimate attributable cancer burden for schistosomiasis.

Estimates of prevalence for infection with *S. mansoni* and *S. haematobium* in African countries were based on information provided by the WHO programme for Control of Neglected Tropical Diseases for 2003–2004. For countries in the Eastern Mediterranean region, the previous 2002 prevalence estimates were used. For the 2004 revision, incidence rates were estimated assuming zero remission rates (except for a period in early adulthood when prevalence rates decline). The estimated durations are much longer than the one year assumed in the GBD 2002 and GBD 1990, and as a result of time discounting, the YLD estimated for the 2004 revision (0.88 million globally) are lower than those

published for 2002 (1.5 million).

The GBD 2002 estimated that schistosomiasis was responsible for around 15 000 deaths globally (excluding attributable cancer deaths), although others have argued that the figure should be much higher (75). Van der Werf et al. (76), using limited data from Africa, estimated that schistosomiasis caused 210 000 deaths annually. A literature review found limited data from studies with small sample sizes, limiting ability to extrapolate to population level. In the absence of usable studies, a back-calculation method was employed to estimate approximate case fatality rates for two populations with significant numbers of schistosomiasis deaths recorded in death registration data.

Egyptian death registration data for 2000 gave an estimate of 3303 schistosomiasis deaths in 2000 after adjustment for incompleteness of reporting. Reported deaths did not distinguish between *S. mansoni* and *S. haematobium*. Estimates of population prevalence for the 1980s and 1990s vary widely (20–40%); see for example Mansour et al. (77). Assuming a prevalence rate of 30% in the 1980s, this gives an approximate case fatality rate of around 0.03%. This method was also applied to Brazil, where only *S. mansoni* is endemic. An analysis of Brazilian death registration data for 1990 to 1995 found that annual numbers of deaths due to schistosomiasis averaged around 570. Based on a conservative estimate of infection prevalence of around 8 million in 1980 (78), this gives a case fatality rate of around 0.007%.

These estimates are generally consistent with those reported in the literature, and also with the known lower fatality rates for *S. mansoni* compared with *S. haematobium*. For the GBD 2004 update, annual case fatality rates for prevalent cases were conservatively assumed to be 0.01% for *S. mansoni*, 0.02% for *S. haematobium*, and 0.03% for *S. japonicum* and *S. mekongi*. Applying these case fatality rates to the revised prevalence estimates gave a revised global estimate for deaths due to schistosomiasis (excluding cancers caused by schistosomiasis) of 41 000 for 2004. The sex ratio of schistosomiasis deaths was assumed to be similar to the 1990 estimates (62.5% male in the African and Eastern Mediterranean regions, 66% in the Americas and Asia, and 80% male in China).

Leishmaniasis

GBD 2002 estimates for visceral and cutaneous leishmaniasis were revised to resolve some inconsistencies between prevalence and mortality estimates, using information provided by the WHO Department of Control of Neglected Tropical Diseases on reported cases by country, and on the presence and endemicity of each form of leishmaniasis infection by country. The regional and global estimates for mortality and DALYs for 2004 remain similar to those for 2002.

Lymphatic filiariasis

GBD 2002 incidence and prevalence of lymphoedema and hydrocele due to lymphatic filiariasis were revised using information provided by the WHO Department of Control of Neglected Tropical Diseases on mapping status, areas endemic and population at risk for countries with endemic lymphatic filiariasis. Lymphatic filiariasis was considered to be eliminated in China and the Republic of Korea for 2004.

Onchocerciasis

The prevalences of onchocerciasis-caused low vision and blindness were updated using country-specific estimates provided by the WHO Programme for Prevention of Blindness and Visual Impairment.

Dengue

The GBD 2002 estimates for dengue were based on country-level estimates of dengue mortality in the year 2000 from the WHO Department of Control of Neglected Tropical Diseases and on an earlier review of nearly 300 population-based incidence studies *(79)*. For the GBD 2004, country-specific mortality estimates were revised, drawing on a review of dengue mortality studies and on deaths reported by DengueNet *(80)*.

The incidence of dengue haemorrhagic fever or dengue shock syndrome was back-estimated from the mortality estimates assuming case fatality rates of 0.025 in China and the Americas, and 0.04 in other regions. The incidence of dengue fever was then estimated assuming that 6% of symptomatic cases were dengue haemorrhagic fever and 94% were dengue fever *(81)*. The disease model was revised to include

two sequelae:

1. Dengue fever with an average duration of 5.5 days, and an average disability weight of 0.2 (from the GBD 1990 weight for dengue haemorrhagic fever).
2. Dengue haemorrhagic fever/dengue shock syndrome with an average duration of 11 days and an average disability weight of 0.5 (adjusted so that disability weight multiplied by duration is the same as for GBD 1990 (0.2 multiplied by 1 month)).

Trachoma

The prevalences of trachoma-caused low vision and blindness were updated using country-specific estimates provided by the WHO Programme for Prevention of Blindness and Visual Impairment *(82)*.

Acute respiratory infections

A single-cause proportional model was used to estimate child mortality due to acute lower respiratory infections (mainly pneumonia) for countries without usable death registration data. Community-based studies with durations of one year or longer, and published since 1980, were used to estimate the proportional mortality from acute respiratory infections in children aged 0–4 years in developing countries *(83)*. Data from seven separate studies that compared verbal autopsies with hospital-based diagnoses were used to adjust for under-identification of acute respiratory infection deaths by verbal autopsy instruments. Estimated acute respiratory infection deaths for 2004 from this model were assumed to exclude neonatal deaths due to pneumonia, and the latter were included in the CHERG neonatal model estimates for severe infection.

Maternal mortality

WHO and UNICEF recently released new estimates of mortality from maternal conditions for WHO Member States for the year 2005 *(84)*. To estimate maternal mortality in 2004, the 2005 country-specific estimates of the proportion of non-HIV deaths of women of reproductive age (ages 15–49 years) that are due to maternal causes (proportion of maternal deaths of females of reproductive age – PMDF) were applied to the 2004 country-specific estimates of the total number of non-HIV deaths of women aged 15–49 years.

Abortion-related mortality occurs mainly as a result of unsafe induced abortion. GBD estimates for 2004 were updated using WHO estimates of incidence and mortality rates due to unsafe induced abortion in 2003 based on published and unpublished reports for more than 130 countries together with other information on legal and social contexts (85, 86).

Protein–energy malnutrition

The prevalences of underweight, stunting and wasting were based on analysis of 388 nationally representative studies for 139 countries from the WHO Global Database on Child Growth and Malnutrition[a]. These were used to estimate prevalence of child stunting and wasting for each country in the world according to the new WHO Child Growth Standards (87–90). In 2004, an estimated 32% of children aged under five years were stunted (height-for-age more than two standard deviations below the standard) and 20% were wasted (weight-for-age more than two standard deviations below the standard).

Iron-deficiency anaemia

The WHO Department of Nutrition for Health and Development has prepared global, regional and national estimates of anaemia prevalence in pre-school-aged children, pregnant women and non-pregnant women, using data collected for the Vitamin and Mineral Nutrition Information System (VMNIS)[b]. These estimates were based on the most recent national and subnational surveys measuring blood haemoglobin concentration carried out in the years 1993–2005 (91, 92). These surveys covered around two thirds of the world's population and were used to calculate regional age- and sex-specific prevalence estimates for mild, moderate and severe anaemia. According to these estimates, 42% of pregnant women and 47% of preschool children

worldwide have anaemia. As for the GBD 2002 estimates, it was assumed that 60% of anaemia was due to iron deficiency in non-malaria areas and 50% in malaria areas.

Cancer

Previous GBD estimates for the site-specific distribution of cancer mortality for Member States without good vital registration data, and for site-specific incidence of cancers, were based on a model for relative interval survival applied to country-level estimates of cancer incidence distributions by site published by the International Agency for Research on Cancer (IARC) in its Globocan 2000 database (93–95). For the GBD 2004, regional site-specific survival probabilities were updated based on regional trends in gross domestic product per capita (in international dollars) and applied to revised site-specific incidence distributions for 2002 published by IARC in Globocan 2002 (96).

Diabetes mellitus

Diabetes prevalence estimates were updated to take account of a number of recently published population surveys that used oral glucose tolerance tests and WHO criteria to measure diabetes prevalence (97–110). For countries and regions for which more recent prevalence studies were not available, previous diabetes prevalence estimates (111) were projected from those for 2000–2004 using projected trends in population body mass index distributions (112) together with recent estimates of the relative risk of diabetes associated with each unit increase in body mass index from a large meta-analysis of the Asia Pacific Cohort Studies (113). These revisions increased the estimated prevalence of diabetes mellitus from 191 million (if GBD 2002 prevalence rates are applied to the 2004 population) to 220 million in 2004.

Depressive disorders

Point prevalence estimates for episodes of unipolar major depression were derived for the GBD

[a] http://www.who.int/nutgrowthdb/
[b] http://www.who.int/vmnis

2000–2002 from a systematic review of all available published and non-published population studies on depressive disorders. This review identified 56 studies, with studies coming from all six WHO regions *(114)*. Variations in the prevalence of unipolar depressive disorders in some European countries, Australia, New Zealand and Japan were estimated directly from relevant population studies *(115)*.

In the GBD 2002, all comorbid cases of depression and alcohol use disorder were included in the burden of depressive disorders. For the GBD 2004, one half of these comorbid cases were included in depressive disorders and the other half in alcohol use disorders. Age-sex-specific prevalence rates from the GBD 2002 were adjusted downwards by one half of the estimated prevalence rate of comorbid cases of depression and alcohol use disorder (see following section) and then applied to the 2004 population estimates to calculate the prevalence and burden of depressive disorders.

Alcohol and drug use disorders

Previous global estimates for alcohol dependence and harmful use (alcohol use disorders) were based on a range of assessment instruments with varying quality including screening instruments such as the CAGE or the AUDIT, which may not be completely comparable across populations *(116)*. A new review was carried out for the GBD 2004 update using only studies conducted after 1990, which used ICD-10, DSM-IIIR or DSM-IV criteria for alcohol dependence and one of the following diagnostic instruments: the Composite International Diagnostic Interview (CIDI), the Schedules for Clinical Assessment in Neuropsychiatry (SCAN) or the Alcohol Use Disorder and Associated Disabilities Interview Schedule-Alcohol/Drug-Revised (AUDADIS-ADR) *(117)*.

Population estimates of the point prevalence of alcohol use disorders in the age range 18–64 years were obtained from 37 studies *(118)*. Published data on alcohol production, trade and sales, and adjusted for estimates of illegally produced alcohol were used to estimate country averages for volumes of alcohol consumed. These preliminary estimates were then further adjusted on the basis of the survey data on alcohol consumption to estimate prevalence

of alcohol use disorders for countries where recent population-based survey data were not available.

Estimated regional prevalence rates for alcohol dependence by age and sex were then adjusted upwards by 39% for men and 61% for women to account for the additional prevalence of harmful use of alcohol. To correct for comorbidity with depression, prevalence was reduced by a proportional subtraction of 9% (males) and 21% (females) for the WHO regions of Europe and the Americas. For all other regions, prevalence was reduced by 5% (males) and 10% (females) to correct for comorbidity with depression. Incidence rates and average durations for alcohol use disorders were estimated from prevalence, relative risk of mortality and remission rates using DISMOD II *(118)*. Instantaneous remission rates of 0.175 were assumed for ages 15 years and over; the relative risk of mortality averaged 1.8 for males and 3.8 for females.

The original GBD 1990 disability weight of 0.18 for alcohol dependence was applied to both alcohol dependence and harmful use in the GBD 2000–2002. Recent analyses of disability associated with harmful use of alcohol from the Australian Burden of Disease Study *(119)* and of health state valuations collected in the WHO Multi-country Survey Study (MCSS) *(120)* suggest that the average disability weight for harmful use of alcohol is much lower than for alcohol dependence. Weights derived from the multi-country study were used for the harmful use proportion of alcohol use disorders resulting in average disability weights for alcohol use disorders of 0.137 (males) and 0.132 (females) in people aged under 30 years, and 0.134 (males) and 0.122 (females) for those aged 30 years and over.

Applying these weights, the overall YLD for alcohol use disorders for 2004 are 22.0 million compared to 19.1 million if GBD 2000 assumptions and estimates were maintained for the 2004 population. However, the revised prevalence estimates have resulted in increases in the estimated burden for China, India and countries of the former Soviet Union, and decreases for high-income countries, Latin America and Africa.

Estimating mortality directly attributable to illicit drug use, such as overdose death, is difficult because of variations in the quality and quantity of mortality data. For some regions where there is known to be a

1

2

3

4

Annex A

Annex B

Annex C

References

substantial prevalence of illicit drug dependence, no deaths are recorded in available data sources as being due to drug dependence. As a result, it is necessary to make indirect estimates, involving estimates of the prevalence of illicit drug use and case fatality rates, and adjustments to death registration data *(121, 122)*. For the GBD 2004, estimates of deaths due to drug use disorders for 2002 were updated using regional trends in the use of illicit opiate drugs reported by the United Nations Office on Drugs and Crime *(123)*.

Mental retardation (lead-caused)

Estimates of YLD for mental retardation caused by environmental lead exposure prepared for the GBD 2000 were updated to 2004 using projected trends in the incidence of lead-caused mental retardation *(124, 125)*.

Causes of vision loss

Prevalence rates for blindness and low vision due to all causes were updated for the GBD 2002 based on data from available population-based surveys since 1980. Low vision and blindness were defined in terms of measured visual acuity in the better eye with best possible correction *(126, 127)*. These revisions were carried out before the regional distributions for causes of vision loss were available.

For the GBD 2004, prevalence estimates for causes with low vision and blindness sequelae were revised to take account of the regional distributions for causes of blindness published by Resnikoff et al. *(127)*. Relevant causes included gonorrhoea, onchocerciasis, trachoma, vitamin A deficiency, injury, diabetic retinopathy, glaucoma, cataract, and macular degeneration and other age-related causes of vision loss not correctable by provision of glasses or contact lenses. The GBD 2002 cause category "Age-related vision disorders" was renamed "Macular degeneration and other" (age-related causes of vision loss).

The GBD 2002 did not include refractive errors (myopia, hyperopia and astigmatism) correctable with spectacles or other refractive corrections. The definition of vision impairment based on "best possible correction" excludes these impairments in people who do not normally use spectacles or other refractive corrections. For the GBD 2004, an additional cause "refractive errors" was added to the sense organ disorders cause group. Prevalence estimates were based on recent WHO estimates of the regional prevalences of uncorrected refractive errors for all ages over five years *(128)*.

The original GBD 1990 weight for low vision (visual acuity less than 6/18 and greater than 3/60) was quite high at about 0.24, and low vision was only included as a sequela for a few infectious causes, but not for glaucoma or cataracts. For the GBD 2004, the disability weight for low vision has been revised to 0.17 based on the Netherlands disability weights study *(129)*. The disability weight for blindness has been maintained at 0.60 for blindness with best possible correction, but the Netherlands study weight of 0.43 used for blindness due to uncorrected refractive errors.

Ischaemic heart disease

The GBD 2000–2002 study developed a model for ischaemic heart disease YLD which included three sequelae: acute myocardial infarction (AMI), angina pectoris and congestive heart failure following AMI *(130)*. The GBD 1990 study estimated a regression relationship between the prevalence of AMI survivors and the prevalence of angina pectoris (both pre- and post-AMI) using data from developed country studies, and then applied this regression relationship in other developing regions. For the GBD 2000–2002 revisions, the same methodology was followed, but the regression relationships were re-estimated using data from the US Burden of Disease Study for 1996 *(131)*. Two recent national burden of disease studies have made estimates of the prevalence of angina pectoris for Australia in 2003, a developed country population *(119)*, and for Thailand in 2004, a developing country population *(132)*. These were used to re-estimate the regression equations, in order to estimate angina pectoris prevalence for each region from updated estimates of the prevalence of 24- hour AMI survivors for 2004. These revisions resulted in an increase in the estimated global prevalence of angina pectoris from 25 million in 2002 to 54 million in 2004.

DISMOD II was used to estimate the incidence

and average duration of angina pectoris for the calculation of YLD from estimated prevalence rates, relative risks of mortality and remission rates (due to revascularization procedures). Mortality relative risks were revised for high-income countries based on a study of mortality by cause following first-ever AMI in the Danish MONICA study *(133)*. Based on the ratio of the regional 28-day case fatality rates, it was assumed that the excess mortality risk was 40% higher in B and C strata, and 50% higher in D and E strata. These letters denote mortality strata used to group countries in the GBD 2002 *(6)*. Disability weights for angina pectoris were also revised based on the revisions in the Australian and Thai studies *(119, 132)*. The revised disability weights ranged from 0.104 in high-income countries to 0.141 in the WHO African Region, compared with a previous range of 0.108–0.207.

The proportion of incident AMI cases who go on to develop congestive heart failure was assumed to be 0.17 in A strata, 0.20 in B and C strata, 0.20 in D strata other than countries in the African Region, and 0.25 in D and E strata in the African Region. Case fatality rates for A strata were based on those estimated in the United States Burden of Disease and Injury Study *(131)*. Case fatality rates were assumed to be 10% higher in B and C strata, and 20% higher in D and E strata.

Cerebrovascular disease

The GBD 2000–2002 study developed a model for stroke based on available population data on case fatality within 28 days for incident cases of first-ever stroke and on long-term survival in cases surviving this initial period in which the risk of mortality is highest *(134)*. For the GBD 2004, estimated prevalence rates for stroke survivors from this model were compared with results from available population studies. GBD estimates for stroke survivor prevalence rates were generally around 10–30% higher than prevalence rates reported in available studies from developing countries, but most of the studies dated from the 1980s or 1990s, and may not fully identify survivors of mild strokes without noticeable neurological problems.

Two recent national burden of disease studies have made estimates of the prevalence of stroke survivors for Australia in 2003, a developed country population *(119)*, and for Thailand in 2004, a developing country population *(132)*. The Australian stroke estimates were based on detailed analysis of linked databases for Western Australia to identify incidence of first-ever stroke, and mortality for cases. Provisional Thai stroke prevalence estimates were based on data from the Third National Health Examination Survey 2004 *(135)*. Data from these studies were used to recalibrate the long-term case fatality rates for first-ever stroke survivors across all regions for the GBD 2004 estimates, resulting in a reduction in the estimated prevalence of stroke survivors from 50 million to 30 million, and a 30% reduction in YLD for cerebrovascular disease.

Edentulism

Regional prevalence estimates for edentulism (loss of all natural teeth) were updated using data from the World Health Surveys for 60 countries in 2002–2004 *(136)*, together with a review of other published prevalence estimates *(137)*.

Conflicts and natural disasters

The GBD 2004 includes estimates of deaths occurring in 2004 for which the underlying cause (following ICD conventions) was an injury due to war, civil insurrection or organized conflict, whether or not that injury occurred during the time of war or after cessation of hostilities. The GBD estimates include injury deaths resulting from all organized conflicts, including organized terrorist groups, whether or not a national government was involved. They do not include deaths from other causes (such as starvation, infectious disease epidemics, lack of medical intervention for chronic diseases), which may be counterfactually attributable to war or civil conflict.

Country-specific estimates of war and conflict deaths were updated to 2004 using information on conflict intensity, time trends and mortality obtained from a variety of published and unpublished war mortality databases *(138–142)*. Murray et al. *(143)* have summarized the issues with estimation of war deaths, and emphasized the very considerable uncertainty in the GBD estimates for conflict deaths.

Additional information from epidemiological

1 2 3 4 Annex A Annex B Annex C References

studies and surveys was also used for certain specific conflicts in the Democratic Republic of the Congo *(144)*, Iraq *(145)* and the Sudan *(146–149)*. Deaths due to landmines and unexploded ordinance were estimated separately by country *(150, 151)*.

Deaths due to major natural disasters in 2004 are included in the external cause of injury category "Other unintentional injuries". Such deaths will not be included in mortality data sources and estimates except for countries with death registration data for 2004. Estimated deaths for natural disasters in 2004 were obtained from the Office of United States Foreign Disaster Assistance/Centre for Research on the Epidemiology of Disasters (OFDA/CRED) International Disaster Database *(152)*. An estimated 226 321 deaths from the Asian tsunami on 26 December 2004 were added to estimated injury deaths for India, Indonesia, Malaysia, Maldives, Somalia, Sri Lanka and Thailand. Additional natural disaster deaths in 2004 were also added to injury deaths for the Dominican Republic, Haiti, Madagascar, Morocco, Paraguay, the Philippines and the Sudan. Age distributions were based on a number of studies of earthquake deaths *(153, 154)* and tsunami deaths *(155, 156)*.

B6. Prevalence of long-term disability

GBD 2004 updates were used to estimate the prevalence of people with long-term disability by age, sex and region for two severity thresholds of disability. The GBD links loss of full health to disease and injury causes through the concepts of cases and sequelae. For incident cases of a given disease or injury in the population, there will be a distribution of current and future health states (conceptualized in terms of functioning capacity in a set of health domains) in the population, aggregated across individuals. The term disability was used in the naming of the DALY to stress the vision of health that goes beyond the absence of disease and the emphasis on difficulties in functioning. Although the term disability has a number of different meanings and connotations and is not seen by some as a synonym or proxy for "loss of health", the GBD uses "disability" to refer to a sub-construct of "diminution of health", where health is conceptualized in terms of functioning capacity in a set of health domains.

The GBD 1990 study established severity weights for 22 sample "indicator conditions" using an explicit "person trade-off" protocol in a formal exercise involving health workers from all regions of the world. These weights were then grouped into seven classes where class I has a weight between 0 and 0.02 and class VII a weight between 0.7 and 1 (see Table 8). To generate disability weights for the remainder of the approximately 500 disabling sequelae in the study, participants in the study were asked to estimate distributions across the seven classes for each sequela. Distributions across disability classes were estimated separately for treated and untreated cases where relevant, and distributions could also vary by age group and sex.

These severity distributions for GBD sequelae, together with updated severity distributions for those sequelae for which disability weights have been revised in the GBD 2004, were used to estimate the prevalence of long-term disability by severity class in 2004. Results are presented here for the prevalence of "severe" disability, defined as severity classes VI and VII (the equivalent of having blindness, Down syndrome, quadriplegia, severe depression or active psychosis) and for "moderate and severe" disability, defined as severity classes III and greater (severity class III is the equivalent of having angina, arthritis, low vision or alcohol dependence). The disability prevalence estimates also excluded conditions with average durations of less than six months.

The GBD prevalence estimates cannot be simply added, because they were calculated without regard for multiple pathologies or comorbidities (that is, it is possible for a given individual to fall within more than one disability level if they have more than one diagnosis). Murray & Lopez adjusted for comorbidity assuming that all conditions were statistically independent and that the probability of having two conditions was the product of the probability of having each condition alone *(3)*. For the disability estimates presented here, a comorbidity adjustment method was used that takes account of the increased probability of having certain pairs of conditions *(23)*. Only very limited data were available on comorbidity, so the resulting disability prevalences have an additional level of uncertainty above the cause-specific prevalence estimates.

Clinically and conceptually it is not usual practice to infer disability from diagnoses. Disabilities are limitations or problems in the performance of actions or tasks. They are identified and assessed in their own right – and in some cases may only subsequently be explained in terms of pathology, or may never be adequately explained at all. In future revisions of the GBD study, increased effort will be devoted to the estimation of the prevalences of impairments and disabilities directly, and to ensuring consistency with the disease- and injury-specific sequelae estimates. The GBD disability prevalence estimates have the virtue of comprehensiveness, and at least some grounding in disease prevalence. However, they are very much approximations, and are subject to very clear limitations in the way they were compiled and in the way that comorbidity was addressed in adding across causes.

B7. Projections of mortality and burden of disease

WHO recently published mortality projections from 2003 to 2030 using methods similar to those applied in the original GBD study and starting from the GBD 2002 estimates (19). A set of relatively simple models were used to project future health trends for baseline, optimistic and pessimistic scenarios, based largely on projections of economic and social development, and using the historically observed relationships of these with cause-specific mortality rates.

Updated projections to the year 2030 have been prepared using the updated GBD 2004 results as a starting-point. The methods used are essentially the same as those previously published (19), with the following changes:

- Projections of income per capita were revised to take account of World Bank revisions to purchasing power parity (PPP) conversion rates (157) and latest World Bank regional projections of real growth per annum in income per capita (21);
- Countries for which low-income regression coefficients were used were revised to take account of revised country income levels and projections;
- The projection regression equations were recalibrated so that back projections of child mortality

rates from 2004 to 1990 matched observed trends for World Bank regions. In the recalibrated projections, the regression coefficient for human capital was left unchanged and the regression coefficient for time (a proxy for technological change) was set to zero for low-income countries in the African, European, South-East Asia and Western Pacific Regions;

- Revised UNAIDS projections for HIV mortality were used, based on projections of current trends in scale-up of antiretroviral therapy coverage;
- Relative risks for diabetes mellitus mortality associated with increasing levels of body mass index (kg/m^2) were revised downwards based on latest information from the Asia Pacific Cohorts study.

B8. Uncertainty of estimates and projections

There remain substantial data gaps and deficiencies, particularly for regions with limited death registration data. The GBD 2004 includes results for these regions, albeit with wider uncertainty ranges, based on the best possible assessment of the available evidence. Uncertainty ranges for all-cause mortality rates for WHO Member States were published in the *World health report 2006 (25)*. Uncertainty analysis for the GBD 2004 cause-specific estimates has not been carried out, but uncertainty ranges are likely to be similar to those assessed for the GBD 2001 *(158)*.

Ninety-five per cent uncertainty ranges for regional cause-specific mortality estimates were calculated using simulation methods based on estimated uncertainty ranges for input data *(158)*. Uncertainty in estimated all-cause mortality for 2001 ranged from ±1% for high-income countries to ±15–20% for sub-Saharan Africa, reflecting differential data availability. Uncertainty ranges were generally larger for deaths from specific diseases. For example, the relative uncertainty for deaths from ischaemic heart disease ranged from ±12% for high-income countries to ±25–35% for sub-Saharan Africa.

Assessments of 2001 YLD uncertainty for specific causes took into account not only typical levels of measurement error in the input data sets, but also expert judgment about the degree of uncertainty arising from the lack of representativeness of the available data for each region. The resulting uncertainty varied considerably across causes, ranging from relatively certain estimates for diseases such as polio, for which intensive surveillance systems are in place, to highly uncertain estimates for those such as osteoarthritis, where for some regions no usable data source was found, and for others the latest available data were decades old. Typical uncertainty for regional prevalence estimates ranged from ±10% to ±90%, with a median value of ±41%, among a subset of diseases for which uncertainty analysis was carried out *(158)*.

Although the GBD 2004 estimates have similarly large uncertainty ranges for some causes and some regions, they continue to provide useful information on broad relativities of disease burden, on the relative importance of mortality and disability, and on regional patterns of disease burden. The analysis of the levels of uncertainty in the GBD 2001 estimates reinforces the need for caution when interpreting global comparative epidemiological assessments and the need for increased investment in population health measurement systems and in improved methods for analysing available population health data.

The projected declining age-specific death rates for most chronic diseases reflect the observed declines in age-specific chronic disease death rates with increasing levels of development in the available death registration data for 107 countries between 1950 and 2002. Adverse trends for some chronic disease risk factors such as overweight and physical inactivity were probably more than offset in these countries by improved control of other risk factors such as high blood pressure, high blood cholesterol and tobacco smoking, and improved access to effective treatment interventions.

Projected chronic disease mortality rates are not highly sensitive to a reasonably broad range of assumptions about future economic growth and trends in the tobacco epidemic. The projected decline in communicable disease mortality rates is more sensitive to these assumptions, and may be optimistic if future trends in economic growth are not as high as projected. The mortality and burden of disease projections are less firm than the base year assessments, and provide "business as usual" projections under specified assumptions that do not specifically take account of trends in major risk factors apart from tobacco smoking and, to a limited extent, overweight and obesity. If risk factor exposures do not generally decline with economic development and with improving health systems in developing countries, then these projections may underestimate future deaths in low- and middle-income countries.

Annex C

Analysis categories and mortality data sources

Table C1: Countries grouped by WHO region and income per capita, 2004   120

Table C2: Countries grouped by income per capita, 2004   121

Table C3: GBD cause categories and ICD codes   122

Table C4: Data sources and methods for estimation of mortality by cause,

     age and sex   126

Table C1: Countries grouped by WHO region and income per capita,[a] 2004

WHO region	Income category[b]	WHO Member States
African Region	LMIC	Algeria, Angola, Benin, Botswana, Burkina Faso, Burundi, Cameroon, Cape Verde, Central African Republic, Chad, Comoros, Congo, Côte d'Ivoire, Democratic Republic of the Congo, Equatorial Guinea, Eritrea, Ethiopia, Gabon, Gambia, Ghana, Guinea, Guinea-Bissau, Kenya, Lesotho, Liberia, Madagascar, Malawi, Mali, Mauritania, Mauritius, Mozambique, Namibia, Niger, Nigeria, Rwanda, Sao Tome and Principe, Senegal, Seychelles, Sierra Leone, South Africa, Swaziland, Togo, Uganda, United Republic of Tanzania, Zambia, Zimbabwe
Region of the Americas	High	Bahamas, Canada, United States of America
Region of the Americas	LMIC	Antigua and Barbuda, Argentina, Barbados, Belize, Bolivia, Brazil, Chile, Colombia, Costa Rica, Dominica, Dominican Republic, Ecuador, El Salvador, Grenada, Guatemala, Guyana, Haiti, Honduras, Jamaica, Mexico, Nicaragua, Panama, Paraguay, Peru, Saint Kitts and Nevis, Saint Lucia, Saint Vincent and the Grenadines, Suriname, Trinidad and Tobago, Uruguay, Venezuela (Bolivarian Republic of)
Eastern Mediterranean Region	High	Bahrain, Kuwait, Qatar, Saudi Arabia, United Arab Emirates
Eastern Mediterranean Region	LMIC	Afghanistan, Djibouti, Egypt, Iran (Islamic Republic of), Iraq, Jordan, Lebanon, Libyan Arab Jamahiriya, Morocco, Oman, Pakistan, Somalia, Sudan, Syrian Arab Republic, Tunisia, Yemen
European Region	High	Andorra, Austria, Belgium, Cyprus, Denmark, Finland, France, Germany, Greece, Iceland, Ireland, Israel, Italy, Luxembourg, Malta, Monaco, Netherlands, Norway, Portugal, San Marino, Slovenia, Spain, Sweden, Switzerland, United Kingdom
European Region	LMIC	Albania, Armenia, Azerbaijan, Belarus, Bosnia and Herzegovina, Bulgaria, Croatia, Czech Republic, Estonia, Georgia, Hungary, Kazakhstan, Kyrgyzstan, Latvia, Lithuania, Moldova, Poland, Romania, Russian Federation, Serbia and Montenegro, Slovakia, Tajikistan, The former Yugoslav Republic of Macedonia, Turkey, Turkmenistan, Uzbekistan, Ukraine
South-East Asia Region	LMIC	Bangladesh, Bhutan, Democratic People's Republic of Korea, India, Indonesia, Maldives, Myanmar, Nepal, Sri Lanka, Thailand, Timor-Leste
Western Pacific Region	High	Australia, Brunei Darussalam, Japan, New Zealand, Republic of Korea, Singapore
Western Pacific Region	LMIC	Cambodia, China, Cook Islands, Fiji, Kiribati, Lao People's Democratic Republic, Malaysia, Marshall Islands, Micronesia (Federated States of), Mongolia, Nauru, Niue, Palau, Papua New Guinea, Philippines, Samoa, Solomon Islands, Tonga, Tuvalu, Vanuatu, Viet Nam
Non-Member States or territories		American Samoa, Anguilla, Aruba, Bermuda, British Virgin Islands, Cayman Islands, Channel Islands, Faeroe Islands, Falkland Islands (Malvinas), French Guiana, French Polynesia, Gibraltar, Greenland, Guadeloupe, Guam, Holy See, Isle of Man, Liechtenstein, Martinique, Montserrat, Netherlands Antilles, New Caledonia, Northern Mariana Islands, Pitcairn, Puerto Rico, Réunion, Saint Helena, Saint Pierre et Miquelon, Tokelau, Turks and Caicos Islands, United States Virgin Islands, Wallis and Futuna Islands, West Bank and Gaza Strip, Western Sahara

LMIC, low- and middle-income countries.

[a] WHO Member States are classified as high income if their 2004 gross national income per capita was US$ 10 066 or more as estimated by the World Bank (159).
[b] LMIC include those with 2004 gross national income per capita less than US$ 10 066.

Table C2: Countries grouped by income per capita,ª 2004

Income group	Countries included
High income	Andorra, Aruba, Australia, Austria, Bahamas, Bahrain, Belgium, Bermuda, Brunei Darussalam, Canada, Cayman Islands, Channel Islands, Cyprus, Denmark, Faeroe Islands, Finland, France, French Polynesia, Germany, Greece, Greenland, Guam, Iceland, Ireland, Isle of Man, Israel, Italy, Japan, Kuwait, Liechtenstein, Luxembourg, Malta, Monaco, Netherlands, Netherlands Antilles, New Caledonia, New Zealand, Norway, Portugal, Puerto Rico, Qatar, Republic of Korea, San Marino, Saudi Arabia, Singapore, Slovenia, Spain, Sweden, Switzerland, United Arab Emirates, United Kingdom, United States of America, United States, Virgin Islands
Upper middle income	American Samoa, Antigua and Barbuda, Argentina, Barbados, Belize, Botswana, Chile, Costa Rica, Croatia, Czech Republic, Dominica, Equatorial Guinea, Estonia, Gabon, Grenada, Hungary, Latvia, Lebanon, Libyan Arab Jamahiriya, Lithuania, Malaysia, Mauritius, Mexico, Northern Mariana Islands, Oman, Palau, Panama, Poland, Russian Federation, Saint Kitts and Nevis, Saint Lucia, Saint Vincent and the Grenadines, Seychelles, Slovakia, South Africa, Trinidad and Tobago, Turkey, Uruguay, Venezuela (Bolivarian Republic of)
Lower middle income	Albania, Algeria, Angola, Armenia, Azerbaijan, Belarus, Bolivia, Bosnia and Herzegovina, Brazil, Bulgaria, Cape Verde, China, Colombia, Cuba, Djibouti, Dominican Republic, Ecuador, Egypt, El Salvador, Fiji, Georgia, Guatemala, Guyana, Honduras, Indonesia, Iran (Islamic Republic of), Iraq, Jamaica, Jordan, Kazakhstan, Kiribati, Maldives, Marshall Islands, Micronesia (Federated States of), Morocco, Namibia, Paraguay, Peru, Philippines, Romania, Samoa, Serbia and Montenegro, Sri Lanka, Suriname, Swaziland, Syrian Arab Republic, Thailand, The former Yugoslav Republic of Macedonia, Tonga, Tunisia, Turkmenistan, Ukraine, Vanuatu, West Bank and Gaza Strip
Low income	Afghanistan, Bangladesh, Benin, Bhutan, Burkina Faso, Burundi, Cambodia, Cameroon, Central African Republic, Chad, Comoros, Congo, Côte d'Ivoire, Democratic People's Republic of Korea, Democratic Republic of the Congo, Eritrea, Ethiopia, Gambia, Ghana, Guinea, Guinea-Bissau, Haiti, India, Kenya, Kyrgyzstan, Lao People's Democratic Republic, Lesotho, Liberia, Madagascar, Malawi, Mali, Mauritania, Moldova, Mongolia, Mozambique, Myanmar, Nepal, Nicaragua, Niger, Nigeria, Pakistan, Papua New Guinea, Rwanda, Sao Tome and Principe, Senegal, Sierra Leone, Solomon Islands, Somalia, Sudan, Tajikistan, Timor-Leste, Togo, Uganda, United Republic of Tanzania, Uzbekistan, Viet Nam, Yemen, Zambia, Zimbabwe
Not included	Anguilla, British Virgin Islands, Cook Islands, Falkland Islands (Malvinas), French Guiana, Gibraltar, Guadeloupe, Holy See, Martinique, Montserrat, Nauru, Niue, Pitcairn, Réunion, Saint Helena, Saint Pierre et Miquelon, Tokelau, Turks and Caicos Islands, Tuvalu, Wallis and Futuna Islands, Western Sahara

ª Income categories for 2004 as defined by the World Bank *(159)*. Countries are divided among income groups according to 2004 gross national income (GNI) per capita. The groups are low income (US$825 or less), lower middle income (US$826–3255), upper middle income (US$3256–10 065), and high income (US$10 066 or more). Note that these income groups differ slightly from those used in the Disease Control Priorities Project (based on GNI in 2001) *(9)*.

Table C3: GBD cause categories and ICD codes

	GBD cause name	ICD-10 code
I.	***Communicable, maternal, perinatal and nutritional conditions*[a]**	***A00-B99, G00-G04, N70-N73, J00-J06, J10-J18, J20-J22, H65-H66, O00-O99, P00-P96, E00-E02, E40-E46, E50, D50-D53, D64.9, E51-64***
	A. Infectious and parasitic diseases	**A00-B99, G00, G03-G04, N70-N73**
	1. Tuberculosis	A15-A19, B90
	2. Sexually transmitted diseases excluding HIV	A50-A64, N70-N73
	a. Syphilis	A50-A53
	b. Chlamydia	A55-A56
	c. Gonorrhoea	A54
	Other STDs	A57-A64, N70-N73
	3. HIV/AIDS	B20-B24
	4. Diarrhoeal diseases	A00, A01, A03, A04, A06-A09
	5. Childhood-cluster diseases	A33-A37, A80, B05, B91
	a. Pertussis	A37
	b. Poliomyelitis	A80, B91
	c. Diphtheria	A36
	d. Measles	B05
	e. Tetanus	A33-A35
	6. Meningitis	A39, G00, G03
	7. Hepatitis B	B16-B19 (minus B17.1, B18.2)
	Hepatitis C	B17.1, B18.2
	8. Malaria	B50-B54
	9. Tropical-cluster diseases	B55-B57, B65, B73, B74.0-B74.2
	a. Trypanosomiasis	B56
	b. Chagas disease	B57
	c. Schistosomiasis	B65
	d. Leishmaniasis	B55
	e. Lymphatic filariasis	B74.0-B74.2
	f. Onchocerciasis	B73
	10. Leprosy	A30
	11. Dengue	A90-A91
	12. Japanese encephalitis	A83.0
	13. Trachoma	A71
	14. Intestinal nematode infections	B76-B81
	a. Ascariasis	B77
	b. Trichuriasis	B79
	c. Hookworm disease (ancylostomiasis and necatoriasis)	B76
	Other intestinal infections	B78, B80, B81
	Other infectious diseases	A02, A05, A20-A28, A31, A32, A38, A40-A49, A65-A70, A74-A79, A81, A82, A83.1-A83.9, A84-A89, A92-A99, B00-B04, B06-B15, B25-B49, B58-B60, B64, B66-B72, B74.3-B74.9, B75, B82-B89, B92-B99, G04
	B. Respiratory infections	**J00-J06, J10-J18, J20-J22, H65-H66**
	1. Lower respiratory infections	J10-J18, J20-J22
	2. Upper respiratory infections	J00-J06
	3. Otitis media	H65-H66
	C. Maternal conditions	**O00-O99**
	1. Maternal haemorrhage	O44-O46, O67, O72
	2. Maternal sepsis	O85-O86
	3. Hypertensive disorders of pregnancy	O10-O16
	4. Obstructed labour	O64-O66
	5. Abortion	O00-O07
	Other maternal conditions	O20-O043, O47-O063, O68-O071, O73-O075, O87-O099

GBD cause name	ICD-10 code
D. Conditions arising during the perinatal period	**P00-P96**
1. Prematurity and low birth weight	P05, P07, P22, P27-P28
2. Birth asphyxia and birth trauma	P03, P10-P15, P20-P21, P24-P26, P29
Neonatal infections and other conditions	P00-P02, P04, P08, P23, P35-P96
E. Nutritional deficiencies	**E00-E02, E40-E46, E50, D50-D53, D64.9, E51-E64**
1. Protein-energy malnutrition	E40-E46
2. Iodine deficiency	E00-E02
3. Vitamin A deficiency	E50
4. Iron-deficiency anaemia	D50, D64.9
Other nutritional disorders	D51-D53, E51-E64
II. Noncommunicable diseases[a]	**C00-C97, D00-D48, D55-D64 (minus D 64.9), D65-D89, E03-E07, E10-E16, E20-E34, E65-E88, F01-F99, G06-G98, H00-H61, H68-H93, I00-I99, J30-J98, K00-K92, N00-N64, N75-N98, L00-L98, M00-M99, Q00-Q99**
A. Malignant neoplasms	**C00-C97**
1. Mouth and oropharynx cancers[b]	C00-C14
2. Oesophagus cancer[b]	C15
3. Stomach cancer[b]	C16
4. Colon and rectum cancers[b]	C18-C21
5. Liver cancer	C22
6. Pancreas cancer	C25
7. Trachea, bronchus and lung cancers	C33-C34
8. Melanoma and other skin cancers[b]	C43-C44
9. Breast cancer[b]	C50
10. Cervix uteri cancer[b]	C53
11. Corpus uteri cancer[b]	C54-C55
12. Ovary cancer	C56
13. Prostate cancer[b]	C61
14. Bladder cancer[b]	C67
15. Lymphomas and multiple myeloma[b]	C81-C90, C96
16. Leukaemia[b]	C91-C95
Other malignant neoplasms[b]	C17, C23, C24, C26-C32, C37-C41, C45-C49, C51, C52, C57-C60, C62-C66, C68-C80, C97
B. Other neoplasms	**D00-D48**
C. Diabetes mellitus	**E10-E14**
D. Endocrine disorders	**D55-D64 (minus D64.9), D65-D89, E03-E07, E15-E16, E20-E34, E65-E88**
E. Neuropsychiatric conditions	**F01-F99, G06-G98**
1. Unipolar depressive disorders	F32-F33
2. Bipolar affective disorder	F30-F31
3. Schizophrenia	F20-F29
4. Epilepsy	G40-G41
5. Alcohol use disorders	F10
6. Alzheimer and other dementias	F01, F03, G30-G31
7. Parkinson disease	G20-G21
8. Multiple sclerosis	G35
9. Drug use disorders	F11-F16, F18-F19
10. Post-traumatic stress disorder	F43.1
11. Obsessive-compulsive disorder	F42
12. Panic disorder	F40.0, F41.0
13. Insomnia (primary)	F51
14. Migraine	G43
Mental retardation attributable to lead exposure	F70-F79
Other neuropsychiatric disorders	F04-F09, F17, F34-F39, F401-F409, F411-F419, F43(minus F43.1), F44-F50, F52-F69, F80-F99, G06-G12, G23-G25, G36, G37, G44-G98

(Table C3 continued)

GBD cause name	ICD-10 code
F. Sense organ diseases	**H00-H61, H68-H93**
1. Glaucoma	H40
2. Cataracts	H25-H26
3. Refractive errors	H524
4. Hearing loss, adult onset	H90-H91
Macular degeneration and other	H00-H21, H27-H35, H43-H61(minus H524), H68-H83, H92-H93
G. Cardiovascular diseases	**I00-I99**
1. Rheumatic heart disease	I01-I09
2. Hypertensive heart disease	I10-I13
3. Ischaemic heart disease[c]	I20-I25
4. Cerebrovascular disease	I60-I69
5. Inflammatory heart diseases	I30-I33, I38, I40, I42
Other cardiovascular diseases[c]	I00, I26-I28, I34-I37, I44-I51, I70-I99
H. Respiratory diseases	**J30-J98**
1. Chronic obstructive pulmonary disease	J40-J44
2. Asthma	J45-J46
Other respiratory diseases	J30-J39, J47-J98
I. Digestive diseases	**K20-K92**
1. Peptic ulcer disease	K25-K27
2. Cirrhosis of the liver	K70, K74
3. Appendicitis	K35-K37
Other digestive diseases	K20-K22, K28-K31, K38, K40-K66, K71-K73, K75-K92
J. Genitourinary diseases	**N00-N64, N75-N98**
1. Nephritis and nephrosis	N00-N19
2. Benign prostatic hypertrophy	N40
Other genitourinary system diseases	N20-N39, N41-N64, N75-N98
K. Skin diseases	**L00-L98**
L. Musculoskeletal diseases	**M00-M99**
1. Rheumatoid arthritis	M05-M06
2. Osteoarthritis	M15-M19
3. Gout	M10
4. Low back pain	M45-M48, M54 (minus M54.2)
Other musculoskeletal disorders	M00-M02, M08, M11-M13, M20-M43, M50-M53, M54.2, M55-M99
M. Congenital anomalies	**Q00-Q99**
1. Abdominal wall defect	Q79.2-Q79.5
2. Anencephaly	Q00
3. Anorectal atresia	Q42
4. Cleft lip	Q36
5. Cleft palate	Q35, Q37
6. Oesophageal atresia	Q39.0-Q39.1
7. Renal agenesis	Q60
8. Down syndrome	Q90
9. Congenital heart anomalies	Q20-Q28
10. Spina bifida	Q05
Other congenital anomalies	Q01-Q04, Q06-Q18, Q30-Q34, Q38, Q392-Q399, Q40-Q41, Q43-Q56, Q61-Q78, Q790, Q791, Q796, Q798, Q799, Q80-Q89, Q91-Q99

GBD cause name	ICD-10 code
N. Oral conditions	**K00-K14**
1. Dental caries	K02
2. Periodontal disease	K05
3. Edentulism	—
Other oral diseases	K00, K01, K03, K04, K06-K14
III. ***Injuries***	V01-Y89
A. Unintentional injuries[d]	**V01-X59, Y40-Y86, Y88, Y89**
1. Road traffic accidents[e]	
2. Poisonings	X40-X49
3. Falls	W00-W19
4. Fires	X00-X09
5. Drownings	W65-W74
6. Other unintentional injuries	Rest of V, W20-W64, W75-W99, X10-X39, X50-X59, Y40-Y86, Y88, Y89
B. Intentional injuries[d]	**X60-Y09, Y35-Y36, Y870, Y871**
1. Self-inflicted injuries	X60-X84, Y870
2. Violence	X85-Y09, Y871
3. War and conflict	Y36
Other intentional injuries	Y35

—, not available; STD, sexually transmitted diseases.

[a] Deaths coded to "Symptoms, signs and ill-defined conditions" (780-799 in ICD-9 and R00-R99 in ICD-10) are distributed proportionately to all causes within Group I and Group II.

[b] Cancer deaths coded to ICD categories for malignant neoplasms of other and unspecified sites including those whose point of origin cannot be determined, and secondary and unspecified neoplasms (ICD-10 C76, C80, C97 or ICD-9 195, 199) were redistributed pro-rata across the footnoted malignant neoplasm categories within each age–sex group, so that the category "Other malignant neoplasms" includes only malignant neoplasms of other specified sites (94).

[c] Ischaemic heart disease deaths may be miscoded to a number of so-called cardiovascular "garbage" codes. These include heart failure, ventricular dysrhythmias, generalized atherosclerosis and ill-defined descriptions and complications of heart disease. Proportions of deaths coded to these causes were redistributed to ischaemic heart disease as described in (23). Relevant ICD-9 codes are 427.1, 427.4, 427.5, 428, 429.0, 429.1, 429.2, 429.9, 440.9, and relevant ICD-10 codes are I47.2, I49.0, I46, I50, I51.4, I51.5, I51.6, I51.9 and I70.9.

[d] Injury deaths where the intent is not determined (E980-989 of ICD-9 and Y10-Y34, Y872 in ICD-10) are distributed proportionately to all causes below the group level for injuries.

[e] For countries with 3-digit ICD10 data, for "Road traffic accidents" use: V01-V04, V06, V09-V80, V87, V89 and V99.
For countries with 4-digit ICD10 data, for "Road traffic accidents" use:
V01.1-V01.9, V02.1-V02.9, V03.1-V03.9, V04.1-V04.9, V06.1-V06.9, V09.2, V09.3, V10.3-V10.9, V11.3-V11.9, V12.3-V12.9, V13.3-V13.9, V14.3-V14.9, V15.4-V15.9, V16.4-V16.9, V17.4-V17.9, V18.4-V18.9, V19.4-V19.9, V20.3-V20.9, V21.3-V21.9, V22.3-V22.9, V23.3-V23.9, V24.3-V24.9, V25.3-V25.9, V26.3-V26.9, V27.3-V27.9, V28.3-V28.9, V29.4-V29.9, V30.4.V30.9, V31.4-V31.9, V32.4-V32.9, V33.4-V33.9, V34.4-V34.9, V35.4-V35.9, V36.4-V36.9, V37.4-V37.9, V38.4-V38.9, V39.4-V39.9, V40.4-V40.9, V41.4-V41.9, V42.4-V42.9, V43.4-V43.9, V44.4-V44.9, V45.4-V45.9, V46.4-V46.9, V47.4-V47.9, V48.4-V48.9, V49.4-V49.9, V50.4-V50.9, V51.4-V51.9, V52.4-V52.9, V53.4-V53.9, V54.4-V54.9, V55.4-V55.9, V56.4-V56.9, V57.4-V57.9, V58.4-V58.9, V59.4-V59.9, V60.4-V60.9, V61.4-V61.9, V62.4-V62.9, V63.4-V63.9, V64.4-V64.9, V65.4-V65.9, V66.4-V66.9, V67.4-V67.9, V68.4-V68.9, V69.4-V69.9, V70.4-V70.9, V71.4-V71.9, V72.4-V72.9, V73.4-V73.9, V74.4-V74.9, V75.4-V75.9, V76.4-V76.9, V77.4-V77.9, V78.4-V78.9, V79.4-V79.9, V80.3-V80.5, V81.1, V82.1, V82.8-V82.9, V83.0-V83.3, V84.0-V84.3, V85.0-V85.3, V86.0-V86.3, V87.0-V87.9, V89.2-V89.3, V89.9, V99 and Y850.

1

2

3

4

Annex A

Annex B

Annex C

References

Table C4: Data sources and methods for estimation of mortality by cause, age and sex

Country	Vital registration data used (year)	Estimated coverage (%)	Other sources of information	Method	Cause-of-death distribution pattern used
Afghanistan			a	CodMod	Egypt 2000, Iran (Islamic Republic of) 2001
Albania	2004	50–74	a	CodMod	Vital registration
Algeria			a	CodMod	AfrD distribution[c]
Andorra			b	Based on 2000 data for selected provinces of Spain	GBD2002 cause-of-death estimates
Angola			a	CodMod	AfrD distribution[c]
Antigua and Barbuda	2000–2002	50–74	b	Vital registration	Vital registration
Argentina	2004	90–100	b	Vital registration	Vital registration
Armenia	2003	50–74	a	CodMod	Vital registration
Australia	2003	90–100	b	Vital registration	Vital registration
Austria	2004	90–100	b	Vital registration	Vital registration
Azerbaijan	2002	50–74	a	CodMod	Vital registration
Bahamas	1999–2000	90–100	b	Vital registration	Vital registration
Bahrain	2000–2001	90–100	b	Vital registration	Vital registration
Bangladesh			a	CodMod	India, Philippines
Barbados	2000–2001	75–89	b	Vital registration	Vital registration
Belarus	2003	90–100	b	Vital registration	Vital registration
Belgium	1997	90–100	b	Vital registration	Vital registration
Belize	1999–2001	90–100	b	Vital registration	Vital registration
Benin			a	CodMod	AfrD distribution[c]
Bhutan			a	CodMod	India
Bolivia			a	CodMod	Peru 2000
Bosnia and Herzegovina	1999	75–89	b	Vital registration	Vital registration
Botswana			a	CodMod	AfrE distribution[c]
Brazil	2004	75–89	a	CodMod	Vital registration
Brunei Darussalam	1998–2000	90–100	b	Vital registration	GBD2002 cause-of-death estimates
Bulgaria	2004	90–100	b	Vital registration	Vital registration
Burkina Faso			a	CodMod	AfrD distribution[c]
Burundi			a	CodMod	AfrE distribution[c]
Cambodia			a	CodMod	Philippines, Thailand
Cameroon			a	CodMod	AfrD distribution[c]
Canada	2003	90–100	b	Vital registration	Vital registration
Cape Verde			a	CodMod	AfrD distribution[c]
Central African Republic			a	CodMod	AfrE distribution[c]
Chad			a	CodMod	AfrD distribution[c]
Chile	2004	90–100	b	Vital registration	Vital registration
China	2005		DSP, a	Combination of DSP and vital registration weighted	Vital registration and DSP
Colombia	2004	75–89	a	CodMod	Vital registration
Comoros			a	CodMod	AfrD distribution[c]
Congo			a	CodMod	AfrE distribution[c]
Cook Islands	1999–2001	90–100	a	Vital registration	GBD2002 cause-of-death estimates
Costa Rica	2004	75–89	b	Vital registration	Vital registration

Country	Vital registration data used (year)	Estimated coverage (%)	Other sources of information	Method	Cause-of-death distribution pattern used
Côte d'Ivoire			Deaths assessed by medical personnel in city hospitals 1973-1992 *(160)*; a	CodMod	AfrE distribution[c]
Croatia	2004	90–100	b	Vital registration	Vital registration
Cuba	2004	90–100	b	Vital registration	Vital registration
Cyprus	1997–99	50–74	a	CodMod	GBD2002 cause-of-death estimates
Czech Republic	2004	90–100	b	Vital registration	Vital registration
Democratic People's Republic of Korea			a	CodMod	India, Philippines
Democratic Republic of the Congo			a	CodMod	AfrE distribution[c]
Denmark	2001	90–100	b	Vital registration	Vital registration
Djibouti			a	CodMod	Egypt 2000, Iran (Islamic Republic of) 2000
Dominica	2001–2003	90–100	b	Vital registration	Vital registration
Dominican Republic	2004	<50	a	CodMod	Vital registration
Ecuador	2004	75–89	a	CodMod	Vital registration
Egypt	2000	75–89	a	CodMod	Vital registration
El Salvador	2004	75–89	a	CodMod	Vital registration
Equatorial Guinea			a	CodMod	AfrD distribution[c]
Eritrea			a	CodMod	AfrE distribution[c]
Estonia	2004	90–100	b	Vital registration	Vital registration
Ethiopia			a	CodMod	AfrE distribution[c]
Fiji	2000	90–100	a	Vital registration	Vital registration
Finland	2004	90–100	b	Vital registration	Vital registration
France	2004	90–100	b	Vital registration	Vital registration
Gabon			a	CodMod	AfrD distribution[c]
Gambia			a	CodMod	AfrD distribution[c]
Georgia	2001	90–100	a	CodMod	Vital registration
Germany	2004	90–100	b	Vital registration	Vital registration
Ghana			Mortality data from hospitals in 20 selected districts and 9 regional hospitals in 2003; a	CodMod	AfrD distribution[c]
Greece	2004	90–100	b	Vital registration	Vital registration
Grenada	1994–1996	75–89	b	Vital registration	GBD2002 cause-of-death estimates
Guatemala	2004	90–100	a	CodMod	Vital registration
Guinea			a	CodMod	AfrD distribution[c]
Guinea-Bissau			a	CodMod	AfrD distribution[c]
Guyana	2001–2003	50–74	b	Vital registration	Vital registration
Haiti	2003	<50	a	CodMod	Vital registration
Honduras			a	CodMod	El Salvador, Guatemala, Nicaragua
Hungary	2004	90–100	b	Vital registration	Vital registration
Iceland	2002–2004	90–100	b	Vital registration	Vital registration

(Table C4 continued)

Country	Vital registra-tion data used (year)	Estimated coverage (%)	Other sources of information	Method	Cause-of-death distribution pattern used
India	1995–1998		a	Proportionate mortality for urban and rural summed up to national estimate	1996 – 1998 (Survey of Cause of Death (rural)), Urban Medical certification of Cause of Death System – 1995
Indonesia			a	CodMod	India, Philippines, Singapore, Thailand
Iran (Islamic Republic of)	2004–2005	50–74	a	CodMod	Vital registration
Iraq			a	CodMod	Egypt 2000, Iran (Islamic Republic of) 2001
Ireland	2004	90–100	b	Vital registration	Vital registration
Israel	2004	90–100	b	Vital registration	Vital registration
Italy	2002	90–100	b	Vital registration	Vital registration
Jamaica	1991	50–74	a	CodMod	Vital registration data for Jamaica and Colombia
Japan	2004	90–100	b	Vital registration	Vital registration
Jordan	2003–2004	<50	Verbal autopsy data for 1995/96 (161); a	CodMod	Vital registration
Kazakhstan	2004	75–89	a	CodMod	Vital registration
Kenya			Hospital data, Ministry of Health, 1996, 1998–2000; a	CodMod	AfrE distribution[c]
Kiribati	2000–2002	75–89	Source: (162); a	Vital registration	GBD2002 cause-of-death estimates
Kuwait	2000–2002	90–100	b	Vital registration	Vital registration
Kyrgyzstan	2004	50–74	a	CodMod	Vital registration
Lao People's Democratic Republic			a	CodMod	Philippines, Thailand
Latvia	2004	90–100	b	Vital registration	Vital registration
Lebanon			a	CodMod	Egypt 2000, Iran (Islamic Republic of) 2001
Lesotho			a	CodMod	AfrE distribution[c]
Liberia			a	CodMod	AfrD distribution[c]
Libyan Arab Jamahiriya			a	CodMod	Egypt 2000, Iran (Islamic Republic of) 2001
Lithuania	2004	90–100	b	Vital registration	Vital registration
Luxembourg	2002–2004	90–100	b	Vital registration	Vital registration
Madagascar			a	CodMod	AfrD distribution[c]
Malawi			a	CodMod	AfrE distribution[c]
Malaysia			a	CodMod	China, Singapore, Thailand
Maldives			a	CodMod	India, Philippines
Mali			a	CodMod	AfrD distribution[c]
Malta	2002–2004	90–100	b	Vital registration	Vital registration
Marshall Islands			a	Regional pattern	GBD2002 cause-of-death estimates
Mauritania			a	CodMod	AfrD distribution[c]
Mauritius	2002–2004	90–100	b	Vital registration	Vital registration
Mexico	2004	90–100	Harvard Initiative for Global Health analyses of cause-of-death in Mexico; b	Vital registration	Vital registration

Country	Vital registration data used (year)	Estimated coverage (%)	Other sources of information	Method	Cause-of-death distribution pattern used
Micronesia (Federated States of)			1999 FSM Statistical Yearbook; a	Regional pattern	GBD2002 cause-of-death estimates
Moldova	2004	75–89	b	Vital registration	Vital registration
Monaco			b	Based on 1998 data from Provence Alpes Côte d'Azur, Department of France	GBD2002 cause-of-death estimates
Mongolia	2003	75–89	a	CodMod	Vital registration
Morocco			a	CodMod	Egypt 2000, Iran (Islamic Republic of) 2001
Mozambique			a	CodMod	AfrE distribution[c]
Myanmar			a	CodMod	India, Philippines
Namibia			a	CodMod	AfrE distribution[c]
Nauru	1994–96	<50	Mortality decline in Nauru. Source: R Taylor & K Thoma, unpublished data, 1998; a	Vital registration	GBD2002 cause-of-death estimates
Nepal			a	CodMod	India, Philippines
Netherlands	2004	90–100	b	Vital registration	Vital registration
New Zealand	2003	90–100	b	Vital registration	Vital registration
Nicaragua	2004	50–74	a	CodMod	Vital registration
Niger			a	CodMod	AfrD distribution[c]
Nigeria			a	CodMod	AfrD distribution[c]
Niue	1998–2000	90–100	a	Vital registration	GBD2002 cause-of-death estimates
Norway	2004	90–100	b	Vital registration	Vital registration
Oman			a	CodMod	Bahrain and Kuwait, 1997–2001
Pakistan			a	CodMod	India
Palau			a	Regional pattern	GBD2002 cause-of-death estimates
Panama	2004	90–100	a	CodMod	Vital registration
Papua New Guinea			a	CodMod	India, Philippines
Paraguay	2004	50–74	a	CodMod	Vital registration
Peru	2000	50–74	a	CodMod	Vital registration
Philippines	1998	75–89	a	CodMod	Vital registration
Poland	2004	90–100	b	Vital registration	Vital registration
Portugal	2004	90–100	b	Vital registration	Vital registration
Qatar	2001	75–89	a	CodMod	GBD2002 cause-of-death estimates
Republic of Korea	2004	75–89	b	Vital registration	Vital registration
Romania	2004	90–100	b	Vital registration	Vital registration
Russian Federation	2004	90–100	b	Vital registration	Vital registration
Rwanda			a	CodMod	AfrE distribution[c]
Saint Kitts and Nevis	1993–95	90–100	b	Vital registration	GBD2002 cause-of-death estimates
Saint Lucia	2000–2002	90–100	b	Vital registration	Vital registration
Saint Vincent and the Grenadines	2001–2003	90–100	b	Vital registration	Vital registration

(Table C4 continued)

Country	Vital registration data used (year)	Estimated coverage (%)	Other sources of information	Method	Cause-of-death distribution pattern used
Samoa			DHS 1999 and 2000 (163–164); a	Regional pattern	GBD2002 cause-of-death estimates
San Marino	1998–2000	75–89	b	Vital registration	GBD2002 cause-of-death estimates
Sao Tome and Principe			a	CodMod	GBD2002 cause-of-death estimates
Saudi Arabia			a	CodMod	Bahrain and Kuwait, 1997–2001
Senegal			Niakhar, Senegal, deaths assessed by verbal autopsy data for Niakhar 1983–1990 (165); a	CodMod	AfrD distribution[c]
Serbia and Montenegro	2002	90–100	b	Vital registration	Vital registration
Seychelles	1998–2000	90–100	b	Vital registration	GBD2002 cause-of-death estimates
Sierra Leone			a	CodMod	AfrD distribution[c]
Singapore	2003	75–89	b	Vital registration	Vital registration
Slovakia	2004	90–100	b	Vital registration	Vital registration
Slovenia	2004	90–100	b	Vital registration	Vital registration
Solomon Islands			a	Regional pattern	Cook Islands, Fiji, Kiribati, Nauru, Marshall Islands, Niue, Samoa, Tonga, Tuvalu, Vanuatu
Somalia			a	CodMod	Egypt 2000, South Africa 2004, Zimbabwe National Burden of Disease Study 1997, Mozambique Maputo Central Hospital Mortuary 1993–2004
South Africa	2004	75–89	National burden of disease estimates for 2000 (42); a	Vital registration	Vital registration
Spain	2004	90–100	b	Vital registration	Vital registration
Sri Lanka	1996	50–74	a	CodMod	Vital registration
Sudan			a	CodMod	Egypt 2000, South Africa 2004, Zimbabwe National Burden of Disease Study 1997, Mozambique Maputo Central Hospital Mortuary 1993–2004
Suriname	1998–2000	50–74	b	Vital registration	Vital registration
Swaziland			a	CodMod	AfrE distribution[c]
Sweden	2004	90–100	b	Vital registration	Vital registration
Switzerland	2004	90–100	b	Vital registration	Vital registration
Syrian Arab Republic	2000	90–100	a	CodMod	Vital registration
Tajikistan	2004	50–74	a	CodMod	Vital registration
Thailand	2002	75–89	Ministry of Health – verbal autopsy study; a	Vital registration corrected by verbal autopsy study	Vital registration corrected by verbal autopsy study
The former Yugoslav Republic of Macedonia	2003	90–100	b	Vital registration	Vital registration
Timor-Leste			a	CodMod	India, Philippines
Togo			a	CodMod	AfrD distribution[c]

Country	Vital registra-tion data used (year)	Estimated coverage (%)	Other sources of information	Method	Cause-of-death distribution pattern used
Tonga	1998	50–74	Report of the Minister of Health for the year 1994 (166); a	Vital registration	GBD2002 cause-of-death estimates
Trinidad and Tobago	1999–2000	75–89	b	Vital registration	Vital registration
Tunisia			a	CodMod	Egypt 2000, Iran (Islamic Republic of) 2001
Turkey	2003	<50	a	CodMod	Turkey National Burden of Disease Study 2000
Turkmenistan	1998	75–89	a	CodMod	Vital registration
Tuvalu			a	Regional pattern	GBD2002 cause-of-death estimates
Uganda			a	CodMod	AfrE distribution[c]
Ukraine	2004	90–100	b	Vital registration	Vital registration
United Arab Emirates			a	CodMod	Bahrain and Kuwait, 1997–2001
United Kingdom	2004	90–100	b	Vital registration	Vital registration
United Republic of Tanzania			a	CodMod	AfrE distribution[c]
United States of America	2004	90–100	b	Vital registration	Vital registration
Uruguay	2004	90–100	b	Vital registration	Vital registration
Uzbekistan	2004	50–74	a	CodMod	Vital registration
Vanuatu			Hospital data, Ministry of Health, 2001; a	Regional pattern	GBD2002 cause-of-death estimates
Venezuela (Bolivarian Republic of)	2004	90–100	b	Vital registration	Vital registration
Viet Nam			a	CodMod	China, India, Thailand
Yemen			a	CodMod	Egypt 2000, Iran (Islamic Republic of) 2001
Zambia			a	CodMod	AfrE distribution[c]
Zimbabwe			a	CodMod	AfrE distribution[c]

CodMod, GBD cause-of-death model; DHS, Demographic and Health Survey; DSP, disease surveillance point system.

[a] Epidemiological estimates obtained from studies, WHO technical programmes and UNAIDS for the following conditions: AIDS, TB, diphtheria, measles, pertussis, poliomyelitis, tetanus, dengue, malaria, schistosomiasis, trypanosomiasis, Japanese encephalitis, Chagas, maternal conditions (including abortion), cancers, drug use disorders, rheumatoid arthritis and war.

[b] Epidemiological estimates based on studies, information from WHO technical programmes and UNAIDS for the following conditions: AIDS, drug use disorders and war where applicable.

[c] South African death registration data 2004, Zimbabwe National Burden of Disease Study 1997 (32), INDEPTH verbal autopsy data from 7 sites in Africa 1999–2002 (33), Antananarivo Madagascar 1976–1995 (34), Mozambique Maputo Central Hospital Mortuary 1993–2004 (35).

References

1. World Bank. *World development report 1993. Investing in health.* New York, Oxford University Press for the World Bank, 1993.

2. Murray CJL, Lopez AD. Evidence-based health policy – lessons from the Global Burden of Disease Study. *Science,* 1996, 274:740–743.

3. Murray CJL, Lopez AD, eds. *The global burden of disease: a comprehensive assessment of mortality and disability from diseases, injuries and risk factors in 1990 and projected to 2020.* Cambridge, Harvard School of Public Health on behalf of the World Health Organization and the World Bank, 1996.

4. Murray CJL, Lopez AD. *Global health statistics.* Cambridge, Harvard School of Public Health on behalf of the World Health Organization and the World Bank, 1996.

5. Murray CJL. Rethinking DALYs. In: Murray CJL, Lopez AD, eds. *The global burden of disease.* Cambridge, Harvard School of Public Health on behalf of the World Health Organization and the World Bank, 1996:1–98.

6. *World health report 2004: changing history.* Geneva, World Health Organization, 2004.

7. *Death and DALY estimates for 2002 by cause for WHO Member States.* Geneva, World Health Organization, 2004 (http://www.who.int/evidence/bod).

8. Jamison DT, Breman JG, Measham AR, Alleyne G, Evans D, Claeson M et al. *Disease control priorities in developing countries,* 2nd ed. New York, Oxford University Press, 2006.

9. Lopez AD, Mathers CD, Ezzati M, Murray CJL, Jamison DT. *Global burden of disease and risk factors.* New York, Oxford University Press, 2006.

10. Murray CJL, Lopez AD, Black RE, Mathers CD, Shibuya K, Ezzati M et al. Global Burden of Disease 2005: call for collaborators. *Lancet,* 2007, 370:109–110.

11. Mathers CD, Lopez AD, Murray CJL. The burden of disease and mortality by condition: data, methods and results for 2001. In: Lopez AD, Mathers CD, Ezzati M, Murray CJL, Jamison DT, eds. *Global burden of disease and risk factors.* New York, Oxford University Press, 2006:45–240.

12. UNAIDS, World Health Organization. *AIDS epidemic update: December 2007.* Geneva, UNAIDS, 2007.

13. United Nations Population Division. *World population prospects – the 2006 revision.* New York, United Nations, 2007.

14. Black RE, Allen LH, Bhutta Z, Caulfield LE, de Onis M, Ezzati M et al. Maternal and child undernutrition: global and regional exposures and health consequences. *Lancet,* 2008, 371:243–260.

15. Murray CJL, Laakso T, Shibuya K, Hill K, Lopez AD. Can we achieve Millennium Development Goal 4? New analysis of country trends and forecasts of under-5 mortality to 2015. *Lancet,* 2007, 370:1040–1054.

16. *The state of the world's children 2008.* New York, United Nations Children's Fund, 2008.

17. Bryce J, Black RE, Walker N, Bhutta ZA, Lawn JE, Steketee RW. Can the world afford to save the lives of 6 million children each year? *Lancet,* 2005, 365:2193–2200.

18. *Preventing chronic diseases: a vital investment: WHO global report.* Geneva, World Health Organization, 2005.

19. Mathers CD, Loncar D. Projections of global mortality and burden of disease from 2002 to 2030. *PLoS Medicine,* 2006, 3:e442.

20. UNAIDS, WHO. *Resource needs for AIDS in low- and middle-income countries: estimation process and methods. Methodological Annex II: Revised projections of the number of people in need of ART.* Geneva, Joint United Nations Programme on HIV/AIDS, 2007.

21. *Global economic prospects 2008.* Washington, DC, The World Bank, 2008.

22. Ahmad O, Boschi-Pinto C, Lopez AD, Murray CJL, Lozano R, Inoue M. *Age standardization of rates: a new WHO standard.* Geneva, World Health Organization, 2001 (GPE Discussion Paper No. 31).

23. Mathers CD, Iburg KM, Begg S. Adjusting for comorbidity in the calculation of health-adjusted life expectancies. *Population Health Metrics,* 2003, 4:4.

24. Mathers CD, Bernard C, Iburg KM, Inoue M, Ma Fat D, Shibuya K et al. *Global burden of disease in 2002: data sources, methods and results.* Geneva, World Health Organization, 2003 (GPE Discussion Paper No. 54).

25. *World health report 2006: working together for health.* Geneva, World Health Organization, 2006.

26. Ahman E, Zupan J. *Neonatal and perinatal mortality: country, regional and global estimates 2004.* Geneva, World Health Organization, Department of Making Pregnancy Safer, 2007.

27. Bannister J, Hill K. Mortality in China, 1964-2000. *Population Studies,* 2004, 58:55–75.

28. Yang GH, Hu J, Rao KQ, Ma J, Rao C, Lopez AD. Mortality registration and surveillance in China: history, current situation and challenges. *Population Health Metrics,* 2005, 3:3.

29. Mari Bhat PN. Completeness of India's sample registration system: an assessment using the general growth balance method. *Population Studies,* 2002, 56:119–134.

30. International Institute for Population Sciences, Macro International. *National Family Health Survey (NFHS-3), 2005–06, Vol. I.* India, Mumbai, International Institute for Population Sciences, 2007.

1

2

3

4

Annex A

Annex B

Annex C

References

31. Salomon JA, Murray CJL. The epidemiologic transition revisited: compositional models for causes of death by age and sex. *Population and Development Review,* 2002, 28:205–228.

32. Chapman G, Hansen K, Jelsma J, Ndhlovu C, Piotti B, Byskov J et al. The burden of disease in Zimbabwe in 1997 as measured by disability-adjusted life years lost. *Tropical Medicine and International Health,* 2006, 11:660–671.

33. Adjuik M, Smith T, Clark S, Todd J, Garrib A, Ashraf A et al. Cause-specific mortality rates in sub-Saharan Africa and Bangladesh. *Bulletin of the World Health Organization,* 2006, 84:181–188.

34. Waltisperger D, Cantrelle P, Ralijaona O. *La Mortalité à Antananarivo de 1984 à 1995.* Les Documents et Manuels CEPED no 7, mai 1998.

35. *Injury Mortality Database.* Department of Legal Medicine, Maputo Central Hospital, Ministry of Health, Mozambique, 2005.

36. Rao C, Lopez AD, Yang G, Begg S, Ma J. Evaluating national cause-of-death statistics: principles and application to the case of China. *Bulletin of the World Health Organization,* 2005, 83:618–624.

37. Jha P, Gajalakshmi V, Gupta PC, Kumar R, Mony P, Dhingra N et al. Prospective study of one million deaths in India: rationale, design, and validation results. *PLoS Medicine,* 2006, 3:e18.

38. Khosravi A, Taylor R, Naghavi N, Lopez AD. Mortality in the Islamic Republic of Iran, 1964–2004. *Bulletin of the World Health Organization,* 2007, 85:607–614.

39. Stevens G, Dias RH, Thomas KJ, Rivera JA, Carvalho N, Barquera S et al. Characterizing the epidemiological transition in Mexico: national and subnational burden of diseases, injuries, and risk factors. *PLoS Medicine,* 2008, 5:e125 (http://medicine.plosjournals.org/perlserv/?request=get-document&doi=10.1371/journal.pmed.0050125, accessed 19 September 2008).

40. *Report on the global HIV/AIDS epidemic – June 2000.* Geneva, Joint United Nations Programme on HIV/AIDS, 2000.

41. Bah S. HIV/AIDS in South Africa in the light of death registration data: In search of elusive estimates. In: Zuberi T, Sibanda A, Udjo E, eds. *The demography of South Africa.* Armonk, ME Sharpe, 2005.

42. Norman R, Bradshaw D, Schneider M, Pieterse D, Groenewald P. *Revised burden of disease estimates for the comparative risk factor assessment, South Africa 2000.* Cape Town, South African Medical Research Council, 2006.

43. Tangcharoensathien V, Faramnuayphol P, Teokul W, Bundhamcharoen K, Wibulpholprasert S. A critical assessment of mortality statistics in Thailand: potential for improvements. *Bulletin of the World Health Organization,* 2006, 84:233–237.

44. Akgün S, Rao C, Yardim N, Basara B, Aydin O, Mollahaliloglu S et al. Estimating mortality and causes of death in Turkey: methods, results and policy implications. *The European Journal of Public Health*, 2007, 17:593–599.

45. *World health report 2005: child and maternal survival.* Geneva, World Health Organization, 2005.

46. Bryce J, Boschi-Pinto C, Shibuya K, Black RE, WHO Child Health Epidemiology Reference Group. WHO estimates of the causes of death in children. *Lancet*, 2005, 365:1147–1152.

47. Morris SS, Black RE, Tomaskovic L. Predicting the distribution of under-five deaths by cause in countries without adequate vital registration systems. *International Journal of Epidemiology*, 2003, 32:1041–1051.

48. Lawn JE, Cousens S, Zupan J. 4 million neonatal deaths: when? where? why? *Lancet*, 2005, 365:891–900.

49. Lawn JE, Wilczynska-Ketende K, Cousens SN. Estimating the causes of 4 million neonatal deaths in the year 2000. *International Journal of Epidemiology*, 2006, 35:706–718.

50. *Global tuberculosis control: surveillance, planning and financing: WHO report 2006.* Geneva, World Health Organization, 2006.

51. Boschi-Pinto C, Velebit L, Shibuya K. Estimating the child mortality due to diarrhoea in developing countries. *Bulletin of the World Health Organization*, 2008, (in press).

52. Crowcroft NS, Stein C, Duclos P, Birmingham M. How best to estimate the global burden of pertussis? *Lancet Infectious Diseases*, 2003, 3:413–418.

53. *WHO/UNICEF estimates of national immunization coverage.* Geneva, World Health Organization, 2007 (http://www.who.int/immunization_monitoring/routine/immunization_coverage/en/index.html, accessed 11 November 2007).

54. Wolfson LJ. *WHO ICE-T: immunization coverage estimates and trajectories,* version 4.0. Geneva, World Health Organization, Department of Immunization, Vaccines and Biologicals, 2007 (http://www.who.int/immunization_financing/analyses/givs_costing_annex1.pdf, accessed 15 January 2008).

55. *Polio case count.* Geneva, World Health Organization, 2008 (http://www.who.int/vaccines/immunization_monitoring/en/diseases/poliomyelitis/case_count.cfm, accessed 16 January 2008).

56. Brenzel L, Wolfson LJ, Fox-Rushby JA, Miller M, Halsey N. Vaccine-preventable diseases. In: Jamison DT, Breman JG, Measham AR, Alleyne G, Evans D, Claeson M et al., eds. *Disease control priorities in developing countries,* 2nd ed. New York, Oxford University Press, 2006:389–411.

57. Wolfson LJ, Strebel PM, Gacic-Dobo M, Hoekstra EJ, McFarland JW, Hersh BS. Has the 2005 measles mortality reduction goal been achieved? A natural history modelling study. *Lancet*, 2007, 369:191–200.

58. Roper MH, Vandelaer JH, Gasse FL. Maternal and neonatal tetanus. *Lancet*, 2007, 370:1947–1959.

59. Wolfson LJ, Vandelaer JH, Gasse FL, Garnier S, Birmingham ME. A model-based approach to monitoring global progress in the elimination of neonatal tetanus. Paper presented to WHO Quantitative Immunization and Vaccines Related Research Advisory Committee, Geneva 27–28 September, 2007.

60. WHO Department of Immunization. Meningitis estimates. Paper presented to the expert review of estimates of morbidity and mortality associated with *Haemophilus influenzae* type b (Hib) and *Streptococcus pneumoniae* (SP), London, 24–25 October 2006.

61. WHO Department of Immunization. General analytic methods. Paper presented to the expert review of estimates of morbidity and mortality associated with *Haemophilus influenzae* type b (Hib) and *Streptococcus pneumoniae* (SP), London, 24–25 October 2006.

62. Korenromp EL. *Malaria incidence estimates at country level for the year 2004 – proposed estimates and draft report*. Geneva, World Health Organization. Roll Back Malaria Monitoring and Evaluation Reference Group & MERG Task Force on Malaria Morbidity, 2005.

63. Roll Back Malaria, World Health Organization, UNICEF. *World malaria report 2005*. Geneva, World Health Organization, 2005.

64. Nahlen BL, Korenromp EL, Miller JM, Shibuya K. Malaria risk: estimating clinical episodes of malaria. *Nature*, 2005, 437:E3.

65. Malaria Epidemiology Reference Group. *Minutes of the MERG Taskforce Meeting on malaria morbidity*, 19–21 October 2004. Geneva, World Health Organization, 2004.

66. *World Malaria Report, 2008*. Geneva, World Health Organization, 2005.

67. Rowe AK, Rowe SY, Snow RW, Korenromp EL, Schellenberg JA, Stein C et al. The burden of malaria mortality among African children in the year 2000. *International Journal of Epidemiology*, 2006, 35:691–704.

68. Breman JG, Mills A, Snow RW, Mulligan J-A, Lengeler C, Mendis K et al. Conquering malaria. In: Jamison DT, Breman JG, Measham AR, Alleyne G, Evans D, Claeson M et al., eds. *Disease control priorities in developing countries*, 2nd ed. New York, Oxford University Press, 2006:413–431.

69. Snow RW, Craig MH, Newton CRJC, Steketee RW. *The public health burden of Plasmodium falciparum malaria in Africa: deriving the numbers*. DCPP Working Paper No. 11. Washington, DC, Fogarty International Centre, National Institutes of Health, 2003.

70. Ross A, Maire N, Molineaux L, Smith T. An epidemiologic model of severe morbidity and mortality caused by Plasmodium falciparum. *American Journal of Tropical Medicine and Hygiene,* 2006, 75:63–73.

71. Odiit M, Coleman PG, Liu WC, McDermott JJ, Fevre EM, Welburn SC et al. Quantifying the level of under-detection of Trypanosoma brucei rhodesiense sleeping sickness cases. *Tropical Medicine & International Health,* 2005, 10:840–849.

72. African trypanosomiasis (sleeping sickness). Geneva, World Health Organization, 2006 (Fact Sheet No. 259) (http://www.who.int/mediacentre/factsheets/fs259/en/, accessed 15 January 2008).

73. Pan American Health Organization, WHO Program on Neglected Tropical Diseases. *Estimación cuantitativa de la enfermedad de Chagas en les Américas* [In Spanish]. Washington, Pan American Health Organization, 2007 (OPS/HDM/CD/425-06).

74. Mott KE. Schistosomiasis. In: Murray CJL, Lopez AD, Mathers CD, eds. *The global epidemiology of infectious diseases.* Geneva, World Health Organization, 2004:349–391 (http://whqlibdoc.who.int/publications/2004/9241592303.pdf, accessed 17 January 2008).

75. Hotez PJ, Bundy DA, Beegle K, Brooker S, Drake L, de Silva NR et al. Helminth infections: soil-transmitted helminth infections and schistosomiasis. In: Jamison DT , Breman JG, Measham AR, Alleyne G, Evans D, Claeson M et al., eds. *Disease control priorities in developing countries,* 2nd ed. New York, Oxford University Press, 2006:467–482.

76. van der Werf MJ, de Vlas SJ. *Morbidity and infection with schistosomes or soil-transmitted helminths.* Rotterdam, Erasmus University, 2001.

77. Mansour NS, Higashi GI, Schinski VD, Murrell KD. A longitudinal study of *Schistosoma haematobium* infection in Qena governorate, Upper Egypt. 1. Initial epidemiological findings. *American Journal of Tropical Medicine and Hygiene,* 1981, 30:795–805.

78. Machado PA. The Brazilian program for schistosomiasis control, 1975–1979. *American Journal of Tropical Medicine and Hygiene,* 1982, 31:76–86.

79. LeDuc JW, Esteves K, Gratz NG. Dengue and dengue haemorrhagic fever. In: Murray CJL, Lopez AD, Mathers CD, eds. *The global epidemiology of infectious diseases.* Geneva, World Health Organization, 2004:219–242.

80. World Health Organization. DengueNet: WHO's internet-based system for the global surveillance of dengue fever and dengue haemorrhagic fever. *Weekly Epidemiological Record,* 2002, 77:297–304.

81. Shepard DS, Suaya JA, Halstead SB, Nathan MB, Gubler DJ, Mahoney RT et al. Cost-effectiveness of a pediatric dengue vaccine. *Vaccine,* 2004, 22:1275–1280.

1

2

3

4

Annex A

Annex B

Annex C

References

82. *Global elimination of trachoma documents.* Geneva, World Health Organization, 2004 (http://www.who.int/blindness/publications/get2020/en/index.html, accessed 18 January 2008).

83. Williams BG, Gouws E, Boschi-Pinto C, Bryce J, Dye C. Estimates of worldwide distribution of child deaths from acute respiratory infections. *Lancet,* 2002, 2:25–32.

84. WHO, UNICEF, UNFPA, World Bank. Maternal mortality in 2005: estimates developed by *WHO, UNICEF, UNFPA and the World Bank.* Geneva, World Health Organization, 2007.

85. Sedgh G, Henshaw SK, Singh S, Åhman E, Shah I. Induced abortion: estimated rates and trends worldwide. *Lancet,* 2007, 370:1338–1345.

86. *Unsafe abortion: global and regional estimates of the incidence of unsafe abortion and associated mortality in 2003.* Geneva, World Health Organization, 2007.

87. de Onis M, Blossner M. The World Health Organization Global Database on Child Growth and Malnutrition: methodology and applications. *International Journal of Epidemiology,* 2003, 32:518–526.

88. de Onis M, Blossner M, Borghi E, Morris R, Frongillo EA. Methodology for estimating regional and global trends of child malnutrition. *International Journal of Epidemiology,* 2004, 33:1260–1270.

89. *WHO child growth standards: length/height-for-age, weight-for-age, weight-for-length, weight-for-height and body mass index-for-age: methods and development.* Geneva, World Health Organization, 2006.

90. de Onis M, Garza C, Onyango AW, Martorell R. *WHO child growth standards. Acta paediatrica,* 2006, 450(Suppl.):1–101.

91. McLean E , Egli I, Cogswell M, de Benoist B, Wojdyla D. Worldwide prevalence of anemia in preschool aged children, pregnant women and non-pregnant women of reproductive age. In: Kramer K, Zimmermann MB, eds. *Nutritional anaemia.* Basel, Sight and Life Press, 2007:1–12.

92. WHO Nutrition Program. *WHO global database on anaemia.* Geneva, World Health Organization (http://www.who.int/vmnis/anaemia/en/, accessed 8 June 2008).

93. Ferlay J, Bray F, Pisani P, Parkin DM. *Globocan 2000: cancer incidence, mortality and prevalence worldwide,* version 1.0. Lyon, IARCPress, 2001.

94. Mathers CD, Shibuya K, Boschi-Pinto C, Lopez AD, Murray CJ. Global and regional estimates of cancer mortality and incidence by site: I. Application of regional cancer survival model to estimate cancer mortality distribution by site. *BMC Cancer,* 2002, 2:36.

95. Shibuya K, Mathers CD, Boschi-Pinto C, Lopez AD, Murray CJL. Global and regional estimates of cancer mortality and incidence by site: II. Results for the Global Burden of Disease Study 2000. *BMC Cancer,* 2002, 2:37.

96. Ferlay J, Bray F, Pisani P, Parkin DM. *GLOBOCAN 2002: cancer incidence, mortality and prevalence worldwide.* Lyon, IARCPress, 2004.

97. Cowie CC, Rust KF, Byrd-Holt DD, Eberhardt MS, Flegal KM, Engelgau MM et al. Prevalence of diabetes and impaired fasting glucose in adults in the U.S. population: national health and nutrition examination survey 1999–2002. *Diabetes Care,* 2006, 29:1263–1268.

98. Aguilar-Salinas CA, Velazquez-Monroy O, Gómez-Pérez FJ, Gonzalez Chávez A, Esqueda AL, Molina Cuevas V et al. Characteristics of patients with type 2 diabetes in Mexico: results from a large population-based nationwide survey. *Diabetes Care,* 2003, 26:2021–2026.

99. Sánchez-Castillo CP, Velásquez-Monroy O, Lara-Esqueda A, Berber A, Sepulveda J, Tapia-Conyer R et al. Diabetes and hypertension increases in a society with abdominal obesity: results of the Mexican National Health Survey 2000. *Public Health Nutrition,* 2005, 8:53–60.

100. Torquato MT, Montenegro Júnior RM, Viana LA, de Souza RA, Lanna CM, Lucas JC et al. Prevalence of diabetes mellitus and impaired glucose tolerance in the urban population aged 30–69 years in Ribeirão Preto (São Paulo), Brazil. *São Paulo Medical Journal,* 2003, 121:224–230.

101. Chodick G, Heymann AD, Shalev V, Kookia E. The epidemiology of diabetes in a large Israeli HMO. *European Journal of Epidemiology,* 2003, 18:1143–1146.

102. Panagiotakos DB, Pitsavos C, Chrysohoou C, Stefanadis C. The epidemiology of type 2 diabetes mellitus in Greek adults: the ATTICA study. *Diabetic Medicine,* 2005, 22:1581–1588.

103. Ubink-Veltmaat LJ, Bilo HJ, Groenier KH, Houweling ST, Rischen RO. Prevalence, incidence and mortality of type 2 diabetes mellitus revisited: a prospective population-based study in The Netherlands (ZODIAC-1). *European Journal of Epidemiology,* 2003, 18:793–800.

104. Szurkowska M, Szybinski Z, Nazim A, Zafraniec K, Edrychowski W. Prevalence of type II diabetes mellitus in population of Krakow. *Polskie Archiwum Medycyny Wewnetrznej,* 2001, 106:771–779.

105. Szybinski Z. Polish Multicenter Study on Diabetes Epidemiology (PMSDE). *Polskie Archiwum Medycyny Wewnetrznej,* 2001, 106:751–758.

106. Lopatynski J, Mardarowicz G, Nicer T, Szczesniak G, Krol H, Matej A et al. The prevalence of type II diabetes mellitus in rural urban population over 35 years of age in Lublin region (Eastern Poland). *Polskie Archiwum Medycyny Wewnetrznej,* 2001, 106:781–786.

107. Aekplakorn W, Stolk RP, Neal B, Suriyawongpaisal P, Chongsuvivatwong V, Cheepudomwit S et al. The prevalence and management of diabetes in Thai adults. *Diabetes Care,* 2003, 26:2758–2763.

108. Gu D, Reynolds K, Duan X, Xin X, Chen J, Wu X et al. Prevalence of diabetes and impaired fasting glucose in the Chinese adult population: International Collaborative Study of Cardiovascular Disease in Asia (InterASIA). *Diabetologia,* 2003, 46:1190–1198.

109. Hussain A, Rahim MA, Azad Khan AK, Ali SMK, Vaaler S. Type 2 diabetes in rural and urban population: diverse prevalence and associated risk factors in Bangladesh. *Diabetic Medicine,* 2005, 22:931–936.

110. Sadikot SM, Nigam A, Das S, Bajaj S, Zargar AH, Prasannakumar KM et al. The burden of diabetes and impaired glucose tolerance in India using the WHO 1999 criteria: prevalence of diabetes in India Study (PODIS). *Diabetes Research and Clinical Practice,* 2004, 66:301–307.

111. Wild S, Roglic G, Green A, Sicree R, King H. Global prevalence of diabetes: estimates for the year 2000 and projections for 2030. *Diabetes Care,* 2004, 27:1047–1053.

112. Strong KL, WHO Global Infobase Team. *The SuRF Report. Surveillance of chronic disease risk factors: country level data and comparable estimates.* Geneva, World Health Organization, 2005.

113. Asia Pacific Cohort Studies Collaboration. Body mass index and risk of diabetes mellitus in the Asia-Pacific region. *Asian Pacific Journal of Clinical Nutrition,* 2006, 15:127–133.

114. Ustun TB, Ayuso-Mateos JL, Chatterji S, Mathers CD, Murray CJL. Global burden of depressive disorders in the year 2000. *British Journal of Psychiatry,* 2005, 184:386–392.

115. Ayuso-Mateos JL, Vazquez-Barquero JL, Dowrick C, Lehtinen V, Dalgard OS, Casey P et al. Depressive disorders in Europe: prevalence figures from the ODIN study. *The British Journal of Psychiatry,* 2001, 179:308–316.

116. Mathers CD, Ayuso-Mateos JL. *Global burden of alcohol use disorders in the year 2000: summary of methods and data sources.* Global burden of disease 2000 working paper. Geneva, World Health Organization, 2003.

117. Kehoe T, Rehm J, Chatterji S. *Global burden of alcohol use disorders in the year 2004.* Report prepared for WHO. Zurich, Switzerland, WHO Collaborating Centre at the Research Centre for Public Health and Addiction, 2007.

118. Barendregt J, van Oortmarssen GJ, Vos T, Murray CJL. A generic model for the assessment of disease epidemiology: the computational basis of DisMod II. *Population Health Metrics,* 2003, 1:4.

119. Begg S, Vos T, Barker B, Stevenson C, Stanley L, Lopez A. *The burden of disease and injury in Australia 2003.* Canberra, Australian Institute of Health and Welfare, 2007.

120. Ustun TB, Chatterji S, Villanueva M, Bendib L, Celik C, Sadana R et al. The WHO multicountry household survey study on health and responsiveness 2000-2001. In: Murray CJL, Evans D, eds. *Health systems performance assessment: debates, methods and empiricism.* Geneva, World Health Organization, 2003.

121. Degenhardt L, Hall W, Warner-Smith M, Lynskey M. Illicit drugs. In: Ezzati M, Lopez A, Rodgers A, Murray CJL, eds. *Comparative quantification of health risks: global and regional burden of disease attributable to selected major risk factors.* Geneva, World Health Organization, 2003.

122. Single E, Robson L, Xie X, Rehm J. *The costs of substance abuse in Canada.* Ottawa, Canadian Centre on Substance Abuse, 2002.

123. *2006 World drug report.* Vienna, United Nations Office on Drugs and Crime, 2007.

124. Fewtrell LJ, Pruss-Ustun A, Landrigan P, Ayuso-Mateos JL. Estimating the global burden of disease of mild mental retardation and cardiovascular diseases from environmental lead exposure. *Environmental Research,* 2004, 94:120–133.

125. Pruss-Ustun A, Fewtrell LJ, Landrigan P, Ayuso-Mateos JL. Lead exposure. In: Ezzati M , Lopez A, Rodgers A, Murray CJL, eds. *Comparative quantification of health risks: global and regional burden of disease attributable to selected major risk factors.* Geneva, World Health Organization, 2004:1495–1542.

126. Thylefors B, Negrel AD, Pararajasegaram R, Dadzie KY. Global data on blindness. *Bulletin of the World Health Organization,* 1995, 73:115–121.

127. Resnikoff S, Pascolini D, Etya'ale D, Kocur I, Pararajasegaram R, Pokharel GP et al. Global data on visual impairment in the year 2002. *Bulletin of the World Health Organization,* 2004, 82:844–851.

128. Resnikoff S, Pascolini D, Mariotti SP, Pokharel GP. Global magnitude of visual impairment caused by uncorrected refractive errors in 2004. *Bulletin of the World Health Organization,* 2008, 86:63–70.

129. Stouthard M , Essink-Bot M, Bonsel G, Barendregt J, Kramers P. *Disability weights for diseases in the Netherlands.* Rotterdam, Department of Public Health, Erasmus University, 1997.

130. Mathers CD , Truelsen T, Begg S, Satoh T. *Global burden of ischaemic heart disease in the year 2000.* Global burden of disease 2000 working paper. Geneva, World Health Organization, 2004 (http://www.who.int/healthinfo/statistics/bod_ischaemicheartdisease.pdf, accessed 6 June 2008).

131. Michaud CM, McKenna MT, Begg S, Tomijima N, Majmudar M, Bulzacchelli M et al. The burden of disease and injury in the United States 1996. *Population Health Metrics,* 2006, 4:11.

132. Lim S, unpublished data, 2007.

133. Bronnum-Hansen H, Jorgensen T, Davidsen M, Madsen M, Osler M, Gerdes LU et al. Survival and cause of death after myocardial infarction: the Danish MONICA study. *Journal of Clinical Epidemiology,* 2001, 54:1244–1250.

134. Truelsen T, Begg S, Mathers CD, Satoh T. *Global burden of cerebrovascular disease in the year 2000.* Global burden of disease 2000 working paper. Geneva, World Health Organization, 2000 (http://www.who.int/healthinfo/ statistics/bod_cerebrovasculardisease.pdf, accessed 6 June 2008).

135. Aekplakorn W, Abbott-Klafter J, Premgamone A, Dhanamun B, Chaikitti-porn C, Chongsuvivatwong V et al. Prevalence and management of diabetes and associated risk factors by regions of Thailand: third National Health Examination Survey 2004. *Diabetes Care,* 2007, 30:2007–2012.

136. Ustun TB, Chatterji S, Mechbal A, Murray CJL, WHS Collaborating Groups. The world health surveys. In: Murray CJL, Evans D, eds. *Health systems performance assessment: debates, methods and empiricism.* Geneva, World Health Organization, 2003.

137. Petersen PE, Bourgeois D, Ogawa H, Estupinan-Day S, Ndiaye C. The global burden of oral diseases and risks to oral health. *Bulletin of the World Health Organization,* 2005, 83:661–669.

138. Heidelberg Institute on International Conflict Research. *Conflict barometer 2003: 12th annual conflict analysis.* Heidelberg, Department of Political Science, University of Heidelberg, 2004.

139. Heidelberg Institute on International Conflict Research. *Conflict barometer 2004: 13th annual conflict analysis.* Heidelberg, Department of Political Science, University of Heidelberg, 2005.

140. Project Ploughshares. *Armed conflicts report 2005.* Waterloo, Canada, Project Ploughshares, 2005 (http://www.ploughshares.ca/, accessed 26 November 2007).

141. Project Ploughshares. *Armed conflicts report 2006.* Waterloo, Canada, Project Ploughshares, 2006 (http://www.ploughshares.ca/, accessed 26 November 2007).

142. Marshall MG, Gurr TR. *Peace and conflict 2005: a global survey of armed conflicts, self-determination movements, and democracy.* University of Maryland, Center for International Development and Conflict Management, 2005.

143. Murray CJ, King G, Lopez AD, Tomijima N, Krug EG. Armed conflict as a public health problem. *BMJ,* 2002, 324:346–349.

144. Coghlan B, Brennan RJ, Ngoy P, Nofara D, Otto B, Clements M et al. Mortality in the Democratic Republic of Congo: a nationwide survey. *Lancet,* 2006, 367:44–51.

145. Iraq Family Health Survey Study Group. Violence-related mortality in Iraq from 2002 to 2006. *New England Journal of Medicine,* 2008, 358:484–493.

146. Hagan J, Palloni A. Death in Darfur. *Science,* 2006, 313:1578–1579.

147. Guha-Sapir D, Degomme O. *Darfur: counting the deaths. Mortality estimates from multiple survey data.* Brussels, Université Catholique de Louvain, Centre for Research on the Epidemiology of Disasters, 2005 (http://www1.cedat.be/Documents/Analysis_Paper/DarfurCountingThe Deaths-withClarifications.pdf, accessed 19 September 2008).

148. Guha-Sapir D, Degomme O. *Darfur: Counting the deaths (2). What are the trends?* Brussels, Université Catholique de Louvain, Centre for Research on the Epidemiology of Disasters, 2005 (http://www1.cedat.be/Documents/ Analysis_Paper/DarfurCountingTheDeaths2.pdf, accessed 19 September 2008).

149. World Health Organization, European Programme for Intervention Epidemiology Training. *Retrospective mortality survey among the internally displaced population, Greater Darfur, Sudan, August 2004.* Geneva, World Health Organization, 2004 (http://www.who.int/disasters/repo/14652.pdf, accessed 18 January 2008).

150. International Campaign to Ban Landmines. *Landmine monitor report 2005: toward a mine-free world.* New York, Human Rights Watch, 2005.

151. International Campaign to Ban Landmines. *Landmine monitor report 2006: toward a mine-free world.* 2006. New York, Human Rights Watch, 2006.

152. EM-DAT: the OFDA/CRED international disaster database [online database]. Belgium, Centre for Research on the Epidemiology of Disasters, 2006.

153. He H, Oguchi T, Zhou R, Zhang J, Qiao S. *Damage and seismic intensity of the 1996 Lijiang earthquake, Vhina: a GIS analysis.* Technical report. Tokyo, Center for Spatial Information Science, University of Tokyo, 2001 (http:// www.csis.u-tokyo.ac.jp/english/dp/dp.html, accessed 18 January 2008)

154. Naghii MR. Public health impact and medical consequences of earthquakes. *Pan American Journal of Public Health,* 2005, 18:216–221.

155. Nishikiori N, Abe T, Costa DG, Dharmaratne SD, Kunii O, Moji K. Who died as a result of the tsunami? Risk factors of mortality among internally displaced persons in Sri Lanka: a retrospective cohort analysis. *BMC Public Health,* 2006, 6:73.

156. Doocy S, Rofi A, Moodie C, Spring E, Bradley S, Burnham G et al. Tsunami mortality in Aceh Province, Indonesia. *Bulletin of the World Health Organization,* 2007, 85:273–278.

157. *2005 International Comparison Programme preliminary results.* Washington, DC, World Bank, 2007.

158. Mathers CD, Salomon JA, Ezzati M, Begg S, Lopez AD. Sensitivity and uncertainty analyses for burden of disease and risk factor estimates. In: Lopez AD, Mathers CD, Ezzati M, Murray CJL, Jamison DT, eds. *Global burden of disease and risk factors.* New York, Oxford University Press, 2006:399–426.

159. *World development report 2004: equity and development.* Washington, DC, World Bank, 2006.

160. Zanou MB. Deaths assessed by medical personnel in city hospitals 1973-1992 (159). Dataset provided by Ecole Nationale de Statistique et d'Economie Appliquée, Abidjan, Cote d'Ivoire, 2000.

161. Khoury SA, Massad D, Fardous T. Mortality and causes of death in Jordan 1995–96: assessment by verbal autopsy. *Bulletin of the World Health Organization,* 1999, 77:641–650.

162. *Third national health family planning and social welfare plan 1992–1995.* Ministry of Health Family Planning and Social Welfare, Kiribati, 1991.

163. *Demographic and Health Survey, 1999.* Department of Statistics, Samoa, undated.

164. *Demographic and Vital Statistics Survey, 2000.* Department of Statistics, Samoa, undated.

165. *Deaths assessed by verbal autopsy, Niakhar, Senegal 1983–1990.* Dataset provided by Centre Population et Développement, Paris.

166. *Report of the Minister of Health, 1994,* Government of Tonga.

Date Due

JAN 2 0 2009			

BRODART, CO.   Cat. No. 23-233   Printed in U.S.A.